Exploring Language Teacher Efficacy in Japan

PSYCHOLOGY OF LANGUAGE LEARNING AND TEACHING
Series Editors: **Sarah Mercer**, *Universität Graz, Austria* and **Stephen Ryan**, *Waseda University, Japan*

This international, interdisciplinary book series explores the exciting, emerging field of Psychology of Language Learning and Teaching. It is a series that aims to bring together works which address a diverse range of psychological constructs from a multitude of empirical and theoretical perspectives, but always with a clear focus on their applications within the domain of language learning and teaching. The field is one that integrates various areas of research that have been traditionally discussed as distinct entities, such as motivation, identity, beliefs, strategies and self-regulation, and it also explores other less familiar concepts for a language education audience, such as emotions, the self and positive psychology approaches. In theoretical terms, the new field represents a dynamic interface between psychology and foreign language education and books in the series draw on work from diverse branches of psychology, while remaining determinedly focused on their pedagogic value. In methodological terms, sociocultural and complexity perspectives have drawn attention to the relationships between individuals and their social worlds, leading to a field now marked by methodological pluralism. In view of this, books encompassing quantitative, qualitative and mixed methods studies are all welcomed.

All books in this series are externally peer-reviewed.

Full details of all the books in this series and of all our other publications can be found on http://www.multilingual-matters.com, or by writing to Multilingual Matters, St Nicholas House, 31-34 High Street, Bristol BS1 2AW, UK.

PSYCHOLOGY OF LANGUAGE LEARNING AND TEACHING: 5

Exploring Language Teacher Efficacy in Japan

Gene Thompson

MULTILINGUAL MATTERS
Bristol • Blue Ridge Summit

DOI https://doi.org/10.21832/THOMPS5396
Library of Congress Cataloging in Publication Data
A catalog record for this book is available from the Library of Congress.
Names: Thompson, Gene, 1978- author.
Title: Exploring Language Teacher Efficacy in Japan/Gene Thompson.
Description: Blue Ridge Summit: Multilingual Matters, 2020. | Includes bibliographical references and index. | Summary: "This book focuses on the individual and collective beliefs of teachers. It discusses personal and collective dimensions of language teacher efficacy, discusses the ways in which efficacy beliefs develop, helps further understanding of factors that may influence teacher self-efficacy and suggests new directions for future research studies"— Provided by publisher.
Identifiers: LCCN 2019021980 (print) | LCCN 2019981510 (ebook) | ISBN 9781788925396 (hardback) | ISBN 9781788925389 (paperback) | ISBN 9781788925419 (epub) | ISBN 9781788925402 (pdf) | ISBN 9781788925426 (kindle edition)
Subjects: LCSH: English language—Study and teaching (Higher)—Japan. | English language—Study and teaching (Higher)—Japanese speakers. | Second language acquisition—Study and teaching—Japan.
Classification: LCC PE1068.J3 T485 2019 (print) | LCC PE1068.J3 (ebook) | DDC 428.0071—dc23
LC record available at https://lccn.loc.gov/2019021980
LC ebook record available at https://lccn.loc.gov/2019981510

British Library Cataloguing in Publication Data
A catalogue entry for this book is available from the British Library.

ISBN-13: 978-1-78892-539-6 (hbk)
ISBN-13: 978-1-78892-538-9 (pbk)

Multilingual Matters
UK: St Nicholas House, 31-34 High Street, Bristol BS1 2AW, UK.
USA: NBN, Blue Ridge Summit, PA, USA.

Website: www.multilingual-matters.com
Twitter: Multi_Ling_Mat
Facebook: https://www.facebook.com/multilingualmatters
Blog: www.channelviewpublications.wordpress.com

Copyright © 2020 Gene Thompson.

All rights reserved. No part of this work may be reproduced in any form or by any means without permission in writing from the publisher.

The policy of Multilingual Matters/Channel View Publications is to use papers that are natural, renewable and recyclable products, made from wood grown in sustainable forests. In the manufacturing process of our books, and to further support our policy, preference is given to printers that have FSC and PEFC Chain of Custody certification. The FSC and/or PEFC logos will appear on those books where full certification has been granted to the printer concerned.

Typeset by Deanta Global Publishing Services, Chennai, India.

Contents

Figures and Tables	ix
Abbreviations and Japanese Terms	xi
About the Author	xiii
Acknowledgments	xiv
Preface	xv

1 Introduction 1
  1.1 Background of the Study 2
  1.2 Why Study Teacher Efficacy? 7
  1.3 Chapter Summary 10

2 Teacher Efficacy as a Form of Self-Efficacy 12
  2.1 A Brief History: Two Views of Teacher Efficacy 12
  2.2 Teacher Efficacy within Social Cognitive Theory 16
  2.3 How Efficacy Beliefs Differ from Other
      Self-Constructs 18
  2.4 The Development of Efficacy Beliefs 21
  2.5 Additional Factors that May Influence Efficacy Beliefs 25
  2.6 Assessment of Efficacy Beliefs 26
  2.7 Chapter Summary 29

3 Language Teacher Efficacy 31
  3.1 Self-Efficacy for Language Teaching 31
  3.2 Dimensions of Language Teacher Efficacy 33
  3.3 Development of Language Teacher Efficacy Beliefs 36
  3.4 Other Factors Related to LTE Beliefs 39
  3.5 Language Teacher Efficacy in Japan 40
  3.6 Chapter Summary 42

4 Approaches for Investigating Language Teacher Efficacy 44
  4.1 Considerations for Teacher Efficacy Researchers 44
  4.2 Approaches for Investigating Foreign Language
      Teacher Efficacy 47
  4.3 Research Design: Exploring JTE Teacher Efficacy 49

	4.4 Chapter Summary	57
5	Developing a Language Teacher Efficacy Scale	59
	5.1 Using a Local Panel to Develop an Efficacy Instrument	59
	5.2 The Expert Panel	60
	5.3 The Exploratory Cycle	61
	5.4 Item Translation Process	66
	5.5 The Evaluative Cycle	67
	5.6 Chapter Summary	72
6	JTE Language Teacher Efficacy Beliefs and Dimensions	73
	6.1 Key Areas of Challenge for Japanese Teachers of English	74
	6.2 Teacher Efficacy Beliefs of Japanese High School English Teachers	76
	6.3 Dimensions of JTE Efficacy	79
	6.4 Variation in Dimensions of Language Teacher Efficacy	82
	6.5 Chapter Summary	84
7	Language Teacher L2 Efficacy and L2 Usage	86
	7.1 Perceived L2 Capability as a Dimension of Language Teacher Efficacy	87
	7.2 Teacher Efficacy Beliefs and English Proficiency	90
	7.3 Use of English as a Teaching Language	93
	7.4 Factors that Influence Efficacy towards the Use of English	96
	7.5 Chapter Summary	99
8	Efficacy for Language Instruction	101
	8.1 Two Dimensions of L2 Instructional Efficacy for the JTE Context	102
	8.2 Factors that Influence Efficacy towards L2 Instruction	104
	8.3 Factors Associated with Communicative Teaching Efficacy	106
	8.4 Predictors of Efficacy towards Student Achievement	111
	8.5 Chapter Summary	114
9	Efficacy Towards Collaborative Practice and Collective Action	116
	9.1 Individual, Collective and Collaborative Teacher Efficacy	117
	9.2 Collective and Collaborative Efficacy in Language Teaching Contexts	119
	9.3 Efficacy towards Collaborative Practice	120
	9.4 Predictors of Efficacy towards Collaborative Practice	124

	9.5 Towards Stronger Efficacy for Collective Action	127
	9.6 Chapter Summary	129
10	Language Teacher Efficacy Belief Development	131
	10.1 Sources of Language Teacher Efficacy	132
	10.2 Personal Experience as a Source of Efficacy Information	136
	10.3 The Social Nature of Teacher Practice	138
	10.4 Efficacy Development Over Time	143
	10.5 Chapter Summary	144
11	Where Next for LTE Research?	147
	11.1 Key Findings	148
	11.2 Where Next: Suggestions for Future Research	150
	11.3 Final Summary	157
	References	159
	Index	179

Figures and Tables

Tables

Table 4.1	Japanese Teacher of English Teacher Efficacy Scale (JTE-TES)	52
Table 4.2	Demographic items used in the survey stages of the study	53
Table 5.1	The expert panel	62
Table 5.2	Steps and processes of the thematic analysis	64
Table 5.3	Initial items for assessment by the experts in the exploratory interviews	65
Table 5.4	Item rating scales used in the 'evaluative' expert interviews	67
Table 5.5	JTE-TES items for the survey stages of the study	71
Table 6.1	Descriptive statistics and efficacy dimensions of the JTE-TES	77
Table 6.2	JTE-TES items informed by the TSES	83
Table 7.1	Correlations between English proficiency and JTE-TES factors	91
Table 7.2	Summary of regression analysis for variables predicting Using English	97
Table 8.1	Summary of regression analysis for variables predicting Communicative Teaching	108
Table 8.2	Summary of regression analysis for variables predicting Student Achievement	111
Table 9.1	Summary of regression analysis for variables predicting Teamwork	124
Table 10.1	Correlation matrix: JTE-TES dimensions and experience with CLT	136
Table 11.1	Suggestions for future research	151

Figures

Figure 2.1	Conceptual framework of self-efficacy assessment	17
Figure 4.1	Summary of the research design	50

Figure 5.1　Processes used to develop the JTE-TES　　61
Figure 7.1　Predictors of the use of English as the language
　　　　　　of instruction　　95
Figure 11.1 Predictors of JTE-TES dimensions　　149

Abbreviations and Japanese Terms

Abbreviations

ALT	Assistant language teacher
AR	Action research
BOE	Board of education
CLT	Communicative language teaching
COS	Course of Study
CTE	Collective teacher efficacy
EAL	English as an additional language
EFL	English as a foreign language
EI	Emotional intelligence
Eiken	Test in practical English proficiency
ESL	English as a second language
IELTS	International English language testing system
JET programme	Japan exchange and teaching programme
JTE	Japanese high school teacher of English
L1	First or native language
L2	Additional, foreign or second language
LTE	Language teacher efficacy
LTSE	Language teacher self-efficacy
MEXT	Japanese Ministry of Education, Culture, Sports, Science and Technology
MOE	Japanese Ministry of Education
PLC	Professional learning community
SCT	Social cognitive theory
SELHi	Super English language high school
TOEIC	Test of English for international communication
TSE	Teacher self-efficacy

Japanese terms

Gakunen kyoin — A term used to denote a group of teachers working together to design materials and assessments for one cohort of students (e.g. first-year students). It is commonly used at high schools to indicate a group of teachers who coordinate activities and teaching.

Hensachi — This index refers to a standardised rank score, which is usually based on the difficulty of the entrance examination to the school. It is commonly used for considering the academic level of a school as higher *hensachi* indicates higher academic level.

Jitsuyo Eigo Gino Kentei — The Japanese name for the test in practical English proficiency, referred to in this text as the 'Eiken' test.

Kyotenko — A term used to designate a school as a 'model' for implementing curricula reforms, usually with support from the Ministry of Education, Culture, Sports, Science and Technology, or the local board of education.

Yakudoku — This term literally means 'translation through reading', and refers to grammar-translation methodology with a long history of use in Japan.

About the Author

Gene Thompson is an associate professor of language and communication in the College of Business at Rikkyo University, Japan. He holds a Doctor of Philosophy in Education from Queensland University of Technology in Brisbane, Australia. He also has a postgraduate diploma in Second Language Teaching and a masters in Applied Linguistics from the University of Waikato, New Zealand.

His research on language learner and teacher cognitions started from his involvement as a teacher educator in Hiroshima, where he worked with pre-service elementary school teachers and consulted for city and prefectural boards of education. Gene continues to examine learner and teacher cognitions about language learning.

This is Gene's first book. He has published in international journals such as *Studies in Higher Education*, *Asia-Pacific Journal of Teacher Education* and the *International Journal of Bilingual Education and Bilingualism*. He maintains an interest in the teaching of English as an international language, and has co-authored a number of entries in the *TESOL Encyclopedia of English Language Teaching*. He has also co-authored a chapter focused on translation fidelity for multilingual data collection and analysis in *The Routledge Handbook of Research Methods in Applied Linguistics*.

Acknowledgments

The research reported in this book could not have been carried out without the help of many busy English teachers across Japan, who kindly volunteered their time to participate in the studies reported in this book.

As much of the work reported in this book is derived from collaborative research efforts, I wish to thank Karen Woodman, Karen Dooley, Rebecca Spooner-Lane and Mayuno Yanagita for their contributions to the research presented here.

I also wish to thank the series editors Sarah Mercer and Stephen Ryan, who gave me valuable feedback and helped make this book more readable.

Finally, thank you to Mayuko and Alec, for putting up with me.

Preface

This book introduces readers to the developing field of language teacher efficacy (LTE) research. Teacher efficacy has been extensively studied within the wider field of education; however, it has received less attention within the field of applied linguistics. This book helps readers to locate language teacher efficacy within the field of teacher efficacy research, and focuses on the Japanese high school language teaching context. It discusses personal and collective dimensions of language teacher efficacy related to personal second language (L2) capability, instructional L2 efficacy and collective capability towards collaboration. This book presents previously unpublished research exploring the factors that influence language teacher efficacy, with discussion about the ways in which these beliefs develop.

Teacher efficacy is discussed in this book as a type of self-efficacy, and refers to the self-beliefs of teachers about their perceived capability to execute actions and achieve valued teaching outcomes, via personal and collective effort (Bandura, 1997, 2006). A variety of terms have been used in the applied linguistics research literature to refer to the self-efficacy for teaching beliefs of language teachers, such as teaching self-efficacy (e.g. Hiver, 2013), English as a foreign language (EFL) teacher self-efficacy (e.g. Hoang, 2018), language teacher self-efficacy (e.g. Wyatt, 2018b) and EFL teacher collective efficacy (e.g. Göker, 2012). This book uses the term language teacher efficacy (LTE) as it aligns with the use of the term 'teacher efficacy' to refer to teacher self-efficacy beliefs in the wider fields of education and psychology; can be used to discuss efficacy as individual or collective beliefs; and can be applied to a variety of language teaching contexts (e.g. English as a second language [ESL], EFL and the teaching of languages other than English).

My Interest in Language Teacher Efficacy

This book, and the research presented here, came about from my experience as a teacher educator in Japan, during a period of curriculum reform that mandated L2-speaking teachers, at the high school level, to use English as the primary language for carrying out their classes. As a contributor to teacher training workshops, I met many highly motivated teachers giving up their weekends to attend seminars and attempt to learn useful new teaching strategies in preparation for the new curriculum. However, I also met teachers – many of whom were forced to attend such workshops – who were the opposite.

I began to see a difference in the respective 'confidence' of teachers towards the different teaching tasks that the new curriculum guidelines encouraged. I began to wonder how confident are they about using English to teach? How confident are they about developing new activities? How can I further investigate confidence towards different teaching tasks?

My focus on teacher 'confidence' further developed out of a collaborative project I carried out with a high school Japanese teacher of English (JTE) during the early 2010s (see Thompson & Yanagita, 2017). The teacher was struggling to understand exactly how to apply communicative language teaching (CLT) in her classes, and as noted in other studies (Cook, 2009; Underwood, 2012), she faced resistance towards implementing change in materials design and teaching from her colleagues, who preferred to rely on the grammar-translation teaching method called *yakudoku*. The teacher asked me to work with her as a mentor, and from my participant-observer status, I became interested in the change in her 'confidence' over the course of the project, as I learned about the broader teaching environment within which she worked.

I surveyed the teacher cognition literature in order to identify a theoretical construct that specifically discussed the interaction between teachers' perceptions of confidence, their teaching behaviour and how these were dynamically influenced by the contexts that they worked within. As a result, I developed an interest in language teacher efficacy, which I define as the beliefs that teachers have about their perceived capability to organise and carry out courses of action in order to effectively support the development of student L2 language ability.

As Bandura (1997) has explained, feelings about experience (i.e. affective states) help shape and determine beliefs, and teacher self-beliefs have been argued as key mediators of teacher behaviour (Borg, 2003, 2006). Given the dynamic relationship between affect, beliefs and practice, the teacher efficacy research reported in this book grew out of a desire to explore what influenced JTEs' self-beliefs about their capability to effectively teach English in their classrooms.

Overview of the Book

This book discusses findings from a sequential mixed method study of the self-efficacy for teaching beliefs of Japanese high school English language teachers. Certain chapters may be of more interest to different readers, and accordingly each is written in such a way that readers can visit and draw on different chapters without needing to read the entire book. I know that I seldom read a research book in full, and certainly not in one sitting, thus I have attempted to write this book as a series of integrated chapters that do not necessarily require the reader to read each page of each chapter.

The book has 11 chapters. The first chapter introduces the reader to the context of the study, including the background of the research discussed in this book, contextual features of the Japanese language teaching environment and how this study of language teacher efficacy developed from an interest in language teacher 'confidence' towards the use of the L2 for language instruction.

Chapter 2 introduces readers to teacher efficacy within the theoretical framework of social cognitive theory (Bandura, 1986, 1997, 2006) by tracing a brief history of teacher efficacy research, discussing the theoretical basis of efficacy beliefs as mediators of behaviour and considering the sources and assessment of efficacy beliefs. Chapter 3 then focuses specifically on language teacher efficacy beliefs, and further discusses the ideas raised in Chapter 2 by focusing on research carried out within the field of language teaching. It highlights the ways in which the current study contributes to knowledge within this developing field, and suggests some areas where further study is needed.

The following two chapters move from the *why* and *what* towards the *how*. Chapter 4 discusses conceptual and measurement considerations for LTE researchers, introduces some approaches for examining language teacher efficacy and, as an example, provides the research design for the study discussed in this book, including discussion about the limitations of the research.

One concern for teacher efficacy researchers is how to design surveys with strong construct and cultural validity that reflect the actual tasks where teacher efficacy beliefs operate in specific settings. Chapter 5 introduces the design process of the efficacy scale used in the research reported in this book. The Japanese Teacher of English Teacher Efficacy Scale (JTE-TES) represents an attempt to design a scale with task and contextual relevance for a specific population (i.e. for Japanese teachers of English). However, given that many of the challenges faced by JTEs are reflective of difficulties faced by language teachers in various contexts, the scale may also have utility for examining language teacher efficacy in other countries and teaching situations.

Chapter 6 discusses efficacy towards different teaching tasks, and introduces various domains of language teacher efficacy. Three of these dimensions are further explored in Chapters 7–9. Chapter 7 examines efficacy towards the use of the L2 as part of the teaching process, Chapter 8 discusses L2 instructional efficacy and Chapter 9 focuses on L2 teacher efficacy beliefs towards collaboration. In each of these chapters, both the dimension of efficacy and factors that may influence these beliefs are examined.

Chapter 10 focuses on the development of language teacher efficacy beliefs. This chapter synthesises findings from interviews with teachers and teacher consultants working in Japan, to discuss the sources of efficacy beliefs and their development. It notes the strong influence of social forces on teacher efficacy beliefs in the Japanese context, contributing to a growing discussion about the potential role of cultural forces as an influence on the development of teacher efficacy beliefs.

Finally, this book concludes by looking forward. Chapter 11 provides a brief summary of the main contributions of this study, before providing suggestions for future language teacher efficacy research. The research presented in this book highlights the multidimensional nature of language teacher efficacy beliefs, and identifies a number of personal and contextual variables that could be explored in future studies, both within Japan and in the wider field of language education.

1 Introduction

Teachers are people; they make choices about the courses of action they pursue in trying to influence student achievement. They have agency. By proactively carrying out and reflecting on actions they take, they not only react to environmental forces, but also have the capacity to exercise control and effect change by setting goals and regulating their teaching behaviours (Bandura, 1991). They work with students, as part of teams, and within the confines of classrooms using the technology and resources available to them. As such, they are crucial contributors to what happens in their classrooms (Bandura, 1997), and in many cases, may be the strongest outside influence on the success of their students (Hattie, 2003). The beliefs and practices of teachers have therefore become a key area of research activity.

Teacher efficacy refers to the confidence that teachers have in their capability to organise and carry out educational activities to influence student learning. The application of teacher efficacy to the language teaching field began during the early 2000s (e.g. Chacon, 2005) and has now reached a point at which reviews of language teacher efficacy (LTE) research are being released (e.g. Hoang, 2018; Wyatt, 2018b). This book introduces the reader to this developing field, with a focus on the LTE beliefs of Japanese high school teachers of English (JTEs).

This book helps readers to locate LTE within its theoretical framework (Chapter 2), explains key findings from LTE research (Chapter 3) and outlines approaches to investigate LTE beliefs (Chapter 4). It then introduces an efficacy scale developed specifically for language teachers (Chapter 5), and highlights the multidimensional nature of LTE beliefs (Chapter 6), before focusing on personal and collective domains of efficacy related to perceived second language (L2) capability (Chapter 7), instructional L2 efficacy (Chapter 8) and language teacher beliefs about collaborative capability (Chapter 9). It finishes by discussing how LTE beliefs can be developed (Chapter 10) and highlights areas for future study (Chapter 11).

This chapter introduces the background to the study, highlighting key difficulties of policy and methodology change within (and beyond) Japan, before discussing the rationale for studying LTE beliefs towards such challenges. Although this chapter focuses on language education reform efforts (and research) from the Japanese context, it also attempts to show how such movements reflect wider trends in the language teaching field.

1.1 Background of the Study

English has become a global language of business, science and education. Foreign language – and specifically English – skill has become a commodity that enables transnational mobility for individuals with sufficient ability (Cameron, 2012). As a result, in many countries where English is used as a foreign language (such as Japan), policies have been introduced during the past 30 years with the specific purpose of encouraging the development of foreign language 'communicative' ability in students (e.g. see Hato, 2005; Kirkpatrick & Bui, 2016; Nunan, 2003).

These policies have generally emphasised oral communication in response to a perceived need for 'communicative' skills during this period of globalisation (Cameron, 2002), often due to requests from business groups, such as the Japan Business Federation (2000), who bemoaned the lack of English language ability in Japan. At the same time, there was a shift within language teaching towards communicative language teaching (CLT), an approach that focuses on meaning and authentic language use during language instruction (Richards, 2006; Richards & Schmidt, 2002). CLT was derived from L2 acquisition research that emphasised the negotiation of meaning as a crucial aspect of language development (Canale & Swain, 1980; Hymes, 1972; Krashen, 1981), resulting in a change in teaching methodology and policy.

Primarily, reform efforts have been introduced as part of new (and revised) national curricula. For example, policies emphasising the teaching of CLT were introduced in China, Hong Kong, Japan, Malaysia, Singapore, South Korea, Taiwan and Vietnam (see Butler, 2011; Nunan, 2003). Beyond Asia, similar efforts have been implemented in countries across Africa, South America and in the Indian subcontinent (see Diallo, 2014; Kamhi-Stein *et al.*, 2017; Obaidul Hamid, 2010). Within Japan, curriculum guidelines are known as the *Course of Study* (COS). New guidelines for secondary schools were introduced in the late 1990s (Ministry of Education, 1999) with further reforms in the early 2000s by the amalgamated Ministry of Education, Culture, Sports, Science and Technology (2002), referred to using the acronym 'MEXT' in this book. These reforms specifically emphasised the importance of CLT as a means of developing the foreign language communicative ability of Japanese.

1.1.1 Challenges to CLT implementation

Unsurprisingly, such reforms created a range of challenges for teachers and administrators, including significant gaps between classroom realities and policy intentions. Similar to the experience of other countries (e.g. Bangladesh, Hong Kong, Senegal, see Diallo, 2014; Mok-Cheung, 2001; Obaidul Hamid, 2010), change in teaching and assessment within Japan has not necessarily followed policy directives. A substantial body of teacher cognition research investigated Japanese teachers' beliefs and practices during the 2000s (e.g. Kurihara & Samimy, 2007; Nishino, 2008; Nishino & Watanabe, 2008; Sakui, 2004; Taguchi, 2002) with a focus on the implementation of CLT at the high school level and the difficulties that teachers had in implementing communicative-focused language learning. A number of structural problems were shown to limit the integration of communicative teaching in Japanese and secondary school classrooms: (1) the continuing orientation on university entrance preparation in classes at the expense of communicative activities (Brown & Yamashita, 1995; Nishino, 2008; Underwood, 2012); (2) the continuation and reliance on teacher-fronted grammar-translation (*yakudoku*) teaching techniques (Gorsuch, 2001; Kikuchi & Browne, 2009; Thompson & Yanagita, 2017); (3) a lack of knowledge about how to implement or adapt CLT to context-appropriate teaching practices (Sakui, 2004; Taguchi, 2002, 2005); (4) resistance to innovation (Cook, 2009; Sato & Kleinsasser, 2004; Underwood, 2012); and (5) poor pre-service and in-service teacher training (Kizuka, 2006; Lamie, 1998; Yonesaka, 1999).

These challenges are not limited to Japan. The difficulty of implementing CLT while attending to examination preparation appears to be broadly transferable to a range of teaching contexts (e.g. see Carless, 2007; Hatipoglu, 2016; Li, 1998). Collaborative action, whether that involves team teaching, text selection or group materials design (e.g. see Honigsfeld & Dove, 2012; Kamhi-Stein *et al.*, 2017; Nunan, 1992), is another domain of activity common to many – if not most – language teaching contexts. Pre-service and in-service training experiences (e.g. see Diallo, 2014; Li & Baldauf, 2011; Obaidul Hamid, 2010), and a reliance on teacher-fronted instruction (e.g. see Li, 1998; Li & Baldauf, 2011; Orafi & Borg, 2009), are also commonly cited factors that have limited 'communicative' curriculum implementation in a variety of language teaching contexts across Asia, Africa and the Middle East.

Another effort to develop greater mutual 'international' understanding and English language skill improvement in Japan was the introduction of the Japan Exchange and Teaching (JET) programme in 1986, which involves having 'native'-speaking (i.e. L1) non-Japanese work as assistant language teachers (ALTs) in English classes at elementary and secondary schools. These instructors work with Japanese teachers in the planning and implementation of lessons, that is, they are involved with collaborative materials design and team teaching. Similar programmes have been introduced in Hong Kong (where such teachers are known as native-speaking English teachers [NETs], see Carless & Walker, 2006; Nunan, 2003), and as part of the English Programme in Korea (EPIK) in South Korea (see Carless, 2006). The successes and difficulties of the JET and associated team teaching programmes represent a book in themselves, but generally speaking ALTs often perceive themselves to be sidelined. Team teaching represents a significant challenge for both the local Japanese and non-Japanese ALT teachers; communication difficulties and differences in the perception of each other's role are two key problems (see Carless, 2006; Mahoney, 2004; Moote, 2003). These issues have been noted in other countries (e.g. in China, see Rao & Chen, 2019), and given that team teaching is now expanding beyond Asia (e.g. Chile, see Barahona, 2017) and may grow in use due to the integration of content and language learning (see Fan & Lo, 2015; MacDonald et al., 2012), team teaching – and the associated challenges of collaborative planning and instruction – may become of greater importance for language education researchers.

1.1.2 English as a medium of instruction

Historically, English classes at Japanese high schools have been mediated in Japanese. Reflecting the movement across Asia towards English medium instruction (see Hu & McKay, 2012), a new *Course of Study* (MEXT, 2011b) was announced in 2011 which mandated that from 2013, high school English classes should be conducted 'primarily' in English. The English translation of the MEXT (2011b: 3) curriculum guidelines stated, 'when taking into consideration the characteristics of each English subject, classes, in principle, should be conducted in English'.

The announcement of the new guidelines led many to speculate that teachers would not or could not make such a shift in teaching practice. In a series of studies, Glasgow (2012, 2013, 2014) showed that JTEs themselves felt underprepared for the introduction of the new curriculum, and lacked 'confidence' in their ability to implement the guidelines. Specifically, teachers discussed a lack of confidence in their perceived L2 ability (Benesse Educational Research and Development Institute, 2011; Glasgow, 2014), and the MEXT itself recognised that only 24% of junior high school and 49% of senior high school teachers had attained the required English proficiency benchmark level (Commission on the Development of Foreign Language Proficiency, 2011). Quite simply, it seemed that many teachers just did not feel that they had sufficient L2 resources, or experiences, to use the L2 as a teaching language. Other research (Underwood, 2012) highlighted the social context of teacher practice, indicating that teacher intentions towards the implementation of the new curriculum were influenced by the teams that they worked with – where social pressure and school culture may lead teachers to reject making changes to their teaching practice.

This shift towards L2-mediated L2 instruction in Japan is similar to reforms being implemented in other countries – with similar difficulties arising. Indonesia, Hong Kong, South Korea and Nepal (see Baldauf *et al.*, 2011; Choi, 2015; Hamid *et al.*, 2013) are examples of countries that are moving towards – or have implemented – English medium instruction during compulsory English language education. South Korea is one of the leaders in this movement and has been steadily introducing curriculum changes regarding the teaching of English as a foreign language (EFL; see Choi, 2015; Kim, 2008). Teachers have been required to use English as the primary teaching language since the mid-2000s, stimulating a significant amount of research about the impact of the policy on teachers (e.g. Choi, 2015; Kim, 2008; Shin, 2012). Research findings highlight the transferability of key challenges across contexts, as similar difficulties have been found in South Korea as those noted above for Japan. For example, teachers have had difficulty in adapting CLT to match the local context (Li, 1998), often because no specific *methodology* is prescribed in the guidelines beyond a mandate to employ a CLT approach (Choi & Andon, 2014). Similar concerns about a lack of L2 proficiency appear to limit the teaching behaviour of Korean teachers (Choi & Lee, 2016; Kim, 2008), while other research (Shin, 2012) has noted that teachers work primarily within teams – many of which may not support curriculum changes – leading to policies not being implemented.

1.1.3 Teacher beliefs and teaching practice

Throughout this process, a wide body of research about teacher cognitions – defined by Borg (2003: 81) as 'what teachers know, believe and think' – has been carried out. This is due to the generally accepted assumption that the beliefs of teachers are a key influence on their judgements of pedagogic practice and teaching behaviours (see Pajares, 1992). However, extant research of the relationship between teacher beliefs and practice from the wider field of education (e.g. Chen, 2008; Fang, 1996; Shi *et al.*, 2014), within the smaller field of language teaching (e.g. Basturkmen, 2012; Basturkmen *et al.*, 2004; Farrell & Bennis, 2013), and of language teachers in Japan (e.g. Sakui, 2004, 2007; Taguchi, 2002, 2005) has often revealed significant inconsistencies between teachers' reported beliefs and behaviours.

With respect to CLT and the integration of the L2 into teaching practice, research from Japan (e.g. Nishino & Watanabe, 2008; Sakui, 2004; Taguchi, 2005) and other language teaching contexts (e.g. Hong Kong and Libya, see Mak, 2011; Orafi & Borg, 2009) has often shown a divergence between (generally) positive teacher beliefs *about* CLT or the integration of 'communicative' activities and teachers *actual* classroom practices, which are often teacher fronted with a focus on knowledge transmission. Conflicting beliefs and contextual influences often appear to account for these inconsistencies. For example, in a study of three EFL teachers in Libya, Orafi and Borg (2009) identified positive beliefs in two participants about pair work; however, due to negative perceptions of student capability, the teachers explained that they avoided such activities. As examinations assessed students' receptive skills, teachers emphasised preparation via translation and knowledge transmission, rather than making use of opportunities for English usage. Similar patterns are noted by Basturkmen (2012), who reviewed the relationship between language teacher beliefs and practices, finding that contextual (e.g. examination pressure and colleague support) and personal (e.g. perceived L2 ability) factors often influenced the extent to which beliefs and practices were in alignment.

Teacher cognition research has highlighted key insights into the (sometimes conflicting) beliefs of language teachers, and has helped identify important personal and contextual challenges that may limit implementation. However, one limitation – particularly in Japan – has been linking teacher self-beliefs with their intentions and/or practice. This may be due to the decontextualised manner in which beliefs have been investigated. To illustrate, some studies have compared teacher beliefs *about* curriculum changes or teaching approaches and their perception of confidence *towards* implementation (e.g. Glasgow, 2014; Hamamoto, 2012), finding that positive attitudes towards such policies or approaches were often not aligned with (negative) teacher confidence to implement them. In other words, although teachers may have positive beliefs about teaching approaches or activities when considered in a general manner, they may have weak confidence about putting them into action. This may be due to teachers assessing the influence of contextual factors (e.g. school setting, social support) and their personal ability (e.g. teaching skill, L2 knowledge) when assessing their confidence for implementation, rather than simply their beliefs about the value of the approach.

1.1.4 Teacher 'confidence'

As greater attention has been turned to teaching via the L2, researchers within and beyond Japan (e.g. Butler, 2011; Glasgow, 2014; Prapaisit de Segovia & Hardison, 2008; Zein, 2017) have discussed a lack of 'confidence' towards teaching in English and the implementation of CLT. Others have discussed how L2 teacher 'confidence' can be developed as part of in-service training programmes, suggesting that teacher confidence directly influences teaching behaviour (e.g. Burns, 2017; Freeman, 2017; Freeman *et al.*, 2015).

However, although research has indicated a link between confidence and teaching practice, few studies have considered the relationship within a theoretical framework of beliefs and practices. For example, a number of studies have discussed a lack of 'confidence' in teachers (e.g. Prapaisit de Segovia & Hardison, 2008; Slaouti & Barton, 2007; Zein, 2017), or examined factors that appear to influence confidence (e.g. Butler, 2011; Glasgow, 2014; Kurihara & Samimy, 2007; Nagamine, 2007), without discussing or defining what is meant *by* teacher confidence. Thus, while it seemed that 'teacher confidence' is an important construct that may influence teaching behaviour – particularly with respect to the implementation of L2 medium instruction – it also seemed clear that a deeper exploration of these beliefs was necessary. This represented the starting point for the research reported in this book, which began with the purpose to examine Japanese high school English teachers' 'confidence' for teaching English, in response to calls for further examination of Japanese teacher self-beliefs against the backdrop of the 2013 *Course of Study* curriculum guidelines (Glasgow, 2014; Nishino, 2012).

1.2 Why Study Teacher Efficacy?

Confidence is a general term that refers to the certainty of a belief (Cramer *et al.*, 2009: 322), not what the belief is about (Bandura, 1997). Furthermore, perceptions of self-confidence reflect beliefs about oneself, rather than beliefs towards the achievement of a task or outcome (Schunk, 1991). Thus, a language teacher with strong 'self-confidence' may believe that they are a competent teacher, but may have little confidence towards implementing English medium instruction in their classroom. As a result, such a belief may not predict their behaviour, as the specific teaching task and context are not necessarily represented by the self-belief.

1.2.1 Teacher efficacy is a type of task-focused confidence

Teacher efficacy, on the other hand, can be considered as the confidence (i.e. perception of certainty) that teachers have in their ability to carry out tasks in the pursuit of teaching outcomes. Teacher efficacy is type of self-efficacy (Bandura, 1977, 1986, 1997), a self-belief construct derived from the field of psychology focused on the cognitive perceptions of individuals to organising and executing the 'courses of action required to produce given attainments' (Bandura, 1997: 3). As Wyatt (2018a) has noted, one value of teacher efficacy is its task and context specificity. Language teachers may feel stronger or weaker confidence towards different tasks or areas of professional practice. For example, English medium instruction policies may require teachers to make radical changes to some of their behaviours. By investigating their efficacy towards different tasks (e.g. giving instructions, correcting student work) or dimensions (e.g. towards classroom management, instructional strategies), research can highlight specific areas of practice where efficacy is strong or weak. Such findings not only contribute to knowledge in the field, but may also be vital for driving development efforts; by identifying areas where teacher efficacy is weak, teacher education programmes can target specific tasks or domains of activity.

1.2.2 Teacher efficacy beliefs and teacher behaviour

Furthermore, efficacy beliefs have generally been shown to be a stronger predictor of behaviour in comparison to other self-belief constructs (e.g. see Pajares & Kranzler, 1995; Pajares & Miller, 1994; Thompson *et al.*, 2019). As a result, teacher efficacy research may help bridge the mismatches identified between teacher self-beliefs and practices. There is significant evidence that teacher efficacy beliefs mediate teacher action, effort and also student achievement. As discussed further in Chapters 2 and 3, research from the wider field of education has shown that teacher efficacy beliefs are associated with greater persistence (Enochs *et al.*, 1995; Mulholland & Wallace, 2001; Woolfolk Hoy & Davis, 2006), openness to innovation and change (Ghaith & Yaghi, 1997; Guskey, 1988; Skaalvik & Skaalvik, 2007) and higher student achievement (Bolshakova *et al.*, 2011; Chang, 2015; Goddard *et al.*, 2000).

Despite such findings, LTE is a relatively underdeveloped area of research (Mercer & Kostoulas, 2018). Although few studies have investigated the link between LTE and teaching practice, two studies have found LTE beliefs to mediate (Nishino, 2012) and moderate (Choi & Lee, 2016) the influence of other self-perceptions and skills on language teaching behaviour. In an important study of teacher beliefs and reported behaviour carried out in Japan, Nishino (2009, 2012) found that positive beliefs about CLT had no direct influence on classroom practices, but that these beliefs did *indirectly* affect classroom practices via teacher efficacy beliefs towards CLT. Furthermore, the study showed interrelationships between contextual (e.g. perceptions of student ability) and personal (e.g. perceived L2 ability) factors. As a result, the construct of teacher efficacy may be useful for helping to connect teacher beliefs with their teaching behaviour and other variables.

1.2.3 Teacher efficacy beliefs operate within a theoretical framework

As a belief construct, self-efficacy developed from a desire to understand and influence behavioural *change* (see Bandura, 1977), and is located within a theoretical system that recognises the interactions between behaviour, context and other self-beliefs (Bandura, 1986, 1997, 2012). As a result, the relative impact of different personal and contextual variables can be examined on these beliefs. By investigating the relationship between such factors on efficacy beliefs and teacher behaviour, knowledge can be used to inform teacher development efforts.

As discussed further in Chapter 2, self-efficacy is a key component of Bandura's (1986) social cognitive theory (SCT), a psychological theory of human agency and learning which views individuals' self-beliefs about their capabilities as crucial for exercising control of their lives. Efficacy beliefs not only influence motivation, effort and action, but can also be strengthened and developed based on attributions from experience, feedback and affective responses (Bandura, 1997; Pajares, 1996; Usher & Pajares, 2009). These attributions inform efficacy assessment, as individuals consider the skills and capability to manage task conditions that they perceive to be available to them (Bandura, 1997; Gist & Mitchell, 1992). Simply put, individuals who perceive themselves to have sufficient skills will be more likely to have stronger confidence towards task success, and vice versa.

As a result, teacher efficacy beliefs are likely to be reliant on individuals perceiving themselves to have appropriate knowledge and skills for successful completion of a task. These may be personal abilities, such as L2 or pedagogic knowledge. Within the small body of LTE research, a common finding has been a positive relationship between L2 proficiency and the strength of teacher efficacy beliefs (Chacon, 2005; Choi & Lee, 2016; Eslami & Fatahi, 2008). For example, in the Nishino study (2009, 2012), teacher 'L2 self-confidence' was also found to influence CLT teacher efficacy beliefs, and therefore indirectly influence teacher practice. Such a relationship between perceived personal language ability, CLT teacher efficacy and teaching behaviour is intuitive. However, it may be an important factor, as teacher L2 proficiency difficulties appear to contribute to the challenge of implementing CLT and English medium instruction, within and beyond Japan (e.g. see Baldauf *et al.*, 2011; Butler, 2011; Hamid *et al.*, 2013).

Successful task completion also involves negotiating contextual difficulties. Teachers may need specific strategies for dealing with the materials or equipment available for use. Language teachers, in particular, may work with highly motivated groups, or learners forced to study a language with little desire to master it (Wyatt, 2018a). Such challenges may strongly impact efficacy (i.e. beliefs about capability to bring about actions to stimulate learner L2 development) as teachers struggle to identify and implement effective teaching behaviours to negotiate contextual demands. Few studies have examined the influence of contextual factors on LTE beliefs; studies have considered the type of school (Chong *et al.*, 2010; Moradkhani & Haghi, 2017; Nishino, 2009) and professional support (Göker, 2006; Shin, 2012), leading to calls for research to examine other potential influences on LTE beliefs (Choi & Lee, 2016; Moradkhani & Haghi, 2017; Nishino, 2011). By better understanding how personal and contextual variables influence beliefs of perceived capability, efficacy research may be able to provide insights for teacher development programmes.

In summary, teacher efficacy research can stimulate knowledge about teacher confidence towards different tasks, and there is strong evidence that these beliefs connect with teacher practice. Research has shown that teacher efficacy beliefs can be strengthened (Bautista & Boone, 2015; Morris & Usher, 2011; Tschannen-Moran & McMaster, 2009), leading to *change* in teaching behaviour (Wyatt, 2013b, 2015; Wyatt & Dikilitaş, 2015). As a result, efficacy beliefs are not only of academic interest, but may also have importance for those with an interest in teacher development and the successful implementation of new policies, such as the English medium instruction initiatives of Japan and other countries.

1.2.4 Need for more teacher efficacy research

There remains much to be learned about LTE. Klassen *et al.* (2011) have suggested that a number of challenges remain for teacher efficacy researchers. The authors highlighted six key areas for efficacy researchers to attend to:

(1) Resolution of conceptual/measurement problems.
(2) Attention to domain specificity.
(3) Investigation of the sources of teacher efficacy.
(4) Increased attention on collective efficacy research.
(5) Internationalisation of teacher efficacy research.
(6) More diverse methodologies.

The research discussed in this book represents one attempt to respond to a number of these challenges. This book discusses a new measure for examining LTE that was created in accordance with Bandura's guidelines for efficacy scale development (i.e. Area 1); explores the dimensions of LTE beliefs (i.e. Area 2); examines factors that may influence LTE efficacy beliefs, including sources of information that inform LTE (i.e. Area 3); identifies and discusses a collective dimension of LTE related to collaborative practice (i.e. Area 4); and represents one of the first studies of LTE beliefs carried out in Japan (i.e. Area 5). The study also uses a sequential mixed method design, drawing on multiple means of data analysis (i.e. Area 6).

Given the predictive role of efficacy beliefs on performance, and the cyclical nature of efficacy belief development, suggestions for teacher development are presented with discussion of key findings. Much work remains for LTE researchers, and Chapter 11 provides a number of suggestions on how knowledge can be extended within this developing field via future research.

1.3 Chapter Summary

The movement within language teaching towards English medium instruction, including government policies for English education that require L2-speaking teachers to use English as the teaching language, has seen a change in the demands placed on teachers. This movement has generated a resurgence in interest about teacher L2 proficiency (e.g. Freeman *et al.*, 2015; Katz, 2017; Richards, 2017), teacher knowledge and instructional strategies (Choi & Andon, 2014; Humphries & Burns, 2015), and how these interact with teacher behaviour (Nishino, 2012). This book contributes to understanding how these factors interact, by providing an in-depth examination of the complex associations between teacher self-beliefs of perceived capability against personal and contextual variables that may influence these beliefs (e.g. personal past experiences).

These topics are discussed with respect to the Japanese high school English language teaching context, and accordingly, some of the findings presented may not be universal to other language teaching environments. Nevertheless, many of the challenges discussed in this book are likely to be present in other language teaching situations. For example, the difficulty of implementing CLT while attending to examination preparation is one faced by teachers across Asia (e.g. Hatipoglu, 2016; Li, 1998; Ramezaney, 2014). Collaborative action, whether that involves team teaching, text selection or group materials design (Honigsfeld & Dove, 2012; Kamhi-Stein *et al.*, 2017; Nunan, 1992), is another domain of activity common to most language teaching contexts.

As a developing field of study that bridges the applied linguistics and education psychology fields, there remains much to be learned about LTE beliefs and how these influence student learning. Research from a variety of teaching contexts has suggested that teacher efficacy beliefs are key mediators of behaviour, and as these beliefs can be developed via effective professional development programmes, the research discussed in this book is not only presented to extend academic knowledge about LTE beliefs, but also to highlight areas where development efforts can be targeted in order to equip language teachers with stronger agency beliefs as they attempt to bring about growth in students.

Within the applied linguistics field of language cognitions research, the use of teacher efficacy as a construct for investigating language teacher 'confidence' has a number of benefits. Teacher efficacy is a beliefs construct that has both theoretical and empirical support; it links beliefs, behaviour and context within a framework that shows how such beliefs can be developed (Bandura, 1986, 1997, 2001; Bandura *et al.*, 1977). The theorised process of efficacy assessment and development also broadly aligns with conceptual frameworks of language teacher cognition (Borg, 2003, 2006). Chapter 2 discusses the theoretical background of teacher efficacy in greater depth, presents a brief history of research within the general field (i.e. beyond language teaching) and shows the cyclical nature of the efficacy development process.

2 Teacher Efficacy as a Form of Self-Efficacy

This chapter helps the reader to locate teacher efficacy within its theoretical framework. As Borg (2003) has noted, definitional and conceptual clarity is an essential aspect of teacher belief research, and the lack of such clarity has been a recurring problem in teacher efficacy research (Klassen et al., 2011). The first section of this chapter introduces teacher efficacy with respect to its historical research context, shows how it is now viewed as a type of self-efficacy and discusses the theoretical underpinnings of efficacy beliefs by showing how teacher efficacy relates to social cognitive theory (SCT). The chapter then clarifies how efficacy beliefs differ from other self-beliefs, before introducing the reader to the process of efficacy belief development. The chapter concludes by providing a conceptual framework by which efficacy beliefs are assessed.

2.1 A Brief History: Two Views of Teacher Efficacy

Although teacher efficacy research now clearly reflects a self-efficacy orientation, it was born from two psychology theories related to control: Rotter's (1966) locus of control and Albert Bandura's (1977) self-efficacy theory. There was an early divergence in views about how the construct of teacher efficacy was viewed; one strand of research followed the locus of control distinction (i.e. the extent to which teachers perceived that they could influence student learning and achievement) while another strand of teacher efficacy research integrated Bandura's theory of self-efficacy (i.e. teacher's perceptions of capability to bring about the actions required for student learning and achievement to occur).

The first study to investigate 'teaching efficacy' was the 1976 Rand Corporation study (Armor et al., 1976) of reading programmes in Los Angeles. Two items were used to investigate differences between teachers regarding their outcome expectations:

(1) When it comes right down to it, a teacher really can't do much – most of a student's motivation and performance depends on his or her home environment

(2) If I try really hard, I can get through to even the most difficult or un-motivated students

(Armor *et al.*, 1976: 73)

The researchers identified that a key teacher factor was their belief that 'they could "get through" even to children with shaky motivation or home background' (Armor *et al.*, 1976: 38). They labelled this 'personal efficacy', and in a later Rand report, it was defined by Berman *et al.* (1977: 137) as 'the extent to which the teacher believes he or she has the capacity to affect student performance'. The Rand studies demonstrated the value of teacher control beliefs, spurred action into teacher efficacy research and later studies using the two Rand items showed significant relationships between stronger 'personal efficacy' and student achievement (e.g. Ashton & Webb, 1986).

At the same time as the Rand study was being carried out, Albert Bandura (1977) was developing his theory of self-efficacy to discuss the role of cognition as a psychological process in learning and regulating behaviour. For Bandura (1997: 3), the crucial aspect of human agency was the individual's beliefs in their personal efficacy, which he later defined as 'beliefs in one's capabilities to organize and execute the courses of action required to produce given attainments'. He argued that such beliefs act as cognitive mediators of behaviour, influencing action, effort, perseverance, resilience and stress coping strategies.

Bandura's self-efficacy theory led to a reevaluation of the Rand items and a reinterpretation of the construct of teacher efficacy. The Rand items were designed to reflect a locus of control orientation, by examining the extent to which respondents perceived internal versus external control of what could be achieved by teachers (see Berman *et al.*, 1977). However, the Rand study authors discussed 'personal efficacy' as a type of 'confidence', and noted that such teachers put forward extra (often special) efforts to help students because they were 'confident that their teaching would yield positive results' (Armor *et al.*, 1976: 38).

A number of researchers (Ashton *et al.*, 1983; Dembo & Gibson, 1985; Gibson & Dembo, 1984) used Bandura's (1977) self-efficacy theory to reinterpret the two Rand study items, arguing that self-efficacy theory provided a clearer conceptual framework. To these researchers, Item 1 'When it comes right down to it, a teacher really can't do much – most of a student's motivation and performance depends on his or her home environment' reflected *outcome expectancy*, while Item 2 'If I try really hard, I can get through to even the most difficult or un-motivated students' oriented towards *self-efficacy*, where such 'beliefs would be teachers' evaluation of their abilities to bring about positive student change' (Gibson & Dembo, 1984: 570).

Bandura (1977) had differentiated between 'outcome expectations' and 'efficacy expectations' by highlighting the difference between the effect on individual behaviour, where

> outcome expectancy is defined as a person's estimate that a given behaviour will lead to certain outcomes. An efficacy expectation is the conviction that one can successfully execute the behaviour required to produce the outcomes. Outcome and efficacy expectations are differentiated, because individuals can believe that a particular course of action will produce certain outcomes, but if they entertain serious doubts about whether they can perform the necessary activities such information does not influence their behaviour. (Bandura, 1977: 193)

In other words, the crucial aspect to Bandura was the extent to which individuals perceived that they have the necessary skills and competence to carry out actions in order to produce outcomes, rather than simply whether people believed that their actions produced outcomes. With respect to the two Rand items, teachers may reject Item 1, as they may believe that teachers can influence student achievement (i.e. strong outcome expectancy), but also disagree with Rand Item 2, as they may not have strong self-beliefs in their capability to effectively help lesser-motivated students (i.e. low personal efficacy). Accordingly, they may not put forth the effort to influence student learning.

Research findings have generally supported this distinction. Gibson and Dembo (1984) developed a 30-item questionnaire and tested this difference, using factor analysis to show that each of the Rand items loaded on separate factors. More recent studies (e.g. Ho & Hau, 2004; Skaalvik & Skaalvik, 2007) have subsequently shown perceived external control and teacher efficacy to be different constructs.

Finally, in a seminal article that brought the two teacher efficacy strands together, Tschannen-Moran et al. (1998: 22) argued that teacher efficacy should be conceptualised as a form of self-efficacy, defining it as the 'teacher's belief in his or her capability to organize and execute courses of action required to successfully accomplish a specific teaching task in a particular context'. Although the authors questioned whether the interpretation of the Rand Item 1 as outcome expectancy was appropriate, it seems clear that the interpretation of the Rand items as two distinct constructs started the realignment of the field towards a view of teacher efficacy as a form of self-efficacy.

Later, Tschannen-Moran and Woolfolk Hoy (2001) introduced the Teacher Sense of Efficacy Scale (TSES), an efficacy scale with long (24 item) and short (12 item) versions, from which exploratory factor analysis had identified three dimensions of teacher efficacy (Student Engagement, Instructional Strategies, Classroom Management). Developed by a team of researchers and graduate students at The Ohio State University (and originally called the Ohio State Teacher Efficacy Scale [OSTES]), this new means of assessing teacher efficacy would have a major impact on the field. Their article may be the most widely cited in the field (see Kleinsasser, 2014), and has stimulated research into teacher efficacy internationally (e.g. Cheung, 2006, 2008; Tsui & Kennedy, 2009), including studies of language teacher efficacy (e.g. Chacon, 2005; Swanson, 2010a; Yilmaz, 2011).

As research developed, it began to be recognised that teachers do not work alone; they work as part of teams. Bandura (1997) has suggested that efficacy beliefs influence the choices of individuals and organisations; therefore, teacher efficacy may be collective. Given the social structure and context of schools as social enterprises with numerous actors working together to help students learn and achieve, Goddard *et al.* (2000: 482) explained that 'collective efficacy is associated with the tasks, level of effort, persistence, shared thoughts, stress levels, and achievement of groups'. In a study of teachers carried out in Norway, Skaalvik and Skaalvik (2007) further explained the potential importance of perceived collective teacher efficacy, stating,

> teachers do not always work alone. In most Norwegian schools, teachers now work in teams sharing responsibility for a larger group of students. The actual instruction is partly done by individual teachers in smaller groups and partly by pairs of teachers in a larger group. Much of the organizing and the planning are done in teacher teams. The individual teachers' self-efficacy may therefore be dependent on the functioning of the team. (Skaalvik & Skaalvik, 2007: 613)

Thus, teacher capability has both individual and collective aspects, incorporating 'an organizational dimension' (Goddard *et al.*, 2004a: 4). Professional practice, teacher influence on instruction, text selection and materials development are examples of activities in which beliefs would be formed about the capability of the teaching faculty. These perceptions may affect the efficacy assessments of teachers, thus individual teacher efficacy may be influenced by team dynamics and beliefs about faculty capability.

Studies have demonstrated positive relationships between individual and collective efficacy (Goddard & Goddard, 2001; Skaalvik & Skaalvik, 2007), and indicated that collective efficacy may be crucial for curriculum change (Goddard *et al.*, 2004b). There is also evidence that stronger perceived collective efficacy is related to student achievement (Goddard, 2002; Goddard *et al.*, 2015; Tschannen-Moran & Barr, 2004). A series of meta-analyses (Hattie, 2012, 2015) have examined the relationship between student achievement and educational activities, identifying collective teacher efficacy to exert one of the strongest positive influences. Accordingly, this type of teacher efficacy appears to be a valuable area for future research and has many avenues for further exploration. Most collective teacher efficacy research has been carried out in the United States or in countries with similar cultural backgrounds (Klassen *et al.*, 2011), thus a greater understanding is needed about the relationship between individual and collective efficacy, and the areas where individual and collective teacher efficacy beliefs operate, in international (i.e. non-Western) contexts.

2.2 Teacher Efficacy within Social Cognitive Theory

The construct of self-efficacy is central to Bandura's (1986) SCT, which views individuals as active agents whose interpretations of the results of their performances inform and alter 'their environments, and self-beliefs, which in turn inform, and alter their subsequent performances' (Pajares, 1996: 542). SCT is based on a reciprocal relationship between behaviour, environment and personal factors (e.g. cognitive, biological), with each dynamically and bi-directionally interacting and influencing the others – what is known as 'triadic reciprocal causation' (Bandura, 1986).

Humans are capable of self-referent thought, with the capacity to regulate their effort and reflect on their activities. Thus, SCT rejects a behaviouralist view of the world, in which individuals primarily respond to their environments; it recognises that individuals can plan and have the capacity for self-influence. As Bandura (1997: 3) has stated, individuals' behaviour (e.g. teaching practice) is dynamically influenced by personal factors (e.g. available pedagogic skills) and the environment they are in (e.g. the school context), where 'people are contributors to, rather than the sole determiners of, what happens to them'. Simply put, individuals can shape and change their environments by using the skills they perceive to be available to them and choosing different courses of action. Thus, teachers can influence, but not determine, the learning that occurs within, and beyond, their classrooms.

An SCT perspective indicates that teacher beliefs (and other personal factors), behaviour and context reciprocally influence each other. In fact, such a view aligns with conceptual frameworks of language teacher beliefs, such as Borg's original (2003) and revised (Borg, 2006) models, which focus on the dynamic relationship between beliefs and contextualised behaviour. Thus, for language teachers, self-beliefs and perceptions of individual ability (e.g. of second language [L2] ability) may influence efficacy beliefs towards (or against) teaching tasks that require the teacher to act as a language model. The teacher's interpretation of the results of the behaviour (i.e. whether they are perceived to be successful or unsuccessful) may then influence beliefs and other individual factors (e.g. stronger perceived capability to achieve the task in the future). Furthermore, both may also be influenced by context (e.g. working at a

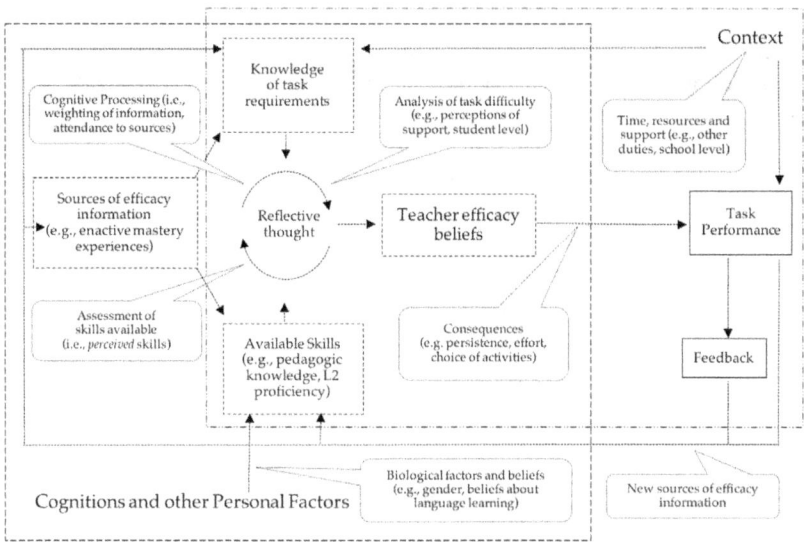

Figure 2.1 Conceptual framework of self-efficacy assessment

school with motivated students versus with students who have no desire or need to speak English). Thus, in the assessment of their efficacy beliefs, individuals are likely to weigh up the difficulty of carrying out the task (e.g. is it possible or valued?) and the expected outcome (i.e. will it be perceived to influence student learning and development?), alongside the skills they perceive available to use in achieving the task (see Figure 2.1).

Accordingly, self-efficacy beliefs are argued to influence agency, motivation and self-regulation, and to mediate states of anxiety. Agency is concerned with individuals' capacity to control and coordinate their actions, beliefs and emotions to reach goals. Therefore, agency is the driver of intentional acts (as opposed to outcomes, which may be unintended). Bandura (2001: 10) claimed that 'efficacy beliefs are the foundation of human agency' and summarised their importance, stating 'whatever other factors may operate as guides and motivators, they are rooted in the core belief that one has the power to produce effects by one's actions'. As self-efficacy beliefs are perceptions of capability, these beliefs influence choice and effort towards goals, that is, individuals 'regulate their level and distribution of effort in accordance with the effects they expect their actions to have' (Bandura, 1986: 129).

Efficacy beliefs have also been consistently shown to have a negative relationship with anxiety (Mills et al., 2006; Pajares & Kranzler, 1995; Swars et al., 2006). Such a relationship is not surprising, as people who perceive a negative emotional and threatening response towards a task (e.g. anxiety towards teaching via English) may also believe themselves less capable of bringing about actions to complete it. Thus, anxiety and other affective responses are likely to be influences on the development of efficacy beliefs. However, research has also indicated that efficacy beliefs mediate the impact of anxiety on performance (Pajares & Kranzler, 1995; Siegel *et al.*, 1985), as individuals with stronger capability to cope with task demands are also more likely to manage the negative influence of anxiety. This may be due to individuals responding to their self-doubts by 'acquiring knowledge and skills', which provide them with stronger perceived capability to manage the threatening situation (Bandura, 1997: 76).

Accordingly, self-efficacy beliefs are hypothesised to be key to motivation (Zimmerman, 2000), and their causal influence has been demonstrated in the wider psychological research literature (Pintrich & Schunk, 1996; Schunk, 1995) for language learning (Kormos *et al.*, 2011; Oxford & Shearin, 1994; Tremblay & Gardner, 1995) and for teaching (Skaalvik & Skaalvik, 2014). In summary, individuals with stronger perceived capability for specific tasks are more likely to choose and expend effort on such activities.

Research within the field of teacher efficacy has supported these ideas, as teachers with stronger efficacy beliefs towards a subject (or subject area) are more likely to be more persistent and spend greater time teaching it (Enochs *et al.*, 1995; Mulholland & Wallace, 2001; Woolfolk Hoy & Davis, 2006), and are likely to have stronger commitment to teaching (Chan *et al.*, 2008; Chesnut & Burley, 2015; Ware & Kitsantas, 2007). On the other hand, low teacher efficacy towards a subject is associated with spending less time teaching that subject area (Enochs & Riggs, 1990). Furthermore, findings have also supported a link between teacher and student efficacy and student achievement (Bolshakova *et al.*, 2011; Chang, 2015), indicating that teacher efficacy beliefs may influence not only teacher motivation and effort, but also student motivation.

2.3 How Efficacy Beliefs Differ from Other Self-Constructs

Although they are intertwined, self-constructs are generally divided by those that are primarily cognitive (i.e. centred on the knowledge and beliefs that individuals have about themselves and their abilities) versus those that are affective (i.e. primarily emotional and based on the feelings that people have about themselves, see Williams *et al.*, 2015). This section briefly discusses how self-efficacy can be differentiated from other self-constructs by orientation, domain and character of evaluation.

As a form of expectancy belief, efficacy expectations represent perceptions of capability to carry out actions in the pursuit of outcomes. Firstly, efficacy beliefs have a future orientation (Zimmerman, 2000); they involve individuals carrying out an evaluation of their personal skills towards (potential) future behaviours. Second, efficacy beliefs are context and task dependent; the strength of these beliefs varies by the teaching task and the situation within which it is carried out (see Wyatt, 2018a). Finally, as explained in Section 2.6 (also see Figure 2.1), they involve individuals carrying out internal cognitive appraisals of the task conditions and the skills that are required for successful completion.

This contrasts efficacy beliefs with other self-constructs, such as self-concept and self-esteem, which do not have a future orientation, but rather a descriptive function concerned with evaluations of one's competence (self-concept) and emotional self-worth (self-esteem). For example, Mercer (2008) explained that self-esteem has the strongest evaluative component, and is primarily affective, as it brings together the positive and negative feelings that people hold of themselves. Although self-esteem is also influenced by self-beliefs, these are primarily attitudinal (Rosenberg, 1965), in that self-esteem integrates a person's self-beliefs of their value or worth. For example, global self-esteem evaluations can be shown by statements such as 'I am a good person' (Leary & Downs, 1995: 124).

Self-concept refers to a 'general self-descriptive construct' that integrates both 'self-knowledge and self-evaluations' (Zimmerman, 2000: 84). Generally, self-concept is viewed as a hierarchy (Marsh & Shavelson, 1985) with 'global' self-concept at the top, which brings together the self-beliefs people have towards their competency in different domains. Self-concept centres around a person's evaluation of their abilities (Williams et al., 2015) and involves individuals comparing themselves with others – and against themselves – with respect to standards of competency and worth (Shavelson et al., 1976). Thus, while both self-concept and self-efficacy include the same central element (perceived competence), Mercer (2008) has explained that self-concept beliefs operate at a higher level, incorporating emotional and cognitive perceptions of competency towards a domain of activity (e.g. towards teaching). The normative assessment of evaluative competency means that self-concept is often assessed with items using 'I am good at …' (Pajares, 1996), reflecting beliefs about 'personal qualities' and competencies (Zimmerman, 2000: 83). A key component of self-concept involves the integration of comparative information about oneself or one's abilities within a domain, either versus others or personal benchmarks. On the other hand, self-efficacy refers to the self-beliefs of capability people have towards tasks, which come about from an assessment of their skills to successfully complete them. As a result, although social comparison plays a part in efficacy development (often vicariously, see Section 2.4), the assessment of self-belief is more focused on skills towards the task rather than beliefs about oneself.

Generally, efficacy beliefs have been shown to be stronger predictors of behaviour in comparison to other self-concept measures (Bandura, 1997; Bong & Skaalvik, 2003; Pajares & Miller, 1994) due to their strong task-focused nature. Bong and Skaalvik (2003) have suggested that self-efficacy is a better predictor of performance due to its future orientation and stronger task-focus specificity. As Zimmerman (2000: 84) has explained, an efficacy item may ask students to 'rate their certainty about solving a crossword puzzle of a particular difficulty level' while a self-concept item may ask them 'how well they expect to do on the puzzle in comparison to other students'. The first provides a measure of internal capability to complete a future task, while the second provides a perception of normative ranking. Accordingly, the relationship between the self-concept belief and actual behaviour may become less pronounced.

Efficacy beliefs can also be differentiated from self-confidence, as they reflect not only the strength of a belief, or of one's general capability, but also perceptions of capability towards a certain task. Confidence primarily 'reflects a degree of certainty about a perception, event, or outcome' (Cramer et al., 2009: 322), thus confidence itself is primarily concerned with belief strength (Merkle & Van Zandt, 2006); it does not necessarily include what the belief is about (Bandura, 1997).

Individual 'self-confidence' represents the strength of an individuals' belief in their personal capability or competence, and given the hierarchical nature of self-concept, self-confidence appears to be contributing towards general self-concept (Schunk, 1991). Thus, teachers with strong 'teacher self-confidence' may have a general belief that they have high competency as teachers (i.e. stronger teacher self-concept). However, such beliefs about self-confidence are not necessarily predictive of behaviour, as these do not consider the teaching task or context. In other words, such beliefs remain 'nondescript' (Bandura, 1997: 382) as they are not focused on capability towards a certain activity, nor are they embedded within a theoretical system that describes how such beliefs may influence behaviour. As a result, researchers (Bandura, 1997; Bong & Skaalvik, 2003; Cramer et al., 2009) have suggested that self-efficacy beliefs are a more appropriate means for investigating task-focused perceptions of perceived capability (e.g. towards L2 teaching activities) in comparison to self-confidence and other self-concept belief constructs.

Furthermore, when some researchers (e.g. Shrauger & Schohn, 1995: 257) have attempted to show how self-confidence at the domain (i.e. a higher-order self-concept belief) level is related to behaviour, they have created new divisions of hierarchy under self-confidence, with 'situation-specific' confidence used to describe confidence at the task level. Pajares (1992) warned that teacher cognition researchers should avoid using different names for existing constructs, and the task-focused situation-specific confidence that Shrauger and Schohn (1995: 257–258) refer to is difficult to separate from Bandura's construct of self-efficacy. Others (e.g. Stajkovic, 2006) accept that self-confidence, as a feature of one's self-concept, is reflective of various underlying beliefs, including one's perceptions of capability to carry out tasks within specific contexts (i.e.

self-efficacy). Indeed, it is now generally accepted that efficacy beliefs do contribute towards self-concept (Mercer, 2008; Williams *et al.*, 2015) as individuals with greater perceived capability towards tasks within a domain may be more likely to have stronger perceptions of ability about their competence towards them. Also, as efficacy beliefs are theorised to contribute towards teacher agency, accordingly they may also influence wider, dynamic constructs such as teacher identity (Beauchamp & Thomas, 2009).

Given its original in psychology, it is important to note that teacher efficacy is a tightly controlled construct; it may not necessarily provide insights about how teachers view themselves or their general competence. The efficacy beliefs that individuals' hold towards different tasks can be grouped together towards certain dimensions of activity (usually via the use of factor analysis on questionnaire data), providing researchers with information about individuals' perceptions of their skills for achieving outcomes within different areas of teaching (e.g. towards instruction, towards discipline). However, the insights gained from such dimensions are tightly limited to the self-beliefs of *capability* towards carry out actions; they do not necessarily provide information about the value that teachers place on them, nor the extent to which teachers appraise them in their self-evaluations of esteem. Thus, a teacher could have strong efficacy for some teaching tasks but also consider themselves to be a poor teacher, due to the different 'self-esteem reactions' (Zimmerman, 2000: 84) that they attend to (e.g. the perceived value of the task) when constructing their self-concept beliefs about their ability as a teacher. As a result, while efficacy may contribute towards other self-beliefs, equally, substantial gaps may be present between efficacy expectations, self-concept beliefs, self-esteem evaluations and broader constructs such as teacher identity.

2.4 The Development of Efficacy Beliefs

Bandura (1977, 1986, 1997) posited that the development of self-efficacy beliefs is based on individuals' interpretations of their experiences, others' reactions and their emotions. He ascribed the development of self-efficacy beliefs to four factors: mastery experiences, vicarious experiences, social persuasion and physiological states.

Mastery experiences are based on perceptions of direct performances, where (perceived) successful performance of a task or activity leads to greater confidence in being able to complete the task proficiently in the future. It is argued that these are the strongest drivers of self-efficacy beliefs. The second factor is vicarious experiences; watching others or self-modelling one's own performance may lead to increased efficacy. Social persuasion constitutes the third factor, as positive feedback or encouragement from others can be useful for overcoming self-doubt.

Finally, an individual's emotional and physical reactions and responses can influence their self-efficacy beliefs. Equally, while these factors may contribute positively (i.e. lead to stronger efficacy), negative attributions (i.e. perceptions of failure) can lead to weaker efficacy beliefs, as the interpretation of the event is crucial. Thus, for some teachers, attributions from perceiving a higher heart rate (i.e. a physical response) prior to a class may be interpreted negatively as a sign of nervousness, while for others it may signal excitement and be interpreted positively. For example, positive physiological states have been shown to be related to stronger teacher efficacy beliefs, with teachers feeling 'excitement while teaching literature' (Mills, 2011: 71) or 'feeling energized' (Morris & Usher, 2011: 238) after class, leading to stronger efficacy beliefs.

Within a teaching context, the development of teacher efficacy beliefs may therefore be influenced by the *interpretations* of teachers about their experiences as a trainee or teacher; self-modelling and observation of others (e.g. participation in seminars); feedback and encouragement from other teachers, students and parents; as well as affective processes such as anxiety or perceived stress. Research has provided support for the four factors theorised to influence self-efficacy beliefs, and *generally* substantiated the claim that mastery experiences tend to be the strongest influence on teacher efficacy beliefs (Morris & Usher, 2011; Mulholland & Wallace, 2001; Tschannen-Moran & Woolfolk Hoy, 2007). For example, in a study of 'novice' and 'career' teachers, Tschannen-Moran and Woolfolk Hoy (2007) found mastery experiences made the strongest contribution to teachers' self-efficacy for teaching. However, Usher and Pajares (2008) also warned that while mastery experiences are usually most influential, sources may become more or less important in different contexts (e.g. for various domains of activity) or for different individuals (e.g. by gender). This point has also been noted by Klassen *et al.* (2011) in their review of teacher efficacy research, where the authors question the extent to which the strength of these four factors is *culturally* specific – a key issue for consideration in studies of language teacher efficacy where respondents are often from different cultural backgrounds.

Furthermore, efficacy sources appear to act in concert with each other. Particularly, mastery experiences and social persuasion have often been found to act simultaneously as sources of efficacy beliefs (Morris & Usher, 2011; Tschannen-Moran & McMaster, 2009), perhaps because many teaching training experiences involve practice teaching (i.e. a potential mastery experience) and feedback from senior teachers, trainers or students about competency (i.e. involving social persuasion). An example comes from Morris and Usher (2011), who used semi-structured interviews to investigate the sources of efficacy for university professors who had been recognised for 'excellence in teaching'. Although the study found that vicarious experiences and affective states were positive influences on teacher efficacy beliefs, mastery experiences and social persuasion were identified to be the most influential sources of self-efficacy. The authors suggested that mastery experiences and social persuasion were closely integrated, as 'in the context of college teaching, appraisals of past performance are almost always informed by social persuasions' (Morris & Usher, 2011: 243). Thus, separating the individual sources and indeed measuring them (see Morris et al., 2016) remain difficulties for teacher efficacy researchers. In fact, other researchers have included perceived mastery experiences *with* social persuasion as one integrated source of efficacy information. For example, in a study of 198 pre-service elementary teachers in Greece, Poulou (2007) combined mastery experiences and social persuasion based on findings of previous studies (Anderson & Betz, 2001; Lent et al., 1996; Matsui et al., 1990), which had identified personal mastery experiences and social persuasion and emotional arousal to cluster together as one factor related to direct personal experience.

Vicarious experiences have also been shown to positively influence teaching efficacy beliefs. There have been mixed results about the influence of mentors and models, with some studies showing a significant influence (Knoblauch & Woolfolk Hoy, 2008; Morris & Usher, 2011; Siwatu, 2011a), but others showing no influence (Rots et al., 2007). Simulated modelling (imagining oneself teaching) has also been identified as a significant source of information influencing positive efficacy development in pre-service science teachers (Palmer, 2006), while Bautista (2011) found that (video) observation could influence teacher efficacy beliefs by providing teachers with new ideas and skills. Furthermore, as the different sources appear to be integrated, it seems that vicarious sources are most effective when they are followed by personal experience, leading to perceptions of mastery. For example, Tschannen-Moran and McMaster (2009) found that professional development lectures could lead to a significant development in teacher efficacy if they were also followed by practice and individual feedback.

Mulholland and Wallace (2001) carried out a longitudinal case study of a teacher making the change from pre-service to in-service teaching, and showed the difficulty of understanding how the various forces influence teacher efficacy beliefs, particularly whether such sources are *always* positive or negative. Using narrative inquiry, the authors examined the development of a novice elementary school teacher's self-efficacy for teaching beliefs towards science, identifying mastery experiences and social persuasion to be, overall, the strongest sources of efficacy information. However, they also noted that the various forms of information (e.g. vicarious experiences, social persuasion) acted in different ways on the teacher, sometimes as a positive influence and sometimes in a negative fashion. The study showed the difficulty of assigning one direction (i.e. positive influence) to different factors, because each factor and each source is *interpreted* and assigned meaning by the individuals themselves.

The separation of these sources may become more difficult as time passes and technology becomes more integrated with teacher training, leading to virtual training opportunities. Generally speaking, simulated modelling is considered a type of vicarious experience (Palmer, 2006). However, when trainees act in a virtual teaching environment with 'avatars' (i.e. computer-generated virtual students), such experiences appear to be much closer to 'real' mastery experiences. Bautista and Boone (2015) suggested that such experiences contributed towards 'cognitive pedagogical mastery' or pedagogic knowledge that can be used during teaching as the simulated experience helped participants to imagine themselves as successful teachers. However, it could be argued these experiences are direct and personal teaching experiences (e.g. when the individuals are confronted by avatars who ask 'why are we doing this?' and the teachers must respond), thus it seems clear that definitional problems may become more apparent as technology progresses and the real and virtual worlds become further interconnected.

Debate continues about whether the original definitions and conceptions of the four sources should be expanded as self-efficacy is considered in different areas, such as teaching development. In order to preserve conceptual clarity, some (e.g. Morris *et al.*, 2016) have argued that perceptions of school support and mentoring should not be considered 'social persuasion' unless the experience specifically involved evaluative feedback. However, others (e.g. Wyatt, 2015: 16) have argued that the source 'verbal persuasion' should be expanded to include any *input* received from others that teachers use to 'reflect, conceptualize or plan', rather than only evaluative feedback. Indeed, as the evaluations of others may be inferred from the 'messages' that teachers receive (Chong & Kong, 2012), rather than the actual words expressed, it seems clear that the focus should be on the extent to which teachers perceive the advice, support or feedback from others as an influence on their efficacy beliefs.

Finally, another key area for attention by teacher efficacy researchers is the extent to which the development of efficacy beliefs is dependent on cultural context (Klassen *et al.*, 2011). Efficacy sources do not automatically influence efficacy beliefs, but are weighed and assessed according to the information that individuals select and deem to be relevant (Bandura, 1997). Some research has indicated that specific sources (such as social persuasion) may be considered more strongly by teachers in different cultures (Phan & Locke, 2015), and is a factor explored in this book. Chapter 10 discusses the ways in which cultural elements of the Japanese teaching environment appear to influence the attendance of teachers towards social factors as sources of efficacy information, likely due to cultural values that emphasise a collective orientation.

2.5 Additional Factors that May Influence Efficacy Beliefs

While there is strong evidence for the four theorised sources of efficacy beliefs outlined in Section 2.4, a number of other factors have been suggested as additional sources of efficacy, or as factors that may influence efficacy. One key source is the role of content and pedagogical knowledge. As Morris *et al.* (2016: 22) have noted, it appears that 'teachers' knowledge, and their beliefs about that knowledge, can play an important role in their development of self-efficacy' as 'knowing the material, and knowing how to teach it well, can improve teachers' sense of efficacy'. The importance of (perceived) content or subject-matter knowledge has been clearly shown in the research literature, with studies of science teachers showing a positive relationship between the number of science classes they had taken and their teacher efficacy beliefs towards teaching that subject (Cantrell *et al.*, 2003; Mulholland *et al.*, 2004). With respect to language teaching (discussed further in Chapter 3), studies have also shown that foreign language proficiency was positively related to efficacy beliefs (Chacon, 2005; Yilmaz, 2011).

However, it is also worth remembering that 'expectation alone will not produce desired performances if the requisite competencies are lacking' (Bandura *et al.*, 1977: 138) as efficacy beliefs are assessed against the skills that individuals perceive to have available to them (Bandura, 1977). In other words, a certain level of knowledge and competency is *required* for individuals to be able to bring about successful performances. Therefore, it seems natural that instruction about content or teaching strategies will influence efficacy beliefs, particularly for those beginning to teach, as these influence the skills that individuals can utilise and draw on. In fact, some researchers (e.g. Raudenbush *et al.*, 1992) have interpreted self-efficacy as 'a cognition that mediates between knowledge and action', thus the key point is not whether instruction influences efficacy, but whether efforts to grow teacher knowledge are likely to have a stronger effect when such activities also attend to efficacy development (i.e. by providing opportunities for enactive mastery).

Furthermore, as Morris *et al.* (2016) have explained, knowledge itself is derived from experience. They argued that knowledge should not be considered a primary *source* of efficacy beliefs, but rather that it is developed via experience and is therefore a mediating factor *appraised* when individuals assess their efficacy beliefs towards a given task. Some examples, which align with the theorised sources of efficacy, are from strategies (i.e. knowledge) developed via personal teaching (i.e. an enactive mastery experience) or from learning teaching skills (i.e. strategies) by observing others or self-modelling (i.e. via vicarious experiences).

In a key study illuminating this discussion, Palmer (2006) investigated the teacher efficacy beliefs of 190 pre-service elementary school teachers at a university in Australia. The author brought together results from three surveys to identify two additional sources of teacher efficacy differentiated from enactive mastery and modelling (i.e. vicarious experiences). Palmer (2006: 349) argued that 'cognitive content mastery' (an understanding of science knowledge that developed from a learning experience) and 'cognitive pedagogical mastery' (a learning experience that influenced understanding of science teaching) were two 'distinctive mastery experiences in their own right' and requirements of enactive mastery. Students in the study directly referred to 'the procedures' or 'great strategies' (Palmer, 2006: 346) that they had learned from the lessons or activities in the course, leading the author to suggest that these should be considered separate, distinct sources of efficacy. However, this returns us to the discussion from the previous paragraph, where such experiences could also be interpreted as vicarious experiences that provided models later integrated into teaching practice. Findings presented in this book (see Chapters 7 and 8) indicate that past *learning* experiences may act as sources of efficacy-forming information; however, these appear to contribute towards knowledge that can be used in a task (i.e. language skills) or may indirectly influence efficacy via attitudes (i.e. affective states) towards different instructional approaches.

Finally, as Morris *et al.* (2016) also noted, not all sources of knowledge conveniently fall into the theorised sources of efficacy beliefs. They provided the example of independent reading as a source of pedagogic knowledge (identified by Buehl & Fives, 2009), which is not, in itself, clearly a modelling or (cognitive) mastery experience. Thus, it seems that there may be additional sources of information that can influence efficacy development, perhaps *indirectly*, by adding to the skills that individuals perceive to have available to them. In summary, it seems that a key area for teacher efficacy researchers is identifying other sources of teacher efficacy, and specifically gaining better understanding of the experiences that lead to the formation of content and teacher knowledge.

2.6 Assessment of Efficacy Beliefs

Efficacy beliefs can be considered with respect to level, generality and strength (Bandura, 1977, 1997, 2006) based on perceptions of personal skill towards specific teaching activities within different contexts. For example, teacher efficacy expectations may vary by level (e.g. carrying out teaching to help students achieve different degrees of examination success), generality (e.g. towards teaching a specific subject versus teaching overall) and strength (e.g. efficacy towards one task or dimension versus another). Accordingly, it seems apparent that different sources of information will be drawn on in the assessment of efficacy beliefs. This section brings the different factors together within a conceptual framework of teacher efficacy assessment based on SCT (Bandura, 1997), and by drawing together frameworks of other researchers (Gist & Mitchell, 1992; Morris *et al.*, 2016; Tschannen-Moran *et al.*, 1998; Wyatt, 2015).

Efficacy beliefs are considered against the level of task demand required, and the contextual situation (Bandura, 1997). Gist and Mitchell (1992) suggested that there are three processes that individuals draw on in the assessment of their efficacy beliefs. First, there is an analysis of the task, including consideration of what a successful performance entails and what is required for such a performance. Task familiarity is the second key attribute assessed, where individuals consider attributions of their experiences, drawing on the four sources of efficacy beliefs, before finally assessing personal (e.g. skill, knowledge, available effort) and situational factors (e.g. distractions) that may influence the skills they have available or the difficulty of the task. Studies have provided some support for the Gist and Mitchell (1992) model, showing the mediating influence of time pressure (Salanova et al., 2003) and task complexity (Bolt et al., 2001; Mangos & Steele-Johnson, 2001) alongside efficacy on performance. Tschannen-Moran and Woolfolk Hoy (2007) extended this model to the context of teaching, explaining that,

> in assessing beliefs about their teaching capability in a particular context, teachers make two related judgments: the requirements of an anticipated teaching task and an assessment of their personal teaching competence in light of those requirements. (Tschannen-Moran & Woolfolk Hoy, 2007: 5)

In other words, teachers assess the personal skills and strategies they can utilise (including any perceived weaknesses, such as a lack of content knowledge) against any constraints within the teaching context (e.g. level of students, level of support) in assessing their efficacy expectations towards teaching tasks in the pursuit of student learning. These factors are presented in Figure 2.1.

The integration of these various sources is a personal process as it relies on each individual's weighting of the different pieces of information (Bandura, 1997), where the 'differential impact of each of these sources depends on cognitive processing what is attended to, what is remembered, and how the teacher thinks about each of the experiences' (Tschannen-Moran et al., 1998: 18). Due to triadic reciprocal causation, the process is theorised to include attributions from *behaviour* (i.e. enactive mastery experience, vicarious experiences, attention to feedback from others and of one's affective states); attention to *contextual* factors that influence perceptions of task difficulty and/or influence individuals' knowledge of and capability to cope with the situation; plus perceptions of *personal knowledge* and skills that individuals can bring to the task.

Research has consistently shown that personal and contextual factors are related to efficacy beliefs. For example, significant relationships have been identified between efficacy beliefs and perceptions of support (Capa Aydin & Woolfolk Hoy, 2005), resources available (Tschannen-Moran

& Woolfolk Hoy, 2007) and school setting (Chong et al., 2010; Knoblauch & Woolfolk Hoy, 2008; Siwatu, 2011b). Beyond content knowledge, other personal variables such as experience (Cheung, 2006; Fives & Buehl, 2009; Tschannen-Moran & Woolfolk Hoy, 2007) and gender (Cheung, 2006; Ross et al., 1996) have been found to be associated with efficacy beliefs.

Discussion continues about how teacher self-efficacy beliefs grow and change. Wyatt (2014) argues that reflection is a crucial aspect neglected in models of efficacy change (such as the model of Tschannen-Moran et al., 1998). However, as Bandura (1997: 51) has noted, 'efficacy beliefs are structured by experience and reflective thought', where reflection is a key aspect related to the cognitive processing that individuals engage in when they consider their efficacy beliefs. Bandura (1997: 79) stated that information from efficacy sources 'is not inherently enlightening. It becomes instructive only through cognitive processing of efficacy information and through reflective thought'. Much of this debate stems from another criticism of the Tschannen-Moran et al. (1998) model by Wheatley (2002), who has emphasised the role of 'efficacy doubt' as an influence on teacher beliefs and behaviour. Simply put, *unsuccessful* experiences can also inform future efficacy via reflection (Cheung, 2006; Wyatt, 2014, 2015). This is a valuable point for consideration, as the role of self-doubt appears to be valuable in driving reflective thought.

Particularly during the 'skill development phase' (e.g. for teachers developing new teaching skills, such as those discussed in Wyatt, 2010a, 2010b, 2013b), Bandura (1997: 76) has suggested that, 'some self-doubt about one's efficacy provides incentives to acquire the knowledge and skills needed to function successfully'. In other words, efficacy beliefs are not only driven by perceptions of success, but may also be mediated by perceptions of failure, anxiety and self-doubt. A number of researchers have highlighted the need for establishing a social environment (Cabaroglu, 2014; Karimi, 2011; Wyatt & Dikilitaş, 2015; Zonoubi et al., 2017) that provides teachers with opportunities for positive efficacy development (e.g. via action research and observation) when they experience such doubts.

Thus, reflection appears to be a key aspect of the cognitive processing that individuals engage in during the assessment of their efficacy beliefs, and is represented as central to the conceptual framework presented in Figure 2.1. Self-reflective thought involves the individual noticing and evaluating information from different sources. In other words, individuals carry out 'strategic thinking about how to manage the environment' and evaluate the 'adequacy' of their 'knowledge, thinking skills, capabilities, and action strategies' (Bandura, 1997: 5). Such considerations integrate the four sources of efficacy information, including the role of task knowledge and perceived skill (Gist & Mitchell, 1992; Morris et al., 2016; Tschannen-Moran et al., 1998), while also recognising that source information may be directly or indirectly related to experience with the task. Thus, an enactive mastery experience may directly influence efficacy beliefs via attributions of perceived success. It may also indirectly contribute to efficacy beliefs via information that is appraised by the individual, such as by providing knowledge of the task demands. The extent to which the source and knowledge are attended to (i.e. the cognitive process) is reliant on the individual, where 'knowledge, competence, and various forms of self-knowledge and self-belief act in concert' (Usher & Pajares, 2008: 790). As Bandura (1986, 1997) and others (Wyatt, 2015) have noted, while self-efficacy beliefs are key mediators of behaviour, they do not work alone and in isolation, thus other personal factors are likely to exert influence on efficacy beliefs (directly and indirectly). Finally, the conceptual framework develops on previous models by emphasising that beliefs and performances are located within and assessed against the contextual situation; significant changes in context are likely to lead to change in efficacy expectations (Wyatt, 2013b, 2014). This framework reflects findings presented later in this book, as efficacy sources, contextual factors and other personal factors (e.g. beliefs about language learning) appear to influence language teacher efficacy beliefs.

2.7 Chapter Summary

As Tschannen-Moran and Woolfolk Hoy (2001: 783) have explained, 'teacher efficacy is a simple idea with significant implications'. Research has suggested that teachers with a lower sense of efficacy experience more stress, that teacher efficacy is negatively correlated with teacher burnout (Betoret, 2006; Brouwers & Tomic, 2000; Skaalvik & Skaalvik, 2007) and that teachers with a higher sense of efficacy are more likely to be committed to teaching (Chan, 2008; Chesnut & Burley, 2015; Ware & Kitsantas, 2007). Furthermore, teachers with stronger efficacy are likely to be more persistent (Enochs *et al.*, 1995; Mulholland & Wallace, 2001; Woolfolk Hoy & Davis, 2006) and more open to innovation and change (Ghaith & Yaghi, 1997; Guskey, 1988; Skaalvik & Skaalvik, 2007). Accordingly, efficacy beliefs appear to act as predicted by SCT, by mediating the reciprocal relationship between self-beliefs, contextual factors and teaching behaviour.

This chapter has discussed the theoretical foundations of teacher efficacy as a form of self-efficacy, and has shown how teacher efficacy research has developed. It has introduced research findings that have provided support for the theorised ways in which teacher efficacy beliefs develop, and has provided a conceptual model for the assessment of teacher efficacy beliefs. The chapter has also highlighted a number of areas where further research is needed, such as developing a better understanding of the relationship between individual and collective efficacy, particularly in 'international' contexts such as many L2 teaching situations; understanding the development of teacher efficacy beliefs in different cultural contexts; and developing a better understanding of the types of information that may directly or indirectly influence efficacy beliefs. The research presented in this book contributes to information about these three areas, and is discussed in Chapters 6 through 10. Chapter 3 focuses specifically on the smaller field of language teacher efficacy. It reviews the knowledge that has been generated from previous language teacher efficacy studies, and suggests areas where future work is needed to develop greater understanding of the relationship between language teacher efficacy and other personal and contextual factors.

3 Language Teacher Efficacy

Chapter 2 outlined the theoretical foundations of teacher efficacy and discussed the ways in which teacher efficacy beliefs develop and are assessed by individuals. This chapter starts by discussing the movement of teacher efficacy research into the field of applied linguistics. Teacher efficacy research in the wider field has generally been focused on North American or other European contexts; however, most language teacher efficacy research has come from West Asian settings, where research from Turkey (Atay, 2007; Cabaroglu, 2014), Iran (Abednia, 2012; Ghanizadeh & Moafian, 2011; Moradkhani & Haghi, 2017) and Oman (Wyatt, 2010b, 2013a, 2013b) has advanced understanding about language teacher efficacy (LTE) development. More recently, LTE research has expanded to East Asian settings (Nguyen & Ngo, 2017; Phan & Locke, 2015; Shin, 2012), and studies have raised interesting questions about the ways in which efficacy beliefs are assessed by teachers from Confucian backgrounds.

This chapter introduces the reader to the growing field of LTE research in order to show what has been learned about the dimensions of LTE, the development of LTE beliefs and what factors are associated with stronger and weaker LTE beliefs. For structured reviews of LTE research, Wyatt (2018b) and Hoang (2018) are recommended. This chapter concludes by discussing the small body of work carried out to examine LTE within Japan.

3.1 Self-Efficacy for Language Teaching

Since the early 2000s, the teacher efficacy beliefs of language educators has received greater attention; the growth in LTE research has followed a parallel body of work that continues to explore the role of self-efficacy for language learners (e.g. Cubukcu, 2008; Graham, 2011; Oxford & Shearin, 1994; Thompson, 2018). Although much of the work in this field has been carried out with teachers of English as a foreign language (EFL; e.g. Chacon, 2005; Göker, 2012; Wyatt & Dikilitaş, 2015), there have also been a number of studies that have examined the efficacy beliefs of teachers of other languages such as French (Mills, 2011; Mills & Allen, 2008) and other foreign languages (Swanson, 2010a, 2010b). Other related research has investigated the efficacy beliefs of teachers working with students who use English as an additional language (EAL) (e.g. Tangen, 2007; Tran, 2015) and EAL teachers (e.g. Spooner-Lane et al., 2009).

One of the first studies to consider the teacher efficacy beliefs of EFL teachers was carried out by Chacon, who used mixed methods to examine the teacher self-efficacy beliefs of Venezuelan middle school English teachers. The study used an adapted version of the Teacher Sense of Efficacy Scale (TSES) (Tschannen-Moran & Woolfolk Hoy, 2001) and highlighted a positive relationship between efficacy beliefs and self-reported English proficiency. Referencing the teacher efficacy assessment process of Tschannen-Moran et al. (1998), Chacon (2005) argued that a

> lack of competency in English influences teachers' self-efficacy because in analyzing the teaching tasks, teachers will make judgments on their teaching competence to teach students speaking, listening, reading, and writing in English. Thus, lower efficacy in teaching English would lead teachers to put less effort in motivating students to learn and value English learning. (Chacon, 2005: 269)

In other words, Chacon highlighted the important relationship between (perceived) English proficiency and teaching behaviour for teachers who use English as a second language (L2). This is a commonly noted issue in contexts where language teachers, as EAL users themselves, have noted L2 proficiency as a key attribute inhibiting their teaching behaviour, especially for language teachers attempting to implement communicative language teaching (CLT; e.g. Li, 1998; Nishino & Watanabe, 2008; Valdes & Jhones, 1991). Later studies have examined the relationship between EFL teacher efficacy beliefs and L2 proficiency (e.g. Eslami & Fatahi, 2008; Nishino, 2012; Yilmaz, 2011), confirming the positive relationship identified by Chacon (2005). The relationship between L2 ability and LTE appears crucial and is discussed further in Section 3.5 and Chapter 7 of this book.

Other important findings from LTE research relate to the difference between teaching a language versus other subjects. In a study of the teacher efficacy beliefs of university graduate students of French literature, Mills (2011) highlighted that the pedagogic knowledge required to effectively teach a language may be considerably different to teaching a related subject (such as French literature). Thus, the instructional strategies and pedagogic knowledge required for language teaching may be domain specific, indicating that LTE may have certain dimensions related to language capability (Nishino, 2012; Swanson, 2008) and L2 teaching strategies (e.g. instructional strategies for CLT, such as in Nishino, 2009, 2012). This domain of LTE is explored further in Chapter 8.

Few studies have explored the collective efficacy beliefs of language teachers, despite calls for such studies (Klassen *et al.*, 2011). Accordingly, little is known about how collective efficacy operates in language teaching contexts. However, in alignment with studies carried out in the general field of teacher efficacy, L2 teacher collective efficacy appears positively related to job satisfaction (Göker, 2012) and teacher empowerment (Baleghizadeh & Goldouz, 2016). For example, in a study that examined the collective teacher efficacy beliefs of 25 EFL instructors at a foundation school in North Cyprus, Göker (2012) used Tschannen-Moran and Barr's (2004) Collective Teacher Efficacy Belief Scale (CTEBS) and found that perceived collective efficacy was positively related with job satisfaction. As collective efficacy beliefs appear to influence individual efficacy, which in turn affects teacher effort and practice, Göker argued for stronger group cohesion and collaboration, suggesting that 'principals should nurture work cultures that value and support their members' learning by modelling, guiding, and facilitating participation in professional communities that value learning'. One implication from the study was that collaboration was an essential element for encouraging stronger collective (and by association) individual teacher efficacy. Few studies have explored teacher efficacy beliefs towards collaborative practice, and this domain of activity is discussed in Chapter 9.

Given that many language teaching environments (e.g. EFL in China, Korea, Japan, Vietnam) involve teachers who may have a stronger collectivist orientation (Phan & Locke, 2015), a factor which has been shown to be a mediating factor related to job satisfaction, stress and collective efficacy (Klassen *et al.*, 2010), it seems clear that more studies are needed to understand the influence of cultural forces on individual efficacy beliefs for L2 teachers in various settings. This theme is discussed in Chapter 10.

3.2 Dimensions of Language Teacher Efficacy

As discussed in Chapter 2, teacher efficacy beliefs can be investigated at the task (i.e. towards a specific teaching activity) and domain (i.e. towards a certain area of teaching, such as instruction versus classroom management) level. In the field of language teaching, much of the research has used variations of Tschannen-Moran and Woolfolk Hoy's (2001) TSES instrument to investigate differing domains of efficacy beliefs. The short (12 item) form of the TSES has been adapted (in one way or another) in a number of studies for use in language teaching contexts (e.g. Atay, 2007; Chacon, 2005; Eslami & Fatahi, 2008; Swanson, 2010a; Tsui & Kennedy, 2009; Yilmaz, 2011), while the longer 24-item form has also been extensively used (e.g. Cabaroglu, 2014; Ghonsooly & Ghanizadeh, 2013; Moradkhani *et al.*, 2017).

A number of studies (e.g. Cabaroglu, 2014; Chacon, 2005; Ghonsooly & Ghanizadeh, 2013; Moradkhani *et al.*, 2017; Yilmaz, 2011) have used the TSES in different cultural contexts without examining the underlying factor structure of the instrument. In other words, such studies have generally accepted that the three factors identified in the original study (Student Engagement, Instructional Strategies, Classroom Management, see Tschannen-Moran & Woolfolk Hoy, 2001) are satisfactory as generalisable dimensions of teacher efficacy. In such studies, researchers have used inferential statistics to compare the strength of teacher efficacy for each factor with correlational analyses (e.g. versus perceived language capability) to highlight different areas of activity where teacher efficacy beliefs appear to be stronger (or weaker). Such studies (e.g. Chacon, 2005; Eslami & Fatahi, 2008; Yilmaz, 2011) have generally found teachers to be more efficacious towards instructional strategies in comparison to student engagement and classroom management.

However, there is also evidence that teacher efficacy beliefs (Ho & Hau, 2004; Tsui & Kennedy, 2009), including those of language teachers (Phan & Locke, 2015), operate in different ways in different contexts, particularly within East Asian Confucian contexts (Ho & Hau, 2004; Phan & Locke, 2015; Tsui & Kennedy, 2009). A study carried out with language teachers in the United States (Swanson, 2010a) used the short 12-item form of TSES to examine LTE belief dimensions, finding the same three-factor structure identified by Tschannen-Moran and Woolfolk Hoy (2001). In another study of 435 Iranian EFL teachers, Karami *et al.* (2019) demonstrated the same three-factor structure for the 24-item TSES, although the authors did identify one item ('How much can you assist families in helping their children do well in school?') with inadequate fit. On the other hand, studies using the TSES in East Asian contexts have had mixed results when the factor structure is examined (e.g. Cheung, 2006, 2008; Tsui & Kennedy, 2009). For example, in a study carried out in Hong Kong, Tsui and Kennedy (2009) found differences in the underlying factor structure. Specifically, a single factor referred to as 'Efficacy in teaching and learning' was identified, which comprised of items that had loaded as two distinct factors ('Student Engagement' and 'Instructional Strategies') in the original TSES. Accordingly, the authors suggested that the underlying dimensions of teacher efficacy were different for Hong Kong teachers, where 'Student Engagement' and 'Instructional Strategies' loaded together because they both reflected general Confucian cultural values regarding the responsibilities of teachers, thus were not separate dimensions of teacher efficacy beliefs for local teachers. Thus, the Tsui and Kennedy study (and others, e.g. Cheung, 2006, 2008; Kennedy & Hui, 2006) has demonstrated that the underlying dimensions of teacher efficacy beliefs may change in different cultural contexts.

Furthermore, teacher efficacy beliefs are not 'monolithic' (Morris *et al.*, 2016: 24); they change by context and domain. Thus, it seems clear that LTE has additional dimensions to those identified by Tschannen-Moran and Woolfolk Hoy (2001) in the TSES. One example specific to LTE beliefs concerns teacher self-beliefs about their capability to use their content knowledge and L2 capability in teaching. Most LTE studies have investigated L2 proficiency as a factor related to (i.e. an influence on) teacher efficacy (e.g. Chacon, 2005; Eslami & Fatahi, 2008; Yilmaz, 2011); however, some studies have considered content and L2 knowledge not only as a skill that is drawn on, but also as a dimension of LTE (Nishino, 2009, 2012; Swanson, 2010a). For example, in a study of foreign language teachers (of mainly Spanish and French) carried out in the United States, Swanson (2010a) adapted and added to the TSES by developing the 10-item Foreign Language Teacher Efficacy Scale (FLTES). Exploratory factor analysis identified two underlying dimensions, which the researcher named 'foreign language teacher knowledge' and 'foreign language teacher as facilitator'. The additional dimensions (i.e. separate from the TSES) focused on teachers' self-beliefs about their capability to *use* the foreign language (foreign language teacher knowledge) and their capability to *use* their language knowledge as a tool to aid student learning (foreign language teacher as facilitator). Another study carried out in Japan (Nishino, 2009, 2012) identified 'L2 confidence' (i.e. L2 self-efficacy) as a separate belief dimension from 'CLT self-efficacy' (i.e. instructional efficacy for CLT practices). Thus, it seems apparent that LTE may have additional dimensions separate from those identified within the wider teacher efficacy field.

Therefore, while the use of established scales has the benefit of comparability with other studies in the field, and develops understanding about teacher efficacy across cultural contexts, the use of such scales may also fail to identify other significant challenges for language teachers in the local contexts where their efficacy beliefs operate, reducing the value of efficacy expectations as predictors of behaviour (Bandura, 1997, 2006). It is vital to remember that efficacy beliefs, as an area of interest, emerged from research concerned with the adaptation and change of human behaviour (Bandura, 1977; Bandura *et al.*, 1977). Indeed, one of the key reasons for understanding the dimensions of teacher efficacy is that it helps teacher educators identify domains of teaching (and associated) activity where efficacy is weak and efforts are needed to help individuals take greater agency. Teachers are not only responsive to their environments – they can help shape them. Thus, gaining a better understanding of the different and various underlying dimensions of LTE may help to identify areas where education interventions may be most effective and are most needed in providing teachers with strategies they can use to be better educators.

In summary, the underlying dimensions of teacher efficacy beliefs may be expected to differ when instruments are adapted for use in contexts that may have significantly different cultural or teaching features. For this reason, LTE researchers should consider research designs that strengthen the cultural and content validity of any scales used – either by adding additional dimensions or by developing context-specific instruments. Chapter 5 provides an example of how this was attempted in the research presented in this book, while Chapter 6 discusses the dimensions of Japanese high school teacher of English (JTE) efficacy beliefs. Results indicate context-specific domains of LTE beliefs in Japan reflecting local teaching challenges.

3.3 Development of Language Teacher Efficacy Beliefs

Gaining a better understanding about how LTE beliefs develop can provide insights into how teacher education programmes can be structured (i.e. towards domains such as discipline or instruction), as well as suggesting the types of instruction or experiences that are needed (e.g. teaching practice, feedback or observation opportunities). Research on LTE development has mirrored the general trends from the wider teacher efficacy field, identifying enactive mastery experiences via personal experience (Atay, 2007; Karimi, 2011; Zonoubi *et al.*, 2017) as the key source of stronger efficacy beliefs. For example, in an experimental study of 60 teachers carried out in Iran (treatment group of 30, control group of 30), Karimi (2011) found that teachers who participated in a professional development course, which involved three modules related to language teaching practice, had significantly higher teacher self-efficacy beliefs at the end of the course in comparison to the control group who received no training. As the course involved a teaching practicum, the researchers attributed the increase to enactive mastery experiences.

Similarly, Zonoubi *et al.* (2017) investigated the influence of participation in a professional learning community (PLC) on 10 EFL teachers in Iran. Teachers participated in two six-month modules and were interviewed using self-efficacy prompts developed by Abednia (2012). Thematic analysis of interview findings identified developments in participants' pedagogic self-efficacy (i.e. towards instruction), as well as perceived language proficiency. The researchers found that all sources of efficacy development were present, as

> the participants' experience of taking part in the PLC interventions afforded them the opportunity to observe accomplishments in their own teaching (mastery experiences) and their peers' (vicarious experiences), to receive positive and constructive feedback from their colleagues and supervisors on their contributions to the PLC discussions, their teaching performance, and their professional growth (social persuasion), and to gain a sense of pleasure and satisfaction as a result of observing their own and peers' professional development (emotional states). (Zonoubi *et al.*, 2017: 9)

Thus, it seems clear that professional development activities provide efficacy development information, as different activities (e.g. teaching practice, observation) may act as specific sources (i.e. enactive mastery experiences, vicarious experiences) of influence on teacher efficacy beliefs. Zonoubi *et al.* (2017) also emphasised the role of peer and supervisor feedback as contributors to stronger efficacy beliefs, and such feedback is often a reinforcement of personal mastery, indicating (as discussed in Chapter 2) that different sources of efficacy development information may be working together in a united fashion.

The relationship between pedagogic skill and efficacy belief development is a common feature of LTE research. In a series of studies, Wyatt (e.g. 2010a, 2010b, 2013b, 2015) emphasised the importance of reflection as part of the process of efficacy belief development. Personal experiences (i.e. enactive mastery experiences) were a key source of efficacy information, due to a focus on experimentation in practice followed by reflection. In some of these studies (e.g. Wyatt, 2010a, 2010b; Wyatt & Dikilitaş, 2015), the participants may have been going through the process of skill development (i.e. were relatively novice teachers who may not have had sufficient knowledge to implement new teaching strategies). For such teachers, both positive and negative personal experiences, including self-doubts (see Wheatley, 2002), may act as drivers of efficacy belief development as they learn about the areas of practice where skill improvement is needed (Bandura, 1997).

Such individuals can be differentiated from teachers who have (supposedly) developed the necessary skills for language teaching. Indeed, in self-efficacy theory, Bandura (1997: 75–76) considered the skill development phase as separate from 'the use of established skills to manage situational demands'. In other words, efficacy doubts may be useful drivers of reflection and may stimulate efficacy development for language teachers who perceive themselves to be lacking in skill. However, at the point where teachers perceive themselves to have the required skills, such doubts may negatively influence efficacy beliefs. This highlights a personal factor that appears to be an important source of efficacy information, which is years of teaching experience. Although time, itself, is not necessarily a specific source, a number of studies (Ghonsooly & Ghanizadeh, 2013; Swanson, 2010a) have shown teaching experience to be positively related to stronger teacher self-efficacy beliefs.

For example, Swanson's (2010a) study of foreign LTE showed significant differences between novice and veteran teachers regarding the dimension of 'foreign language teacher as facilitator'. Teacher efficacy beliefs are proposed to develop and strengthen over time (Tschannen-Moran & Woolfolk Hoy, 2001), becoming more stable as educators have a broad range of experience from which to interpret sources of efficacy-forming information (Pajares, 1992). One implication is that novice teachers have fewer experiences that they can draw on and which they may interpret as successful (i.e. fewer enactive mastery experiences). Furthermore, research has demonstrated that contextual variables affect novice teachers' efficacy beliefs more strongly (Tschannen-Moran & Woolfolk Hoy, 2007), perhaps due to less experience managing the various constraints of teaching. However, 'novice' in this sense may be concerned not only with total teaching time, but also relevant teaching experiences. An example with respect to LTE comes from Wyatt (2010a), who introduced a case study of a teacher transitioning to a new school, where a more student-centred teaching approach utilising group work was required, which the individual had little experience implementing in their prior teaching practice. The individual's failure to deal with the new constraints appears to have negatively influenced their teacher efficacy beliefs.

Efficacy belief development is reliant on individuals considering and weighting different sources of information. It has been suggested that the interpretations of the evaluative judgements of others may be given greater weight in more group-oriented societies. There is growing evidence that social feedback may be a stronger influence than personal experience for teachers in such contexts. For example, in a study of EFL teachers in Vietnam, Phan and Locke (2015) have provided support for the idea that the four theorised sources of teacher efficacy are influenced by the cultural context. In their study of eight EFL teachers at a technical university in Vietnam, Phan and Locke (2015) identified all four sources of efficacy as influences on the individuals' efficacy beliefs. However, feedback from colleagues was the strongest source of teacher efficacy beliefs identified via thematic analysis of interview data. The authors warned that the interview technique (particularly the follow-up questions used) may have pushed participants to focus more on feedback as a source of efficacy. Nevertheless, teachers in the study appeared to give 'more weight to other-oriented (social persuasion) than self-oriented evaluation (mastery experiences) when constructing their self-efficacy as EFL teachers' (Phan & Locke, 2015: 80). The authors concluded that the Vietnamese teachers' development of LTE beliefs is influenced by a cultural context that emphasises collectiveness, leading individuals to closely attend to social persuasion. The study noted that such feedback was not always positive, and discussed the negative influence on participants attributed to a *lack* of feedback from school leaders. Thus, in the way in which information is attended to (i.e. the cognitive processing of information and self-reflective thought of individuals), the authors suggested that cultural features influence efficacy belief development.

In another study of EFL teachers carried out in Iran, social persuasion was also found to be the strongest source of efficacy beliefs for teachers working in private schools, while personal mastery experiences were found to be stronger for teachers in public schools (Moradkhani & Haghi, 2017). The study found that student (and other stakeholder) feedback was a stronger source of information for private school teachers – although it should be noted that the authors included 'collegial support' within this source, perhaps moving beyond the specific features of social persuasion as evaluative feedback (Morris *et al.*, 2016). Nevertheless, the study is of interest because it suggests that the strength of different sources may change according to context-specific factors related to the educational environment.

The relatively small body of work carried out thus far has highlighted key areas for further investigation, by identifying that cultural context may be a key feature that influences the development of teacher efficacy beliefs. Specifically, it seems that social persuasion may be a stronger influence on the self-efficacy beliefs of teachers in East Asian Confucian contexts with collectivist orientations, such as Japan (the setting of the study discussed in this book). By extending knowledge about the development of teacher efficacy in Japan, the current study contributes to this growing field of research. However, it is also clear that to form a better understanding of how cultural features influence LTE belief development, future studies are needed from a range of diverse contexts.

3.4 Other Factors Related to LTE Beliefs

It seems clear that L2 ability is positively associated with L2 teacher efficacy beliefs (Chacon, 2005; Phan & Locke, 2015; Yilmaz, 2011). However, one limitation has been the way in which L2 proficiency was measured in some studies. For example, in a number of studies (e.g. Chacon, 2005; Eslami & Fatahi, 2008; Yilmaz, 2011), the self-reported English proficiency of teachers was examined using self-report items written with 'I can' phrasing – a feature of self-efficacy items – rather than separate, independent measurements of language knowledge or ability. Each of these studies found statistically significant correlations between teachers' efficacy beliefs and reported language proficiency. For example, Yilmaz (2011: 99) explained that 'the more proficient the EFL teachers perceived themselves to be across the four basic skills the more efficacious they felt'. Thus, it seems clear that *perceived* English proficiency is a factor that influences teacher efficacy beliefs. However, equally one could argue that perceived English proficiency (particularly when measured using 'I can' items) represents a measure of L2 self-efficacy, rather than of language proficiency. Few studies have investigated the relationship between teacher efficacy and language proficiency using more objective measures, such as the International English Language Testing System (IELTS) or Test in Practical English Proficiency (Eiken). The current study contributes knowledge towards this relationship by examining the relationship between efficacy beliefs, L2 proficiency and the use of English (see Chapter 7).

Professional development, ongoing study and action research appear to be other indirect sources of efficacy information (i.e. sources of information that contribute to the skills that teachers appraise in their assessment of their efficacy) as these may arise from 'cognitive' mastery experiences (see Palmer, 2006) that help the development of pedagogic knowledge (Atay, 2007; Zonoubi *et al.*, 2017). Studies have shown that action research participation is associated with stronger teacher efficacy (Cabaroglu, 2014; Wyatt & Dikilitaş, 2015), as participants were able to develop practical knowledge (i.e. skills that teachers can bring to the task) while experimenting with different teaching approaches. Indeed, in some cases these skill developments came from direct enactive mastery experiences (e.g. social interaction with students in class), and in others via indirect sources, such as carrying out a literature review about alternative teaching methods.

Although Bandura (1997) has suggested that efficacy expectations become stable over time, LTE beliefs appear to be highly context dependent. Wyatt (2010a, 2013b) has shown how change in the teaching environment influences the teacher efficacy beliefs of individuals, using examples of school movement, requirements to teach different years and via alternative methods, to show the strong influence of context on efficacy expectations. The professional lives of language teachers often require movement to very different teaching contexts (Johnston, 1997), which suggests that contextual variation may be a critical aspect for investigation in LTE research. Thus, the strength of individuals' LTE may vary by teaching contexts (e.g. school type). For example, in a study of Iranian EFL teachers that used the TSES, Moradkhani and Haghi (2017) found that teachers in private schools had significantly higher teacher efficacy beliefs for all three dimensions, in comparison to teachers in public schools. The authors attributed the 'unfavorable educational setting' of many public schools as a primary cause for the difference, as teachers at such schools faced high class sizes, limited resources, time constraints and variable student level. In other words, the study identified a number of situational factors that may influence perceptions of task difficulty and subsequently teacher efficacy.

Research has also identified contextual features that positively influence LTE. A number of studies (Wyatt, 2010b; Zonoubi *et al.*, 2017) have noted that teacher efficacy tends to be stronger when teachers perceive themselves to be in a supportive environment. However, there has generally been less of a focus on identifying contextual factors that may influence efficacy directly or indirectly, and due to the variability in language teaching contexts, this also constitutes an area for future studies to explore. The current study contributes to this developing area of interest by highlighting the predictive influence of school academic level on L2 instructional efficacy beliefs in Japan, alongside other environmental factors (see Chapters 8 and 9).

3.5 Language Teacher Efficacy in Japan

This chapter concludes by reviewing the small body of work that has investigated LTE in Japan. Japan has a long history of teacher cognition research (e.g. Nishino, 2008; Sakui, 2004; Underwood, 2012), with a number of studies examining teacher confidence and development (e.g. Glasgow, 2014; Kurihara & Samimy, 2007; Nagamine, 2007), and some specifically discussing 'teaching efficacy' (Nishino, 2009, 2012). Research has highlighted the lack of 'confidence' of high school English teachers in integrating more communicative approaches towards instruction (Thompson & Yanagita, 2017), and in using English as a teaching language (Glasgow, 2014). Kurihara and Samimy (2007) identified that participation in an overseas teaching training programme had a positive impact on the participants' English language skills and 'confidence' for teaching, indicating that professional development programmes provide opportunities for the development of these beliefs. However, few studies appear to have investigated teacher efficacy as a type of self-efficacy within a social cognitive theoretical framework.

In one of the most comprehensive studies of high school English teachers' beliefs in Japan, Nishino (2009, 2012) used principal components analysis and developed a path model to explore the dimensions of a teacher beliefs instrument designed by the researcher. Nishino (2009) hypothesised that teaching efficacy was an important construct related to the implementation of curriculum innovation, after noting the predictive value that self-efficacy beliefs had in Smylie's (1988) study on change in teacher practice. Nishino designed a number of items to reflect 'perceived teaching efficacy', and identified two dimensions of teacher efficacy from these items, which were called 'L2 self-confidence' (i.e. English efficacy) and 'CLT self-efficacy' (i.e. instructional efficacy). The Nishino (2009, 2012) study found that positive beliefs towards CLT and L2 self-confidence indirectly affected classroom practices via stronger CLT self-efficacy beliefs.

Using path analysis, Nishino (2012) tested her framework of teachers' beliefs and practices, and results showed a dynamic relationship between teacher beliefs, contextual factors and practice, indicating that CLT self-efficacy beliefs mediated self-concept beliefs on teaching practice. These beliefs also mediated the influence of teacher training experiences and perceptions of L2 self-confidence, indicating that teacher perceptions of L2 capability were also indirectly influential on practice. Furthermore, teacher perceptions of student capability (which Nishino called 'Student-related Communicative Conditions') were also found to influence teaching behaviour. This implies that teachers made judgements about practice, based on their perceptions of student capability and expectation, suggesting that contextual constraints were an influence on their behaviour. As discussed in Chapter 2, teachers assess their capability in relation to their particular context, where 'considerations include such factors as the students' abilities and motivation' and 'the availability and quality of instructional materials' (Tschannen-Moran et al., 1998: 20). The interaction between teacher beliefs about personal capability (i.e. CLT self-efficacy), teacher behaviour (i.e. frequency of

CLT activities) and perceptions of contextual constraints (i.e. perceived level of students) can be interpreted via triadic reciprocal causation (i.e. reciprocal interaction between beliefs, context and behaviour), indicating that efficacy beliefs acted in accordance with social cognitive theory (Bandura, 1986, 1997).

However, one limitation of the Nishino study concerns the way in which teacher efficacy beliefs were investigated. Specifically, the items were not written in such a way as to capture teacher judgements of future capability in accordance with a self-efficacy perspective (Bandura, 2006), but were interpreted to reflect teacher efficacy from the results of the path analysis. For example, the four items that comprised the CLT self-efficacy variable in the final path model (see Nishino, 2009: 340) were: (1) 'I supervise the classroom adequately when students are doing pair work or group work'; (2) 'I provide activities in which my students can enjoy communicating in English'; (3) 'I adequately facilitate my students' English communicative activities'; and (4) 'I give students autonomy when they do communicative activities'. These items are written as judgements and evaluations of current practice, rather than future capability. As discussed further in Chapter 4, such item wording is a common measurement problem in the field of teacher efficacy research, as researchers should use 'phrasing reflecting forward-looking capability' (Klassen et al., 2011: 26) in accordance with Bandura's (2006) guidelines for constructing efficacy scales. Thus, for LTE researchers, some caution is needed in interpreting Nishino's (2009, 2012) findings.

In summary, the small body of research carried out to investigate LTE in Japan provides some evidence to suggest that efficacy beliefs act as theorised by social cognitive theory. However, due to the inconsistent theoretical grounding of the previous studies, it also appears that an instrument with a clearer self-efficacy orientation is required. This book presents an instrument designed to meet this need, and further explores LTE beliefs in the Japanese context.

3.6 Chapter Summary

This chapter has discussed the growing body of teacher efficacy research that is specifically focused on language teachers and educators working in language education settings. It has outlined some key findings from the small body of work in this developing field, which has indicated that LTE has content dimensions (i.e. perceived L2 capability is a domain of LTE), and that the development of LTE beliefs may be culturally dependent.

It has also raised a number of questions for researchers to investigate further, such as the case of the L2, which appears to be both (1) integrated into a dimension of efficacy (i.e. efficacy towards the use of English); and also (2) a skill to be appraised (i.e. L2 capability influences efficacy in the use of English and other teacher efficacy beliefs). A number of researchers (Chacon, 2005; Nishino, 2012; Yilmaz, 2011) have called for research that examines the relationship between English proficiency and LTE beliefs, and it seems to be a key area for further research. Indeed, despite the growth in LTE research, more knowledge is needed about teacher efficacy in various EFL contexts. The chapter has also highlighted the role of contextual factors, and it is suggested that future studies should explore local factors as potential sources of efficacy information that may contribute to efficacy development or influence perceptions of task difficulty.

The following chapters move from the *'what'* and *'why'* aspects of LTE towards *'how'* LTE beliefs can be examined and what processes can be used for efficacy scale development. Chapter 4 introduces different methods for investigating LTE and provides the design of the research presented in this book. This chapter has highlighted the need for research to reflect the key dimensions of efficacy for the local context, and Chapter 5 specifically focuses on the *process* of LTE scale design.

4 Approaches for Investigating Language Teacher Efficacy

Given its psychological orientation, teacher efficacy research has relied on the use of quantitative scales. However, recent reviews (Hoang, 2018; Morris *et al.*, 2016; Wyatt, 2018b) have noted the growth in studies employing mixed methods, utilising data gained via interviews, observations and case studies. Such reviews also discuss a number of continuing problems with teacher efficacy research, suggesting that conceptual and measurement inconsistencies are a common issue in many studies. The purpose of this chapter is threefold: (1) to discuss some key considerations for researchers when investigating teacher efficacy; (2) to briefly review some approaches that have been used to examine teacher efficacy; and (3) to provide an overview of the design of the research discussed in this book.

4.1 Considerations for Teacher Efficacy Researchers

As discussed in Chapter 2, teacher efficacy, as a form of self-efficacy, differs from other self-constructs such as (teacher) self-concept and locus of control. However, even within the field of teacher efficacy, a common problem concerns the *way* in which the teacher efficacy construct is examined. Thus, this section briefly introduces a number of conceptual considerations for teacher efficacy researchers.

4.1.1 Conceptual alignment with self-efficacy theory

In some efficacy research, misalignments between the underlying theoretical framework and the instrumentation employed can be identified. This is often due to a gap between the construct supposedly being investigated and the means of gathering data – often via questionnaire items, but also through vignettes and interview prompts. Early teacher efficacy research integrated a locus of control orientation focused on whether teachers had control of outcomes. Scales from that time (e.g. Gibson & Dembo, 1984; Riggs & Enochs, 1990) often focused on whether teachers could influence learners (i.e. locus of control), rather than self-beliefs about perceived capability to carry out actions in the pursuit of outcomes. For example, the item 'effectiveness in science teaching has little influence on the achievement of students with low motivation' (Riggs & Enochs, 1990: 27) examines beliefs about the extent to which teachers perceive themselves to be able to influence learners (i.e. locus of control), not self-efficacy expectations.

Other studies have investigated teacher efficacy using scales that reflect beliefs of teacher self-concept (e.g. Evers et al., 2005; Somech & Drach-Zahavy, 2000) or attributions of past experience (e.g. Tournaki & Podell, 2005). For example, in a study by Somech and Drach-Zahavy (2000: 653), items such as 'I doubt my ability to do my job' and 'few teachers in my school can do a better job than I can' were employed to examine teacher efficacy. The items used appear to evoke affective self-esteem reactions, and have an 'evaluative character' (Shavelson et al., 1976: 414) with a normative reference (i.e. the comparison of oneself to others). Accordingly, they appear to be more focused on teacher self-concept, as they examine the view that individual teachers have of themselves.

Efforts to develop language teacher efficacy (LTE) scales have had similar problems. For example, Akbari and Tavassoli (2014) developed a scenario-based scale to reflect seven dimensions of LTE beliefs. After adopting a theoretical framework following Tschannen-Moran and Woolfolk Hoy (2001), that is self-efficacy within social cognitive theory, they then adapted the Ashton vignettes (Ashton et al., 1984), using 39 situations from which participants were asked to report 'the extent to which each item applied to them' (Akbari & Tavassoli, 2014: 35). The scale uses language that may evoke self-esteem reactions, rather than perceptions of capability. For example, with respect to each situation, participants were asked, 'to what extent does the teacher's feeling describe that of yours?' (Akbari & Tavassoli, 2014: 44–50). As a result, one limitation is that the respondents may not necessarily interpret the scenarios by drawing on their perceptions of capability towards each task.

These examples show that aligning theoretical orientation with instrumentation remains a continuing challenge for researchers. They also point towards two crucial aspects for researchers to consider: domain specificity and the wording of efficacy items or prompts.

4.1.2 Attention to domain specificity

Domain specificity is another challenge for teacher efficacy researchers to consider. The Gibson and Dembo (1984) Teacher Efficacy Scale (TES) received criticism from Bandura (1997, 2006) due to the global focus of the scale. Bandura (2006: 307) explained that 'the efficacy belief system is not a global trait but a differentiated set of self-beliefs linked to distinct realms of functioning'. In other words, Bandura questioned the broad nature of the TES, suggesting that in order to have greater predictive power, teacher efficacy measures require a degree of context specificity, such as beliefs towards teaching activities, rather than about teaching generally.

Teacher self-efficacy beliefs are assessed in relation to specific tasks and teaching contexts, and the past 20 years has seen a movement towards greater domain specificity in teacher efficacy research, with scales designed to focus on particular subjects (e.g. science, see Enochs & Riggs, 1990; Enochs et al., 1995; Mulholland & Wallace, 2001) and specific areas of teacher activity (e.g. the three dimensions of teacher activity related to engagement, instruction and classroom management in the Teacher Sense of Efficacy Scale (TSES), see Tschannen-Moran & Woolfolk Hoy, 2001). As discussed in Chapters 2 and 3, the efficacy beliefs of teachers vary according to subject and contexts, including their perceptions of efficacy towards different dimensions of efficacy. Thus, regardless of whether the researcher uses an efficacy scale or other data collection methods, a key difficulty for teacher efficacy researchers is 'pinpointing the range of teachers' work' (Wyatt, 2014: 179) in order to collect data that reflects the crucial areas of functioning for the target population.

Thus, for teacher efficacy researchers, the problem is reminiscent of Goldilocks – finding domains of activity and investigating teacher efficacy in a manner that is neither too specific nor too general. As studies and scales become more specific, they may become more predictive for the target population (e.g. towards language teaching), but become less generalisable to other settings, such as towards the broader teacher population (Klassen et al., 2011; Pajares, 1996). Thus, researchers must seek a balance between the level of domain specificity and the utility of findings towards the general field.

4.1.3 Inconsistency of wording

Teacher efficacy beliefs are future-oriented self-beliefs about capability. A common problem with many studies is the *wording* of items or the manner in which efficacy is introduced to participants. A number of studies have interpreted items of intention or current behaviour as efficacy, such as the Nishino (2009: 340, 2012) study discussed in Chapter 3, in which items used phrasing such as 'I provide activities in which my students can enjoy communicating in English' that clearly reflect a judgement of current practice, rather than a self-belief about future capability. Bandura (2006: 308) has stated that 'items should be phrased in terms of can do rather than will do. Can is a judgment of capability; will is a statement of intention'. Accordingly, the phrasing of items (i.e. within efficacy scales) or prompts (i.e. for interviews or focus groups) is another key consideration for teacher efficacy researchers.

4.2 Approaches for Investigating Foreign Language Teacher Efficacy

Teacher self-efficacy research has relied extensively on the use of questionnaires to investigate beliefs about capability (e.g. Chacon, 2005; Swanson, 2010a; Tschannen-Moran & Woolfolk Hoy, 2001; Tsui & Kennedy, 2009; Yilmaz, 2011). However, as the field has matured, a greater diversity of research methods has been used to examine efficacy beliefs, underlying latent constructs, the relationship between efficacy and other factors (e.g. second language [L2] proficiency) and sources of teacher efficacy. Wyatt (2014: 184) argues that a greater focus is needed on mixed methods, as a combination of methods allows key areas of efficacy to be highlighted and examined in detail in order to 'provide the insights that can make research into TSE beliefs of real use to teacher educators'. As different methods allow for greater transferability or provide a thicker description of the lived experience of educators, the combination of methods appears important for triangulating findings and enhancing their significance.

4.2.1 Use of efficacy scales

One of the most commonly used survey instruments is Tschannen-Moran and Woolfolk Hoy's (2001) Teacher Sense of Efficacy Scale, a questionnaire with long (24 item) and short (12 item) versions. Other scales have been specifically designed for use with foreign language teachers, such as Swanson's (2010a) Foreign Language Teacher Efficacy Scale (FLTES), and the Japanese Teacher of English Teacher Efficacy Scale (JTE-TES) developed for the current study (Thompson & Woodman, 2019).

Two data reduction techniques have been commonly used to identify underlying latent dimensions of teacher efficacy beliefs: exploratory factor analysis (EFA) and confirmatory factor analysis (CFA). Generally, EFA is an appropriate technique for exploring data and generating theory (Henson & Roberts, 2006). Thus, EFA is commonly used when studies have examined the factor structure of a new scale (e.g. Swanson, 2010a; Tschannen-Moran & Woolfolk Hoy, 2001). Some studies have used EFA with an existing scale, usually in exploratory research with new populations or new versions of the scale, such as Tsui and Kennedy (2009), who examined the factor structure of a translated form of the TSES. However, other studies have applied existing scales to similar populations and used CFA to test the 'fit' of a model (or models) for that population (e.g. Mulholland et al., 2004; Skaalvik & Skaalvik, 2007). Factor analysis can identify underlying dimensions of efficacy beliefs, highlighting the strength of beliefs towards different domains of practice. As a result, findings may be used to identify areas where professional development interventions are needed (e.g. towards different areas of teaching). Furthermore, such findings can be presented to teachers as part of pre-service or in-service training programmes, as a means of raising awareness and challenging teachers to examine their beliefs (Borg, 2011).

4.2.2 Correlational designs

Correlational designs are common in efficacy research, with a number of studies investigating the relationship between efficacy beliefs and personal/contextual factors such as L2 proficiency (Chacon, 2005; Swanson, 2010a; Yilmaz, 2011). However, without supplementary data (e.g. interviews), the inferences that can be drawn from such studies are limited, as they often focus on the quantity of experiences that individuals have, but do not necessarily attend to the quality of those experiences, nor the mediation of the cognitive process involved in the development of efficacy beliefs (see Morris *et al.*, 2016). An example is the use of correlational analysis to identify a positive relationship between (greater) experience and efficacy beliefs (e.g. Cheung, 2006; Fives & Buehl, 2009; Tschannen-Moran & Woolfolk Hoy, 2007). Such studies have indicated that greater experience provides *opportunities* for efficacy development, thus highlighting a relationship for further exploration. However, such studies do not necessarily attend to the perceived *quality* of the experience, which is also important for understanding whether or not experiences were meaningful for individuals, and in what ways they were valuable.

4.2.3 Regression and structural equation modelling

The use of regression analyses and structural equation modelling (SEM) has grown as researchers have started to examine potential direct and indirect predictors of teacher efficacy. Sometimes discussed as first (exploratory) and second (confirmatory) generation methods, each has been used to provide insights into the relationship between efficacy expectations and other factors. For example, Tschannen-Moran and Barr (2004) used multiple linear regression to explore the influence of collective teacher efficacy on student achievement, identifying a significant predictive relationship. Other studies have used more advanced multiple regression techniques (e.g. sequential multiple regression with interaction, see Choi & Lee, 2016) to investigate the influence and interaction between variables on teacher self-efficacy. SEM techniques (including path analysis) have been used to test theoretical models of the relationship between different variables and teacher efficacy. For example, Nishino (2009, 2012) used path analysis to examine the relationship between different teacher self-beliefs (including teacher efficacy) and teacher behaviour, while Goddard *et al.* (2015) used multilevel SEM analysis to examine instructional leadership, collaboration and collective efficacy on student learning. Findings from such research have provided evidence for proposed theoretical relationships; however, relatively large samples (e.g. higher than 200) are required (see Tomarken & Waller, 2005).

4.2.4 Interviews

A number of studies have used qualitative analysis of interviews (Mills & Allen, 2008; Phan & Locke, 2015) to examine the efficacy beliefs of language teachers. These techniques have also been valuable for identifying cultural or contextual elements that may influence the interpretations of teachers about their efficacy, such as the greater attendance to feedback from others for Vietnamese EFL teachers (e.g. Phan & Locke, 2015). Thus, such studies have extended understanding about the *quality* of different sources of efficacy, or about the *construal* of efficacy sources (Bandura, 1997) by individuals in different contexts. However, one challenge for teacher efficacy researchers is relating findings back to the theoretical framework of self-efficacy within social cognitive theory, and studies have used a combination of inductive data analysis with interpretation via thematic analysis (Phan & Locke, 2015) or by interpreting findings with respect to models of teacher efficacy (Mills & Allen, 2008).

4.2.5 Examining efficacy development

As Klassen *et al.* (2011) and others (Morris *et al.*, 2016; Wyatt, 2014) have noted, a reliable scale for investigating the sources of teacher efficacy is yet to be generated, and studies that have developed scales (e.g. Poulou, 2007) have had difficulty isolating the different sources using psychometric analyses. This may be due to the interactive and interconnected nature of efficacy sources, and remains a key area for future research. Generally, studies that have used qualitative analysis of interview and case study data have had greater success in understanding the quality of sources of teacher efficacy, due to the greater depth that attributions can be explored (Morris *et al.*, 2016). For example, in a series of longitudinal case studies, Wyatt (2010a, 2010b, 2013b) analysed interviews and classroom observations to detail the change in the teacher efficacy of participants in a teacher training programme. Such research has been valuable for teacher educators by highlighting key features that are attended to by individuals, and showing how efficacy change is also related to change in other teacher beliefs and knowledge.

4.3 Research Design: Exploring JTE Teacher Efficacy

Up to this point, the chapter has discussed a number of considerations for teacher efficacy researchers, and has presented a number of methods that have been commonly used in LTE studies. The final section of this chapter introduces the research design of the exploratory study discussed in this book. The section concludes by outlining some limitations of the research design.

The current study used a mixed method design to investigate the teacher efficacy beliefs of Japanese high school teachers of English (JTEs) and factors that may influence the efficacy beliefs of JTEs. The research presented in this book centred on exploring the following two questions:

(1) What are the underlying dimensions of JTE efficacy beliefs?
(2) What factors appear to influence JTE efficacy beliefs?

4.3.1 Summary of the research design

The research design of the study reported in this book (see Figure 4.1) included the collection of interview and questionnaire data, with qualitative and quantitative analysis of the data. The study used a quantitative-dominant sequential mixed method design (Collins et al., 2007) with three stages: (1) the first stage of the study focused on the design of the JTE-TES questionnaire and an exploration of the sources of Japanese teacher efficacy beliefs; (2) the second stage pilot tested the JTE-TES; and (3) the final stage surveyed JTEs from 27 prefectures across Japan. In other words, the principal method of inquiry in this study involved survey-style research, using statistical analysis of the data collected (e.g. descriptive, exploratory, inferential) via an online questionnaire. However, these analyses were influenced and supported by preliminary interviews.

4.3.2 Instrument design and piloting of the online questionnaire

Few studies have investigated teacher efficacy beliefs in the Japanese context. To strengthen instrument fidelity (Collins et al., 2006), the study started by exploring the domains of teacher challenge, which involved the collection of interview data that was analysed in a qualitative fashion. In other words, to 'contextualize' (Barcelos, 2006) the teacher efficacy

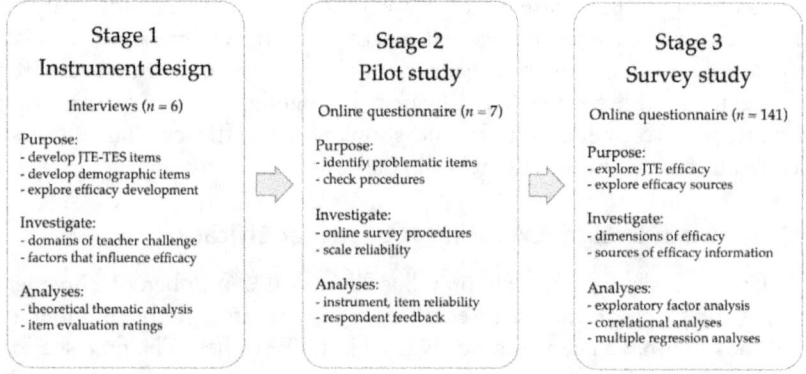

Figure 4.1 Summary of the research design

questionnaire to the Japanese context, the preliminary qualitative stage informed the development of a culturally and linguistically sensitive instrument with stronger construct validity (see Morgan, 1998; Onwuegbuzie et al., 2010).

Individual interviews were carried out with six participants in two cycles (i.e. two interviews per person). Interviews were conducted (primarily) in English, with occasional switches to Japanese. All were audio-recorded and transcribed professionally by an English–Japanese bilingual. A 'verbatim' transcript was produced for analysis, although examples introduced in this book have been edited for grammar and syntax.

The first interview had two stages: (1) a semi-structured format was used to explore the dimensions of teacher challenge within the Japanese context and sources of efficacy information; and (2) the participants were asked to use their expertise of the Japanese language teaching context to evaluate the appropriateness of instruments used in previous teacher efficacy studies (Nishino, 2009; Swanson, 2010a; Tschannen-Moran & Woolfolk Hoy, 2001). This design is consistent with approaches to self-efficacy inventory development. For example, Bandura (2006: 43) suggested that the collection of open-ended data from a small number of participants is important for ensuring validity when developing instruments. Specifically, he stated that 'interviews, open-ended surveys, and structured questionnaires' are an essential part of designing effective self-efficacy scales.

In order to enhance understanding of survey findings related to the second research question, interviews were analysed to identify key factors that influence JTE efficacy beliefs and to develop understanding about *how* such factors act as sources of information that influence JTE efficacy beliefs. In other words, a secondary purpose for the use of mixed methods was concerned with significance enhancement (see Collins et al., 2006). The use of interviews added 'real' examples and facilitated a thicker, richer set of data – crucial when investigating sources of teacher efficacy, as the interpretation of different sources is reliant on the individual, making them difficult to investigate via questionnaires (Morris et al., 2016). Key findings from the interviews have been presented by Thompson and Dooley (2019b) and are summarised in Chapters 6 and 10.

Interview findings were used to design efficacy items, which were translated using the collaborative serial translation approach (see Thompson & Dooley, 2019a), and evaluated by the experts in the second interviews. Their ratings were used to identify 25 items for use in the pilot stage of the study, from which a total of seven responses were collected from a convenience sample of 30 JTEs from three prefectures in Japan (Chiba, Tokyo, Kanagawa). Reliability analyses were carried out, indicating that the questionnaire had satisfactory internal reliability ($\alpha = 0.94$), and based on respondent feedback, small changes were made to the wording of five items before the main study.

4.3.3 Survey of JTEs

The third stage of the research used convenience and random sampling to collect 141 responses (52 male, 57 female, 32 did not report) to the survey from high school teachers from 27 prefectures across Japan. The online questionnaire comprised 25 efficacy items (i.e. the JTE-TES scale, see Table 4.1), using a six-point Likert-style response scale that asked participants to choose their level of confidence from 'not confident at all' to 'very confident'. The online questionnaire also included 33 demographic items (see Table 4.2), where respondents self-reported their

Table 4.1 Japanese Teacher of English Teacher Efficacy Scale (JTE-TES)

	How confident are you that you can
(1)	Give clear instructions to students in English?
(2)	Use English to communicate with your students?
(3)	Use English to have a conversation with an assistant language teacher?
(4)	Use English to plan and carry out a lesson with an assistant language teacher?
(5)	Adequately identify and correct your students' mistakes?
(6)	Provide information and explanations to students when they are confused, using language appropriate to their level?
(7)	Maintain and improve your English ability?
(8)	Manage the classroom adequately when students are doing pair work or group work?
(9)	Provide activities in which your students can enjoy communicating in English?
(10)	Provide student-centred lessons?
(11)	Use technology effectively in your lessons? (when possible and appropriate)
(12)	Develop appropriate assessments for evaluating your students' English ability? (e.g. tests, assignments)
(13)	Motivate students who show low interest in learning English?
(14)	Help students to increase their English proficiency?
(15)	Help your students develop English skills to pass university entrance tests?
(16)	Teach according to the Course of Study?
(17)	Adequately prepare for your classes?
(18)	Share teaching ideas and materials with colleagues?
(19)	Balance your teaching, administration and club responsibilities?
(20)	Manage your time in order to complete all required duties?
	How confident are you about your team/department/school's capability to
(21)	Communicate ideas effectively?
(22)	Develop teaching materials, syllabus and assessments collaboratively?
(23)	Support novice teachers effectively?
(24)	Support each other to develop new skills?
(25)	Implement communicative teaching approaches and ideas?

Table 4.2 Demographic items used in the survey stages of the study

Categorical variables

(1)	What is your gender?
(2)	Have you ever studied or lived abroad? (Please specify the length of your time abroad)
(3)	Please indicate your university programme major (Please specify)
(4)	Do you belong to a teachers' association? (If yes, please specify)
(5)	Where is your high school? (Please specify)
(6)	In what type of school (public/private) are you currently teaching?
(7)	Are you working fulltime?
(8)	Are you designated as a homeroom teacher?
(9)	What courses are you currently teaching? (Please specify)
(10)	Are you responsible for a club? (If yes, please specify)
(11)	In the last 10 years, has your school had a special designation, such as Super English High School? (If yes, please specify)
(12)	What administrative committees are you assigned to? (Please specify)

Interval variables

(13)	Please indicate the extent to which you use English as the language of instruction in your classes

Ordinal variables

(14)	What is your age?
(15)	How many years have you been teaching English?
(16)	What is your most recent test of English for international communication (TOEIC) score?
(17)	What is your most recent Eiken score?
(18)	Please estimate your current Eiken level.
(19)	What is the highest degree you have attained?
(20)	Please indicate the (*hensachi*) level of your school compared to other schools in your area.
(21)	How many fulltime teachers are there in your school's English department?
(22)	Please indicate the average age of teachers in your English department.
(23)	How often do you teach with an assistant language teacher?
(24)	Please indicate the amount of time each week you spend preparing for your English classes.
(25)	Please indicate the amount of time each week you spend checking and grading student work for your English classes.
(26)	Please indicate the amount of time each week you spend carrying out duties not related to classes, preparation or grading (such as homeroom, club or administration duties).
(27)	Please indicate the extent of your experience studying English communicatively in classes at elementary school, junior high school, high school, university or in other institutions
(28)	Please indicate the extent of your pre-service experience studying about communicative language teaching, *before* becoming a teacher.
(29)	Please indicate the extent of your pre-service experience observing lessons using communicative language teaching approaches and methodologies, *before* becoming a teacher.

(Continued)

Table 4.2 Demographic items used in the survey stages of the study (*Continued*)

(30)	Please indicate the extent of your experience conducting practice lessons using communicative language teaching approaches and methodologies, *before* becoming a teacher.
(31)	Please indicate the extent of your experience learning about communicative language teaching approaches and methodologies (e.g. attending seminars) *since* becoming an English teacher.
(32)	Please indicate the extent of your experience observing lessons using communicative language teaching approaches and methodologies (e.g. demonstration lessons) *since* becoming an English teacher.
(33)	Please indicate the extent of your experience conducting lessons using communicative language teaching approaches and activities (e.g. demonstration lessons or in your regular classes) since becoming an English teacher.

English proficiency, use of English as a teaching language and experiences with communicative language teaching (CLT).

EFA was carried out to identify underlying latent constructs of JTE teacher efficacy beliefs. Key findings have been presented elsewhere (see Thompson & Woodman, 2019) and are summarized in Chapter 6 of this book. Generally, extracted factors should be represented by three or more items (Costello & Osborne, 2005; MacCallum *et al.*, 1999; Pituch & Stevens, 2016). However, as explained by Thompson and Woodman (2019), the factor *Managing Workload* was only represented by two items, making it a 'weak' factor. Accordingly, this factor should be considered cautiously and future studies should further explore this domain of teacher efficacy.

Correlational and multiple regression analyses were also carried out to investigate the strength of relationships between dimensions of JTE foreign language teacher efficacy beliefs and key variables identified from the expert interviews (such as English language proficiency, years of teaching experience and experience with CLT), and identify any personal or contextual variables that may predict stronger or weaker teacher efficacy beliefs (i.e. variables that could be further investigated as sources of efficacy or as factors that influence the appraisal of teacher efficacy). Dummy variables were created for dichotomous items with multiple possible responses (e.g. demographic Items 9–11), and also for those who reported meeting the minimum mandated English proficiency level of 'Pre-1' on the *Jitsuyo Eigo Gino Kentei* (Test in Practical English Proficiency, commonly referred to in Japan as the 'Eiken' test, see Eiken Foundation of Japan, 2016b). Pearson, Spearman and point bi-serial correlational analyses were calculated for the JTE-TES factors (extracted via regression) against variables measured at interval and ratio (Pearson), ordinal (Spearman) and dichotomous (point bi-serial) level.

Finally, multiple regression analyses were carried out to investigate (1) which variables acted as predictors of JTE-TES dimensions (see Chapters 7–9), and (2) which variables predicted teacher use of English as a language of instruction (see Chapter 7). A forward regression technique was used, with a criterion for entry of $F < = 0.05$. Firstly, responses from seven participants were removed as they had not answered a majority of the demographic items. Next, a total of 53 missing values from 30 items (demographic Items 1, 5 and 9 excluded) for the remaining 128 respondents were replaced using fully conditional specification with predictive mean matching (FCS-PMM). Due to potential collinearity, pre-service (demographic Items 28–30) and in-service (demographic Items 31–33) variables were combined for the regression analyses (based on principal factor analysis). The assumptions for multiple regression were confirmed: linearity, independence, homoscedascity and normal distribution of errors (Keith, 2015). Influential cases were investigated, and in two cases (*Using English*, *Student Achievement*), outliers were identified and removed.

While the sample size for each analysis satisfied *minimum* requirements of five responses per predictor, such samples have been noted to have a 'high probability of not yielding significance unless the effect size is extremely large' (Green, 1991: 509). In other words, due to the limited sample size, the multiple regression analyses may have only identified predictor variables with large effect sizes. Accordingly, future studies could attempt to use larger samples to further explore predictors of efficacy beliefs.

4.3.4 Limitations of the research design

All studies have limitations and constraints. The study reported in this book has a number of limitations concerned with the development of the JTE-TES instrument, the sampling and instrumentation of the survey and the analysis of questionnaire data.

The survey design stage explored the perceptions of six participants, defined by the author as 'expert' in the JTE context, and these findings informed the design of questionnaire items. Participants were chosen following guidelines for the use of an expert panel (Beecham *et al.*, 2005) and based on the researcher's perception of their skills and experiences, thus the demographics and size of the panel may be influences that limit the transferability of findings to the JTE population and beyond. Also, the processes employed have potential limitations. For example, during the evaluative cycle of the expert panel interviews (discussed in Chapter 5), only items ranked as 'crucial' were selected, in order to reduce the total number of items in the scale. Furthermore, the demographic items used in the current study also reflected the key factors discussed by the experts during the survey design stage. For example, class size, a factor discussed in other studies (Nishino, 2009; Sakui, 2004, 2007), was not examined in the current study as it was not discussed by the interview participants as a contextual variable that varied significantly across their respective teaching contexts. Accordingly, other variables could be further examined in future studies.

The study is also limited in the way in which it investigated sources of efficacy. The interviews asked participants to discuss efficacy sources, and follow-up questions explored the attributions and influence of those sources. This allowed for source interpretation to be considered, including the quality and construal of the events towards efficacy beliefs (Morris et al., 2016). However, the demographic items used in the survey stage were not written in a manner that required teachers to interpret or judge the influence of a variable. Thus, while the survey stage investigated the quantity of experiences (e.g. of CLT teaching) that teachers reported, it did not investigate teachers' perceptions about the perceived quality of these experiences, nor the construal of these sources (i.e. the way in which individuals make meaning from these experiences). As a result, the survey stage study findings illuminate *potential* sources of efficacy information that can be further explored in future studies.

The sample size and demographics of the survey stage participants are another potential limitation. Although the total number of responses was similar to previous studies (e.g. Nishino, 2012), the survey stage of the research drew on a relatively small sample of responses. As Underwood (2013) has noted, attempts to survey teachers across Japan on a wide scale are becoming increasingly difficult due to data protection and privacy laws. Furthermore, only official Ministry of Education, Culture, Sports, Science and Technology (MEXT)-sanctioned research can use official distribution networks (Interview participant 'Maki', personal communication, 1 November 2013). This study used a combination of random and convenience sampling to attempt to address the difficulty of reaching teachers. However, some limitations include: (1) low rates of response and (2) responses from teachers with extreme views. The use of an online format allowed the questionnaire to be easily accessed across a wide geographical area; however, (1) respondents needed internet access; and (2) there was the risk of a digital divide (Tourangeau, 2004) that may have discouraged older teachers or teachers with less technological skills.

Analysis of the demographics of the sample against national data (MEXT, 2012a, 2012b, 2012c) indicates that the respondents are somewhat representative of the wider teaching population with respect to age. For example, 20% of respondents reported their age between 20 and 29 (13% nationwide), 27% between 30 and 39 (31% nationwide), 34% between 40 and 49 (31% nationwide) and 1.5% as over 60 (2.2% nationwide). On the other hand, it also appears that other factors may be over or under-represented. For example, private schools appear to be under-represented with only 11% of the respondents reporting that they work in private schools, in comparison to the percentage of approximately 26% nationwide (see MEXT, 2012c). Females may also be over-represented. A total of 57% of respondents to this study identified their gender as female, which is above the national average for *all subjects*, in which females account for 29% of all teachers (MEXT, 2012a). Furthermore, 29% of respondents identified their teaching context as being from a school with a 'special' designation. Of those, 8% identified their school as previously being a 'Super English language high school' or SELHi. According to MEXT (2010, 2012c) data, SELHi schools accounted for approximately 3.5% of all schools in 2009 (when they were discontinued), indicating that the sample may have an over-representation from 'special' schools, specifically schools with strong English programmes, and therefore likely also from teachers with a keener interest in language education.

As data was from self-report items, single source bias could influence the generalisability of findings. While self-reported achievement data has been shown to accurately reflect actual behaviour (Cole & Gonyea, 2010), participants may have over-reported their English proficiency to meet MEXT guidelines for teachers. For example, some studies have found evidence of systematic over-reporting of scores by participants at lower levels of ability (Cole & Gonyea, 2010; Kuncel *et al.*, 2005). However, Japanese respondents have been shown to be relatively accurate in self-report studies, such as when reporting their weight and height, with little difference between reported and actual values (Gorber *et al.*, 2007; Nakamura *et al.*, 1999; Wada *et al.*, 2005). To minimise such response bias effects, the survey was anonymous and confidential, thus respondents did not have any incentive to misreport information. Another issue was the availability of English proficiency scores. High school English teachers are not required to take a 'standard' English proficiency test regularly or at all. To offset this limitation, participants were asked to report their highest score and perceived current level on the *Jitsuyo Eigo Gino Kentei* (Test in Practical English Proficiency), referred to in this book as the 'Eiken' test. This test was chosen because it is officially recognised by the MEXT as the benchmark test for English instructors (Eiken Foundation of Japan, 2016b); it is culturally appropriate for the Japanese context; and because high school teachers have significant knowledge about the test due to its popularity with high school students.

4.4 Chapter Summary

This chapter has introduced issues for researchers to consider when designing teacher efficacy studies, such as the need to (1) establish conceptual clarity of the efficacy construct; (2) locate the research within an appropriate domain of specificity; and (3) develop questionnaire items and interview prompts that operationalise efficacy as future-oriented judgements of capability. The range of research methods used to investigate teacher efficacy is expanding, and this chapter has suggested that mixed method designs are becoming more important as efficacy research becomes more domain specific. As an example of a mixed method research design, this chapter has introduced the sequential methodology used in the current study, which used multiple data sources and means of analysis to investigate LTE in Japan. The *process* of scale development becomes the focus of Chapter 5, which explains how both qualitative and quantitative analysis of interview data was used to aid the design of the JTE-TES.

5 Developing a Language Teacher Efficacy Scale

Teacher efficacy measures require a degree of context specificity. For researchers using questionnaires or other prompts, a key difficulty is identifying the main challenges for the population of interest, and designing a scale that links the operations that teachers can control (i.e. the tasks) with teaching outcomes (Bandura, 2006). As discussed in Chapter 4, conceptual misalignment is a problem noted in many teacher efficacy studies – including many studies where the research is carried out using a common language. The threat of misalignment may be stronger for studies in which the construct of teacher efficacy is being adapted cross-culturally and uses another language for data collection, as researchers must not only design an appropriate scale (or interview prompts) for the respondents, but also attempt to ensure conceptual equivalence in another language. Research within the field of language education is commonly carried out in multiple languages, thus a particular concern for language teacher efficacy research is establishing the content, cultural and linguistic validity of efficacy scales used in multilingual contexts.

This chapter provides an example of the *processes* followed in the design of the Japanese Teacher of English Teacher Efficacy Scale (JTE-TES). The study was carried out with Japanese teachers of English, a research context where few teacher efficacy studies have been implemented. Thus, a key concern was achieving an appropriate level of task and contextual specificity for the population of interest. Furthermore, another validity concern focused on establishing conceptual equivalency with the construct of teacher efficacy in the translated scale. To develop survey items with context specificity and to strengthen instrument fidelity, two cycles of interviews (exploratory, evaluative) were carried out with six participants, defined as 'experts' by the researcher, during the instrument design stage of the study.

5.1 Using a Local Panel to Develop an Efficacy Instrument

The use of local experts in the development and modification of research instruments is a means of supporting the content and cultural validity of the final instrument. Emic perspectives provide valuable insights, because consulting with local participants informs understanding about the setting in which the instrument will be used, and allows local informants to help guide the creation of culturally sensitive items (Onwuegbuzie *et al.*, 2010). As Bandura (2006: 3) has explained, 'comprehensive' self-efficacy assessment requires an understanding of the different areas of functioning over which individuals can exercise control. By drawing on the voices of individuals working with and as Japanese high school teachers of English (JTE), the survey design stage aimed to identify the spectrum of areas where teachers can exercise control (exploratory stage), and then reduce the focus of the inquiry to the crucial tasks for JTEs (evaluative stage).

The use of experts strengthened the content validity of items by helping to ensure that items relevant to JTEs were included; that items irrelevant to the JTE context were not included; and that there was 'mutual understanding' of the constructs being measured by the items (Hyrkäs *et al.*, 2003: 620). The use of local participants was also important for ensuring linguistic validity, as a simple back-translation process may lead to items with similar semantic meanings, but different conceptual interpretations (Hunt *et al.*, 1991; Phillips, 1959). Furthermore, as misconceptions may be culturally derived due to idiomatic or experiential dissimilarity (Guillemin *et al.*, 1993), input from the local panel strengthened the cultural validity of the JTE-TES items by aligning them with terms used by JTEs (e.g. such as using the appropriate term for a teaching team, an example identified during the evaluative interview stage, see Section 5.5.3). In summary, given the conceptual difficulties identified in many previous teacher efficacy studies (see Chapter 4: Section 4.1 for discussion), the use of participants with local expertise helped establish a stronger conceptual equivalence to the efficacy construct and teaching tasks in the final, translated items.

Figure 5.1 shows the processes used in the development of the JTE-TES items during the first stage of the study. One-hour semi-structured interviews were conducted with each participant in two cycles. The exploratory cycle of interviews and analysis focused on developing a model of the domains of challenge for JTEs (i.e. the main areas where they exercise control), and the *generation* of teacher efficacy items. On the other hand, the evaluative cycle of interviews used both qualitative and quantitative analysis of interview data and expert item ratings to identify the items perceived to have the strongest content, linguistic and cultural validity.

5.2 The Expert Panel

As Hyrkäs *et al.* (2003) have explained, 'expert assessment can be qualitative or quantitative in nature', and in the current study, both were carried out during different stages of the survey design process. Two

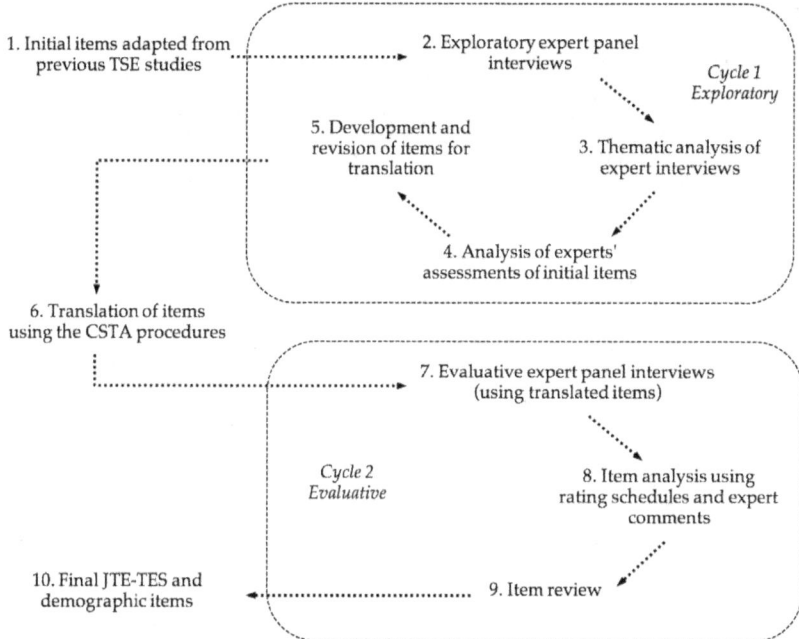

Figure 5.1 Processes used to develop the JTE-TES

cycles of individual interviews (exploratory, evaluative) were carried out with six individuals (two male, four female) identified to have expertise with the language teaching context in Japanese high schools. For the purposes of this study, experts were defined as bilingual educational professionals, with experience at the high school level in Japan as English teachers, curriculum specialists, consultants or researchers. The six members were selected purposively in order to allow them to represent a range of positions (e.g. novice to experienced) and experiences (e.g. current teachers, consultants, curriculum designers). A brief description of each of the members is provided in Table 5.1, using their assigned pseudonyms.

In order to allow the members of the expert panel to evaluate the cultural and content validity of the items for the pilot study, all participants were native speakers of Japanese, proficient users of English and had experience working at high schools as English teachers or working with high school English teachers as administrators, consultants, researchers or trainers. Five of the six were registered as high school English teachers, and the final member had more than 15 years working with teachers (including teaching and observation).

5.3 The Exploratory Cycle

The first exploratory interviews started by investigating the key areas of control and challenge for JTEs, including variables that participants

Table 5.1 The expert panel

Pseudonym	Details about the participant
Ken	A 26-year-old male high school English teacher at a *kyotenko* (schools that emphasise English for communicative purposes and often carry out open days for lesson observations by teachers from other schools), Ken had earned an undergraduate degree in English language before gaining his teacher licence. He had experience teaching at two schools, which had wide differences in academic ranking.
Maki	A 48-year-old female teacher consultant from a board of education (BOE) in a regional city in the south-western area of Japan, Maki organised professional development opportunities for teachers within her area and consulted about the implementation of the Japanese Ministry of Education, Culture, Sports, Science and Technology (MEXT) curricular changes. Before becoming a BOE consultant, she had approximately 20 years of experience as a high school English teacher, and had worked at two public co-educational schools.
Riho	A 31-year-old female university researcher with a specialty in applied linguistics, Riho carried out teacher training events and contributed to licence renewal courses for local and regional BOEs. She had trained as a high school English teacher, had completed her teaching licence and had more than 4 years of experience as a BOE teacher trainer.
Saki	A 28-year-old female high school English teacher with 4 years of experience, Saki had completed a graduate degree in applied linguistics and was working at a school that emphasised English for examination purposes. She had experience teaching at two schools, including one with a relatively low and another with a relatively high academic ranking.
Taka	A 59-year-old male university professor with a specialty in applied linguistics, Taka had more than 25 years of experience as a teacher and teacher trainer. At the time of the research, he was consulting for a number of high schools, as well as multiple local and regional BOEs. He had more than 20 years of policy-making experience as a MEXT curriculum designer and consultant.
Yuri	A 57-year-old female high school English teacher with approximately 35 years of experience, Yuri had taught at five schools in semi-rural and urban areas, including co-educational and single-sex schools. She had worked at a school with a special designation for English language education (known as a SELHi or Super English Language high school), and had taught at both lower and higher academically ranked schools.

perceived to influence their 'confidence' towards teaching English. The first part of the interview had four questions, and within each question the researcher followed up with probes to draw more information from the participants about their specific experiences and how these influenced their efficacy. The four questions that were used to structure the interviews were:

(1) What is it like to be an English teacher at a Japanese high school? Can you tell me about the different parts of the job? What kind of things do English teachers need to be able to do?
(2) Can you tell me about the kinds of challenges that face JTEs in the classroom?
(3) Can you tell me about the kinds of challenges that face JTEs outside the classroom?
(4) From your experience, what kind of things do you think would be likely to affect JTE confidence for teaching English?

The second part of the exploratory interviews involved asking the experts to consider, from their experience of teaching at Japanese high schools, the appropriateness of items used in other teacher efficacy studies. Prior to the first interviews, a total of 29 items (see Table 5.3) were adapted from three scales used in previous studies of language teacher efficacy: (1) the short form of Tschannen-Moran and Woolfolk Hoy's (2001) Teachers Sense of Efficacy Scale (TSES); (2) Swanson's (2010a) Foreign Language Teacher Efficacy Scale (FLTES); and (3) Nishino's (2009) 'Perceived teaching efficacy' items. Due to variations in specificity and the way they were written, items were reworded to a standard format that aligned with a self-efficacy orientation and the language teaching context (e.g. How confident are you that you can motivate students who show low interest in learning English?). Participants assessed the appropriateness (i.e. is the situation faced by JTEs?) and relevance (is the task important?) from their experience of high school teaching, with follow-up probes about items identified to be problematic.

5.3.1 Interview analysis

As reported by Thompson and Dooley (2019b), a 'theoretical' thematic analysis was carried out on the data set derived from the first part of the exploratory interviews. Used in other studies of teacher efficacy (e.g. Phan & Locke, 2015), thematic analysis 'involves the searching across a data set', such as a number of interviews, 'to find repeated patterns of meaning' (Braun & Clarke, 2006: 86). The purpose of the analysis was to (1) identify key domains of teacher challenge, from which efficacy items could be developed; (2) identify personal and contextual variables that influenced teacher efficacy; and (3) examine the key sources of efficacy-forming information. Table 5.2 shows the steps and processes followed in the theoretical thematic analysis, based on the model provided by Braun and Clarke (2006).

As summarised in Chapter 6 (and discussed elsewhere, see Thompson & Dooley, 2019b), findings identified eight domains of teacher challenge: *Classroom Management, Student Engagement, Communicative Language Teaching (CLT) Instructional Strategies, English for Teaching, Student Performance, Coping with Workload, Working with Colleagues* and *Team Efficacy*. Results also highlighted a number of factors that may act as sources of efficacy beliefs (e.g. feedback from colleagues, student learning experiences), and contextual areas that may influence the assessment of efficacy beliefs (e.g. school level, school designation). These findings were used for item development.

5.3.2 Item development and review

The items presented to the experts during the second stage of the exploratory interview are shown in Table 5.3. Following the thematic

Table 5.2 Steps and processes of the thematic analysis

---

(1) Familiarisation with the data
- The interviews were transcribed, corrected, read and re-read.

---

(2) Generation of initial codes
- Transitive verbs and nouns were used to code challenges. For example, when participants discussed the difficulty of making tests, it was coded with 'develop assessments'.
- Factors influencing efficacy were coded with nouns and in a different colour. For example, when a participant mentioned the importance of teacher knowledge for CLT implementation, the code 'knowledge' was used.
- Instances of efficacy change or development were coded with a symbol (e.g. + or −) and an abbreviation (e.g. mastery experience = ME). For example, '+VE' was used to indicate a modelling experience that the participant interpreted as a positive influence on their efficacy.

---

(3) Search for themes
- Codes were collated into themes. For example the 'development' theme combined two challenges: 'develop assessment' and 'develop materials'. Patterns across efficacy sources were also grouped according to common features, such as the 'teacher observation theme', which grouped positive and negative examples of modelling.

---

(4) Review of themes and development of initial dimensions
- Themes were reviewed to create dimensions. Examples from the research literature (Goddard *et al.*, 2000, 2004a; Skaalvik & Skaalvik, 2007; Swanson, 2010a; Tschannen-Moran & Woolfolk Hoy, 2001) were used to help name and define dimensions. Thus, themes related to interactions with students such as 'Relationships' and 'Motivation' were grouped into the dimension *Student Engagement*.

---

(5) Review, definition and naming of dimensions
- After a number of iterations (i.e. checking notes, theorising relationships and refining the theme), dimensions were examined and grouped into final domains.

---

(6) Produce a report
- A report was generated that included a table of the codes, themes and dimensions for both key challenges and sources of efficacy.

---

analysis, the experts' comments about the items used in previous TSE studies were collated, with a focus on identifying items considered inappropriate and/or irrelevant (see Desimone & Le Floch, 2004). A total of four items (4, 11, 15 and 29) were removed because two or more experts indicated that they were inappropriate for use with JTEs. For example, Item 11 '*How confident are you that you can assist families in helping their children do well in English?*' was considered 'weird' by Saki and questioned by Ken, who explained that in his experience, teachers generally 'don't have any contact with their family'.

Next, the initial items were mapped onto the eight dimensions of teacher challenge identified from the thematic analysis and reviewed based on comments made during the exploratory interviews. A total of 15 items were reviewed, using the experts' comments and codes from the interviews. In some cases, wording was changed (e.g. for Item 5, the word 'craft' was replaced by the word 'develop'), while in others the item was specified more closely to the Japanese context. For example, two participants explained that for JTEs, most interactions with native-like speakers occur with a non-Japanese assistant language teacher (ALT), thus Item 16 '*How confident are you that you can have a conversation*

Table 5.3 Initial items for assessment by the experts in the exploratory interviews

Source	How confident are you that you can:
TSES (Tschannen-Moran & Woolfolk Hoy, 2001)	1. Control disruptive behaviour in your classroom? 2. Motivate students who show low interest in learning English? 3. Get students to believe they can do well in learning English? 4. Help your students value learning English? 5. Craft communicative activities for your students? 6. Get your students to follow classroom rules? 7. Calm a student who is disruptive or noisy? 8. Establish a classroom management system in your classes? 9. Use a variety of strategies for assessing your students' English? 10. Provide alternative explanations or examples when your students are confused about English problems? 11. Assist families in helping their children do well in English? 12. Implement alternative strategies in your classroom?
FLTES (Swanson, 2010a)	13. Read and understand an English newspaper? 14. Understand an English movie? 15. Write a personal letter to a pen pal from another country in English? 16. Have a conversation with a native English speaker? 17. Increase students' English proficiency? 18. Help your students learn effectively at the level you teach? 19. Help your students pass university entrance tests?
Nishino's (2009) 'Perceived teaching efficacy' items	20. Speak English to an acceptable level for a high school English teacher? 21. Understand and explain English grammar to an acceptable level for a high school English teacher? 22. Explain aspects about the culture of English-speaking people and countries to your students? 23. Supervise the classroom adequately when students are doing pair work or group work? 24. Provide activities in which your students can enjoy communicating in English? 25. Implement and facilitate communicative activities in your classroom? 26. Give clear instructions to your students in English? 27. Use MEXT-authorised textbooks to teach English communicatively? 28. Provide student-centred lessons? 29. Encourage your students to take control of their learning?

with a native English speaker?' was reworded as '*How confident are you that you can use English to have a conversation with an ALT?*'

Drawing on the thematic analysis findings, a total of 34 new items were then developed. For example, experts had discussed the difficulty for JTEs of communicating with students (a problem also noted in other studies of JTEs, e.g. Glasgow, 2014; Nishino, 2012). Accordingly, a new item '*How confident are you that you can use English to communicate with your students?*' was developed for translation. A number of challenges related to coping, instructional decisions and collective efficacy were also identified in the thematic analysis. As shown in Table 5.2, examples from the research literature (Goddard *et al.*, 2000, 2004a; Skaalvik & Skaalvik, 2007) were also consulted, and items from these studies were drawn on to develop four new items. For example, many JTEs carry out team teaching activities with ALTs, and this was discussed by a number of experts as a key difficulty (also mentioned in studies of JTEs, e.g. Glasgow, 2013). During his interview, Ken discussed a situation at his school, where a colleague did not want to carry out team teaching with the ALT. Accordingly, an item from Skaalvik and Skaalvik's (2007: 624) TSE study representing efficacy to 'cooperate effectively and constructively with other teachers' was adapted for translation and evaluation during the second cycle of interviews as '*How confident are you that you can cooperate effectively and constructively with other teachers, for example, in team teaching?*'

A final set of 60 items was developed for translation, including 34 new items, a total of 16 items accepted from other scales without change and 10 items derived from other measures (i.e. revised from those shown in Table 5.3). The new items included seven items focused on perceived collective and collaborative efficacy, as one key finding from the interviews concerned the importance of tasks and activities that were carried out by teams.

Finally, a number of the key ideas identified in the thematic analysis related to contextual or personal factors that the experts identified as influencing their (and their colleagues) beliefs. These ideas were used to review and revise the demographic items, drawing on specific comments and examples from the interviews. Four new demographic items were added related to school level, school designation and non-teaching duties. For example, as a teacher who had previously worked at a school designated a Super English Language high school (SELHi), Yuri suggested that the contextual situation of teachers at such schools would be very different in comparison to regular schools, due to extra professional development opportunities and a significant difference in (higher) student motivation. Accordingly, an item '*Does your school currently have (or had had within the last 10 years) a special designation?*' was added to the demographic items for translation.

5.4 Item Translation Process

Following the first expert panel cycle, English language items were generated. As Thompson and Dooley (2019a) have explained, translation is a key process for consideration when researchers are working in different languages, as maximising the linguistic and cultural validity of instruments is vital. In the current study, the 'collaborative serial translation approach' (CSTA), a four-step translation and back-translation procedure, was used (see Thompson & Dooley, 2019a), which involved two teams of translators working first individually, then together, to produce a final forward translation (team one) and back-translation (team two). The authors suggested that the researcher (or research team) audit the forward and back-translated content, and revise items with further rounds of translation as required. Accordingly, translations were reviewed by the researcher and by the expert panel during the second (evaluative) interviews. The experts provided alternative translations for any problematic items, which the researcher integrated into the final scale.

5.5 The Evaluative Cycle

The second expert panel interviews had a stronger evaluative function focused on assessing the linguistic, cultural and content validity of the items for local participants. This stage of the design process had the purpose of identifying the most relevant and appropriate items for the JTE context.

During each one-hour semi-structured evaluative interview, participants were asked to consider the appropriateness of the efficacy items by rating each item using two scales. A three-point scale was used to assess the appropriateness of the item (inappropriate, revision needed, acceptable). For all items not rated as 'acceptable', panel members were asked to provide an explanation of the weaknesses of the item, or changes they deemed necessary if the item needed review. If they considered the item appropriate (or acceptable with review), they were then asked to consider the content 'value' of the item for understanding key areas of JTE teacher capability using a content scale (1 = relevant, 2 = important, 3 = crucial). Table 5.4 shows the scales used in the rating process.

5.5.1 Analysis and item review procedures

Items were accepted for use (without change), deleted or revised based on the level of agreement between the participants. Depending on the number of participants involved, agreement rates are generally 70% or 80% (see Beecham et al., 2005; Hyrkäs et al., 2003), and both were used in the current study. Items with 80% or greater agreement were automatically accepted or accepted for revision, while items with 70% or greater were reviewed by the researcher to confirm that items were not discarded due to misunderstandings.

The following process was used to analyse the evaluative interviews and review items:

(1) Key findings: Interviews were read and re-read to identify common problems with content, linguistic and cultural validity of the scale items.
(2) Collate ratings: Expert ratings for items were collated into a table.
(3) Item deletion: Items with ratings of 'inappropriate' or 'unacceptable' were reviewed using an 80% agreement threshold. Thus, if two experts rated an item as unacceptable, it was automatically removed.

Table 5.4 Item rating scales used in the 'evaluative' expert interviews

Process	Rating (symbol used)			
(1) Appropriateness	Inappropriate (I)	Revise (R)		Acceptable (A)
(2) Content rating	Unacceptable (0)	Relevant (1)	Important (2)	Crucial (3)

Items with one 'unacceptable' and one 'revise' rating (i.e. 70% or greater agreement) were also reviewed.

(4) Identify key items: Content ratings for the remaining items were then examined. The total for each item was collated, and an 80% agreement threshold was used to identify key items. Items with collated content ratings above 15 met the 80% threshold, as this indicated that the item was judged by half of the experts as 'important' and the remaining half as 'crucial'. Using these content ratings, 25 items were identified.

(5) Item revision and combination: Ratings for appropriateness were examined using an 80% threshold. Items with five or more 'acceptable' ratings were not changed (6 items). Items with two or more 'revise' ratings were reviewed using any suggestions noted in the transcripts (19 items). Expert comments were examined to identify items that could be combined, using an 80% or greater agreement. Two items were combined.

(6) Analysis of items with agreement of 70%: Items with 70% agreement for *content* rating (i.e. with collated ratings 13 or higher) were reviewed (7 items). One item was revised and added back to the scale, using suggestions from the experts noted in the transcripts. Accordingly, the final JTE-TES had 25 items.

(7) Final review of the scale: Findings related to the linguistic, content and cultural validity of the scale (e.g. instructions) and demographic items were integrated. Expert comments were used to revise the wording for the instructions of the scale. Demographic items were assessed using an 80% agreement. One item was removed and 11 other items were reviewed, using expert suggestions noted in the transcripts.

5.5.2 Key findings from the second expert panel interviews

The second expert interviews provided an opportunity to determine how different individuals judged the same item. The purpose of the survey design process was to identify a set of items that were collaboratively viewed as 'important' to 'crucial' by the experts, indicating *common* cultural, content and linguistic validity. In a number of cases, items were judged as crucial by some experts, but unacceptable by others, reflecting different interpretations of the task or the focus of the item.

One key issue involved the forward translation of 'can', as the final forward translation used two different expressions: *dekimasu*, and *dekiteimasu*. Prior to the second interviews, all back-translated items were checked by the researcher, who noticed the differences in the wording used to express the concept of 'can' for a number of items. As conceptual clarity of efficacy items is crucial, these items were noted for review by the expert panel in the second interviews, with specific discussion about the extent to which the different wordings aligned with the efficacy conceptual framework as forward-oriented expressions of perceived capability. However, even before being brought up by the researcher, this issue was raised by a number of experts in the second interviews (e.g. Yuri, Maki and Riho started by discussing this issue). It was clear that *dekimasu* was perceived as a more appropriate means for introducing 'can' as it relates to confidence for *future* perceived capability, while *dekiteimasu* was considered to also include current practice. For example, Riho explained that *dekiteimasu* includes the concept of ability, but also current practice, stating 'are you actually doing it?' Accordingly, to reflect a forward-oriented 'can' construct in accordance with Bandura's (2006) guidelines, all *dekite imasu ka* (are you doing?) items were changed to *dekimasu ka* (can you?) during the review process.

Secondly, the experts identified confusion with a number of items that investigated different levels of task difficulty. Following the first interviews, a number of items had been revised to include level of difficulty (Bandura, 2006), specifically capability towards completing the task using Japanese versus using English. However, the added complexity made items confusing for a number of the experts. Accordingly, items were reviewed and levels of difficulty (i.e. carrying out the task using English or using Japanese) were removed, in order to make each item clearly focused on one task and the survey faster for respondents to complete. It is suggested that future studies could consider levels of task difficulty for specific task domains (e.g. L2 self-efficacy), as such an item design may provide clarification about the extent to which language knowledge (for example) influences efficacy beliefs towards a specific task. For example, future studies could focus specifically on instructional tasks (e.g. giving instructions to a group of L2-speaking high school students; providing feedback to an individual student about a grammatical error), and ask respondents to rate the strength of their efficacy for carrying out the task in the L1 or L2.

5.5.3 Item review

The experts' ratings were collated and used to select items to remain in the survey for the survey stages of data collection. A total of seven items did not meet the 80% agreement threshold for appropriateness, and were removed. For example, the item '*How confident are you that you can provide activities to students with different abilities?*' was removed as it was seen to be irrelevant for most teaching contexts. In her interview, Saki explained that the item was confusing, as in her experience, all classes were required to use the same materials and tests.

Next, items with agreement ratings above 70% were reviewed (i.e. one expert had rated as 'unacceptable' and one or more experts had rated 'revise'). Sixteen items were removed due to cultural, content and linguistic reasons. For example, the item *'How confident are you that you can use English to have a discussion with other Japanese English teacher colleagues?'* was removed as a number of experts suggested that such a task was extremely rare. Another example is the item *'How confident are you that you can establish a classroom management system in your English classes?* The item was questioned by a number of experts due to cultural and linguistic inappropriateness. In her interview, Saki stated, 'I'm not really sure what it asks me about', while both Taka and Ken had problems with the linguistic translation of 'classroom management' and very different understandings of what was meant by 'management system'.

After item removal, the content ratings for the remaining 37 items were reviewed. A total of 25 items met the 80% threshold for acceptance. The appropriateness ratings (i.e. accept without change or needs revision) were then examined, and six items were accepted for use in the survey stage without any revision (i.e. they met the 80% threshold for both appropriateness and content). For example, the item *'How confident are you that you can use English to communicate with your students?'* received 5 'acceptable' ratings with a content total of 17. A total of 19 items met the content rating threshold, but were flagged for review by two or more experts. Of these items, 14 items had problems with the forward translation of 'can', and 5 items had wording problems. Suggestions from the experts were used to review the items. Finally, the comments of the experts were examined to identify any items that could be combined. Two items concerned with team capability to develop materials, syllabi and assessments were combined into one item *'How confident are you about your team/departments' capability to develop teaching materials, syllabus, and assessments collaboratively?'*

During the final step in item revision for the JTE-TES, the researcher reviewed seven items with content ratings meeting the 70% content agreement threshold (i.e. 13 or greater). The expert comments about each item were examined, and one item was identified to have a poor rating from one expert due to confusion about the levels of task difficulty. In her interview, Maki explained that the item *'How confident are you that you can give clear instructions to students? In English? In Japanese?'* was confusing as she couldn't see why teachers would give the same instructions in English and Japanese. As these levels of task difficulty were removed (see Section 5.5.2), this item was added back into the final scale as *'How confident are you that you can give clear instructions to students in English?'* Accordingly, a final set of 25 items was generated for the survey stages of the research. Table 5.5 shows the JTE-TES items ordered by 'individual' (1–20) and 'collective' (21–25) challenge.

After completing the analysis and finalising the efficacy scale items, the experts' perceptions about the appropriateness of the demographic items were examined. One item was deleted due to five inappropriate ratings, and 11 items were reviewed. Finally, general comments about

Table 5.5 JTE-TES items for the survey stages of the study

How confident are you that you can:	
(1)	Give clear instructions to students in English?
(2)	Use English to communicate with your students?
(3)	Use English to have a conversation with an ALT?
(4)	Use English to plan and carry out a lesson with an ALT?
(5)	Adequately identify and correct your students' mistakes?
(6)	Provide information and explanations to students when they are confused, using language appropriate to their level?
(7)	Maintain and improve your English ability?
(8)	Manage the classroom adequately when students are doing pair work or group work?
(9)	Provide activities in which your students can enjoy communicating in English?
(10)	Provide student-centred lessons?
(11)	Use technology effectively in your lessons? (when possible and appropriate)
(12)	Develop appropriate assessments for evaluating your students' English ability? (e.g. tests, assignments)
(13)	Motivate students who show low interest in learning English?
(14)	Help students to increase their English proficiency?
(15)	Help your students develop English skills to pass university entrance tests?
(16)	Teach according to the Course of Study?
(17)	Adequately prepare for your classes?
(18)	Share teaching ideas and materials with colleagues?
(19)	Balance your teaching, administration and club responsibilities?
(20)	Manage your time in order to complete all required duties?
How confident are you about your team/department/school's capability to:	
(21)	Communicate ideas effectively?
(22)	Develop teaching materials, syllabus and assessments collaboratively?
(23)	Support novice teachers effectively?
(24)	Support each other to develop new skills?
(25)	Implement communicative teaching approaches and ideas?

the scale were reviewed. Two experts (Ken, Saki) had commented on the translation of the item introduction for collective efficacy items. The item introduction in English, *'How confident are you about your team/ department/school's capability to...?'* was not considered linguistically or culturally appropriate for the JTE context due to inappropriate wording for 'team/department/school'. The experts suggested that generally teachers consistently work with one group of teachers for each year and class level (e.g. for first-year students taking 'English Communication I'). Accordingly, Saki's suggestion of *'gakunen kyoin'* was used for 'team' as this is a specific term for teachers working together on curriculum development for a specific course.

5.6 Chapter Summary

This chapter has outlined the development process of the JTE-TES language teacher efficacy scale. It has shown how input from a panel of local respondents with expertise in the teaching context was used to develop a contextualised instrument. As Hyrkäs *et al.* (2003) have explained, expert validity is a type of content validity, and different means of data collection and analysis were used instrumentally to strengthen understanding about the crucial domains of teacher activity and challenge in the JTE context to design the JTE-TES scale. Initial items were adapted from existing instruments, and edited according to Bandura's (2006) guidelines for instrument development to reflect the context and future orientation of self-efficacy theory. Items were edited and new items developed based on the findings of the exploratory expert panel interviews. Next, two agreement scales were used in evaluative interviews with the expert panel to identify the crucial tasks for the Japanese high school context. As discussed in Chapter 4, the scale was pilot tested before use in the main study. This process shows how a number of techniques (adaptation, integration of exploratory thematic analysis, evaluative feedback) can be combined to enhance construct validity and contextualise teacher efficacy for different contexts.

In summary, the use of expert ratings and comments during the survey design process can enhance the content and cultural validity of efficacy scales by ensuring that the instrument is (1) aligned with the construct of teacher efficacy as a future-oriented perception of capability framework (i.e. meeting conceptual requirements for teacher efficacy research); and (2) focused on the key areas of control for the local (JTE) teaching context. Accordingly, this process could be adapted to other contexts.

The process of scale development highlighted a range of challenges for language teachers in Japan related to specific classroom activities and broader areas of teacher action such as collaboration, including regulatory challenges related to workload management. This book now moves to discussion of JTE efficacy beliefs and the dimensions of language teacher efficacy for Japanese high school teachers.

6 JTE Language Teacher Efficacy Beliefs and Dimensions

Teacher efficacy is context dependent and multidimensional. A significant amount of research has identified various dimensions of teacher efficacy towards different areas of teaching practice (e.g. Skaalvik & Skaalvik, 2007; Swanson, 2010a; Tschannen-Moran & Woolfolk Hoy, 2001), while other studies have indicated that the strength of teacher self-beliefs varies by teaching domain. For example, a number of studies (Chacon, 2005; Eslami & Fatahi, 2008; Yilmaz, 2011) have examined the strength of language teachers' efficacy towards the three dimensions of Tschannen-Moran and Woolfolk Hoy's (2001) Teacher Sense of Efficacy Scale (TSES), showing stronger efficacy towards Instructional Strategies in comparison to Student Engagement and Classroom Management.

Other studies have suggested that the latent dimensions of teacher efficacy are context dependent (Cheung, 2006, 2008; Tsui & Kennedy, 2009), and research has suggested that language teacher efficacy has content dimensions (Hiver, 2013; Nishino, 2012; Swanson, 2010a). For example, Swanson (2010a) designed a 10-item scale specifically for foreign language teachers, finding two dimensions related to knowledge (i.e. perceived capability to use the second language [L2]) and facilitation of learning (i.e. perceived capability to use language knowledge to aid student learning).

This chapter introduces and discusses key findings related to the first research question explored in this study of Japanese high school teacher of English (JTE) efficacy:

(1) What are the underlying dimensions of Japanese high school English teacher efficacy beliefs?

The chapter draws on analysis of semi-structured interviews carried out with the six members of the expert panel, and exploratory factor analysis (EFA) of the online questionnaire responses from 141 JTEs. While some of the findings introduced in this chapter have been discussed separately elsewhere (see Thompson & Dooley, 2019b; Thompson & Woodman,

2019), other results (e.g. the relationship between efficacy beliefs and effort) are presented for the first time.

6.1 Key Areas of Challenge for Japanese Teachers of English

Theoretical thematic analysis of interviews identified eight dimensions of teacher challenge for Japanese high school English teachers. The analysis involved the grouping of repeated patterns within the interview data set into themes that represented different 'difficulties' for teachers. A total of five domains of teacher challenge were related to teacher activity in class: *Classroom Management*, *Student Engagement*, *Communicative Language Teaching (CLT) Instructional Strategies*, *Student Performance* and *English for Teaching*. *Coping with Workload* related to teacher stress and the workload demands placed on teachers. Finally, *Working with Colleagues* related to individual beliefs about the challenges of working in teaching teams. This dimension overlapped with a collective dimension, named *Team Efficacy*, which focused on the challenges that teachers face as teams and their capability towards them.

As Thompson and Dooley (2019b) have explained in their summary of the exploratory interviews, key themes emerging from the thematic analysis were that (1) a number of the challenges faced by JTEs align with dimensions of efficacy identified in other studies; (2) some important domains of teacher control for JTEs are outside the classroom; (3) there are individual and collective challenges, which indicates that teacher beliefs about collective capability may be an important aspect for further study; and (4) some domains of challenge reflect local realities of language teaching.

For example, findings indicated that the first three domains broadly aligned with the three dimensions of the TSES (Student Engagement, Instructional Strategies, Classroom Management), indicating that these dimensions are applicable to the language teaching environment in Japanese high schools. Furthermore, other dimensions of challenge can be interpreted by comparison to previous studies (such as Goddard *et al.*, 2000; Skaalvik & Skaalvik, 2007; Swanson, 2010a). For example, the dimension *English for Teaching* comprised of four themes (use of English with students, demonstration of English knowledge, use of English with colleagues and maintenance of ability) and aligned with the *Teacher as Facilitator* dimension of Swanson's (2010a) Foreign Language Teacher Efficacy Scale (FLTES) in that it focused on how teachers draw on their language knowledge for using English with students and other teachers to support student learning.

Three domains of challenge (*Coping with Workload*, *Working with Colleagues* and *Team Efficacy*) included activities carried out not only in classrooms. These three areas of activity related to similar dimensions identified by Skaalvik and Skaalvik (2007) in their study of teacher efficacy in Norway (e.g. Coping with Change, Working with Colleagues and Collective Efficacy). Specifically, respondents discussed the difficulty of 'coping' with duties outside class and changes to the curriculum, the need for effective collaborative work and the reality that many challenges are reliant on group action. Overall, results indicated that there are various areas of activity over which teachers can bring about actions in the pursuit of increased student learning, and this finding supports a wider view of language teacher efficacy; agency is not limited to classroom action. Indeed, interviewees indicated that a number of important challenges are collective. In support of prior research (e.g. Goddard *et al.*, 2004a), tasks viewed as collective challenges included the selection of textbooks; the difficulty of designing and using shared resources; the response of the school to national curriculum changes; and support of novice teachers (see Thompson & Dooley, 2019b).

Interview findings indicated that many of these challenges are reflective of difficulties faced by teachers in the wider education and language teaching fields. For example, individual dimensions related to instruction (Skaalvik & Skaalvik, 2007; Swanson, 2010a) and L2 capability (e.g. Swanson, 2010a) appear to be reflective of challenges faced by teachers, regardless of their environment. However, specific tasks within each domain may also reflect contextual constraints and difficulties, such as the issue for JTEs of team teaching (from *Working with Colleagues*) and the difficulty of using English as a teaching language (from *English for Teaching*). The relevance of such activities may depend on the respective policies of countries towards team teaching or English medium instruction. As a result, these challenges appear to align with movements in language teaching across Asia (Baldauf *et al.*, 2011; Hamid & Nguyen, 2016; Hamid *et al.*, 2013).

Furthermore, as Thompson and Dooley (2019b) have suggested, certain domains of challenge may reflect key local contextual challenges. Specifically, the domain *Student Performance* was identified as a crucial issue for JTEs, as interview findings indicated that a key difficulty for teachers was preparing students for university entrance examinations that rely on esoteric grammatical and pronunciation knowledge. To illustrate, in the Skaalvik and Skaalvik (2007) study of Norwegian teachers, adapting instruction to *individual* student needs was considered an important area of teacher activity. On the other hand, results from this study indicated that a key challenge was *balancing* instruction between the two (perceived) competing aims of university examination preparation and communicative competency development – a result with significant support in the extant JTE language teacher cognition literature (e.g. Butler, 2011; Kikuchi, 2006; Nishino & Watanabe, 2008; Sakui, 2004). Thus, while there appears to be some generality in the domains of control over which teachers exert action, including similarity and transferability in some of the dimensions of efficacy, there also appears to be variation in the specific tasks and domains of challenge for different teacher groups. Future research could further explore the overlapping areas of challenge and identify context-specific domains for different teaching groups.

6.2 Teacher Efficacy Beliefs of Japanese High School English Teachers

In the third stage of the study, 141 responses to the 25-item Japanese Teacher of English Teacher Efficacy Scale (JTE-TES) questionnaire and demographic items were collected via an online format, where respondents rated their confidence towards each task using a six-point Likert-style response format. A total of six participants did not complete a majority of the JTE-TES and were removed prior to analysis. Descriptive statistics were generated (see Table 6.1) and scale reliability was examined (Cronbach $\alpha = 0.94$), indicating strong internal consistency. Efficacy scale findings, as shown in Table 6.1, indicated significant variation in the strength of efficacy towards different tasks. These findings highlight some of the key contextual challenges for JTEs related to workload and the motivation of students.

From examination of measures of central tendency, it seems clear that JTE efficacy is weakest towards non-teaching duties related to workload regulation. The two items with the lowest median and mean ratings were Item 19 'Balancing teaching, administration, and club responsibilities' (Med = 3, $M = 3.40$, $SD = 1.19$) and Item 20 'Managing time in order to complete all required duties' (Med = 3, $M = 3.52$, $SD = 1.30$). This finding provides support for comments made by participants in the interview stage of the study, in which they suggested that the influence of challenges outside the classroom (i.e. balancing the requirements of all required duties) may be the biggest challenge for JTEs due to their heavy workload.

For example, Thompson and Dooley (2019b) report an example from Ken, who explained that he commonly worked 14-hour days in order to attend to his teaching and non-teaching duties (including a significant amount of time on administration and sports coaching). Ken suggested that due to this heavy burden, he could not always attend to teaching preparation. To expand on their discussion, Saki also mentioned the time required to be in charge of a sports club, particularly a sport that she had absolutely no experience of playing, while Yuri discussed the time burden and stress of managing the administration of overseas trips for students. Finally, Riho discussed her time serving on the 'life guidance' committee, which involved her spending her mornings (before school) checking students' uniforms as they arrived at school. She stated 'if you have that time to be checking hundreds of students' socks, every morning... I think you would rather, to be honest, want to be planning your lessons or practicing your own language'.

Table 6.1 Descriptive statistics and efficacy dimensions of the JTE-TES

Item	n	Med	M	SD	Dimension
Efficacy for					
(1) Giving clear instructions to students in English.	135	5	4.61	0.97	UE
(2) Using English to communicate with students.	133	5	4.75	0.91	UE
(3) Using English to have a conversation with an ALT.	135	5	4.76	0.98	UE
(4) Using English to plan and carry out a lesson with an ALT.	135	5	4.71	1.06	UE
(5) Adequately identifying and correcting student mistakes.	133	5	4.56	0.84	SA
(6) Providing information and explanation to students using language appropriate to their level.	134	5	4.47	1.03	
(7) Maintaining and improving your English ability.	134	4	4.46	1.05	
(8) Managing the classroom adequately when students are doing pair work or group work.	135	5	4.71	0.95	CT
(9) Providing activities in which students can enjoy communicating in English.	135	4	4.28	0.98	CT
(10) Providing student-centred lessons.	135	4	4.03	1.03	CT
(11) Using technology effectively in lessons.	134	4	3.81	1.17	
(12) Developing appropriate assessments for evaluating student English ability.	135	4	4.02	0.94	
(13) Motivating students who show low interest in learning English.	135	4	3.87	0.99	
(14) Helping students to increase their English proficiency.	135	4	4.51	0.80	SA
(15) Helping your students develop English skills to pass university entrance tests.	135	4	4.40	1.05	SA
(16) Teaching according to the Course of Study.	135	4	4.19	1.01	
(17) Adequately preparing for your classes.	135	5	4.57	0.95	
(18) Sharing teaching ideas and materials with colleagues.	134	5	4.58	0.92	TW
(19) Balancing your teaching, administration and club responsibilities.	135	3	3.40	1.19	MW
(20) Managing your time in order to complete all required duties.	134	3	3.52	1.30	MW
Efficacy in teaching team's capability for					
(21) Communicating ideas effectively.	135	4	4.04	0.96	TW
(22) Developing teaching materials, syllabus and assessments collaboratively.	135	4	3.95	1.07	TW
(23) Supporting novice teachers effectively.	134	4	3.93	1.11	
(24) Supporting each other to develop new skills.	135	4	4.30	1.03	
(25) Implementing communicative teaching approaches and ideas.	135	4	4.27	1.10	

Notes: ALT = assistant language teacher; UE = using English; CT = communicative teaching; TW = teamwork; SA = student achievement; MW = managing workload.

Findings also indicated weaker efficacy beliefs towards some key teacher classroom actions, such as perceived capability to encourage motivation in students with a low interest in learning English (Item 13: Med = 4, $M = 3.87$, $SD = 0.99$). A number of studies in Japan (e.g. Humphries & Burns, 2015; Nishino & Watanabe, 2008; Sakui, 2007) have discussed the difficulty of low student motivation towards language learning, and correlational analyses showed that teachers with stronger efficacy towards this activity were, unsurprisingly, more likely to work at a school with a special designation. Students at such schools are more likely to have higher motivation towards the study of English, in contrast to schools at the other end of the spectrum, such as technical colleges, where student motivation is low and many students may even sleep during class (Humphries & Burns, 2015). Other demographic variables associated with stronger perceived capability to encourage motivation were experience studying or living overseas ($r = 0.28$, $p < 0.01$), experience studying via CLT as a student ($r = 0.25$, $p < 0.05$), experience carrying out in-service professional development activities ($r = 0.19$, $p < 0.05$) and experience conducting CLT in their current classes ($r = 0.45$, $p < 0.01$). Overall, the amount of experience that teachers had with CLT appeared to be a key demographic factor associated with stronger efficacy beliefs towards teaching tasks (discussed further in Chapter 8). This appears to be a key source of information informing efficacy belief change, and is discussed further in Chapter 10, as it has implications for teacher development.

An interesting result concerned tasks that involved the use of English (i.e. Items 1–4), as measures of central tendency indicated that teachers generally had stronger efficacy towards the use of English for communicating with students (Item 2: Med = 5, $M = 4.75$, $SD = 0.91$) and colleagues (Item 3: Med = 5, $M = 4.76$, $SD = 0.98$) in comparison to other teaching and non-teaching activities. This is a somewhat surprising result, as teacher language competency is commonly focused on as a crucial area where teachers lack skills (Freeman *et al.*, 2015; Glasgow, 2014; Nishino & Watanabe, 2008). Given that teacher efficacy assessment involves drawing on perceptions of competency, this finding may indicate that L2 proficiency is not the main area where teacher skills are lacking. Results indicate that JTE efficacy is relatively strong towards tasks that involve the use of the L2 as against duties beyond the classroom, such as workload regulation. Development initiatives may need to consider how teachers are armed with coping strategies for workload regulation or instructional strategies for working with difficult and unmotivated students, rather than L2 skills development.

In a related finding, there is support for the contention that teachers with stronger efficacy are more likely to expend greater effort and persistence (Enochs *et al.*, 1995; Mulholland & Wallace, 2001; Woolfolk Hoy & Davis, 2006). Effort was assessed via two items that asked participants to self-report the number of hours they spent (1) preparing for class and (2) attending to grading. A weak but significant positive correlation was noted between reported effort and perceived capability to adequately prepare for class (i.e. JTE-TES Item 17: $r = 0.21$, $p < 0.05$). Results also indicated that teachers who reported greater effort were more likely to have stronger capability to implement the new national curriculum (i.e. JTE-TES Item 16: $r = 0.22$, $p < 0.05$). Studies have suggested that teachers with stronger efficacy display greater commitment to innovation (Ghaith & Yaghi, 1997; Guskey, 1988; Skaalvik & Skaalvik, 2007) and are more likely to have greater commitment to teaching (Chan, 2008; Chesnut & Burley, 2015; Ware & Kitsantas, 2007). Taken together, these findings indicate that efficacy beliefs act in accordance with self-efficacy theory as teachers with stronger efficacy reported greater effort and stronger perceived capability for implementing curriculum change.

6.3 Dimensions of JTE Efficacy

As reported by Thompson and Woodman (2019), EFA was carried out to investigate the underlying dimensions of Japanese high school English teacher efficacy beliefs. The authors explained that an iterative process was followed to find a solution with 'clean' factors (i.e. without significant cross-loadings), where items with low loading coefficients and low extracted communalities were removed. They used principal axis factor extraction and promax rotation to identify five dimensions of teacher efficacy from 15 JTE-TES items. As shown in Table 6.1, the five extracted factors were labelled *Using English* (UE), *Communicative Teaching* (CT), *Teamwork* (TW), *Student Achievement* (SA) and *Managing Workload* (MW). Factors were named by interpretation of the common elements of items loading on each dimension.

The dimension *Using English* is focused on teachers' beliefs about their self-efficacy for the use of English with students and other teachers. International studies of language teaching efficacy beliefs have shown the importance of teacher language proficiency as a dimension of teacher efficacy beliefs (Swanson, 2010a) or as a variable influencing efficacy beliefs (Chacon, 2005; Eslami & Fatahi, 2008; Yilmaz, 2011). Teacher language use has been noted as a significant challenge for Japanese teachers (Nishino, 2008; Nishino & Watanabe, 2008; Sakui, 2004). Findings indicate that JTE language teacher efficacy has a dimension concerned with perceived capability to use the L2 as part of teaching in the pursuit of educational outcomes. The identification of the dimension *Using English* in this study of the Japanese context is consistent with and expands on results from previous studies. Swanson's (2010a) two-factor Foreign Language Teacher Efficacy Scale (FLTES) instrument for language teachers showed a distinction between teacher efficacy beliefs *for* proficiency and teacher language beliefs *about* language instruction, which is supported by findings from the current study with a distinction between (1) teacher efficacy beliefs for language usage (i.e. *Using English*) and (2) teacher efficacy beliefs for teaching (i.e. *Communicative Teaching, Student Achievement*). Thus, the factor structure of the JTE-TES suggests that perceived L2 capability represents a separate dimension of teacher efficacy beliefs, in accordance with other studies (Swanson, 2010a) and as proposed in some models of teacher beliefs, such as Nishino's (2012) path model. It is suggested that this dimension may be generalisable to the wider language teaching field, given that studies from a variety of different teaching contexts (e.g. South Korea, Japan, the United States, see Hiver, 2013; Nishino, 2012; Swanson, 2010a) have identified this dimension using various means of analysis (qualitative and statistical). This dimension of perceived capability and the use of the L2 for teaching is discussed further in Chapter 7.

The dimension *Communicative Teaching* represents a methodological factor focusing on encouraging communication, managing activities and providing student-centred learning. Another pedagogic dimension, *Student Achievement*, groups teacher beliefs related to the encouragement of student language skills – specifically for university entrance examinations. Accordingly, Thompson and Woodman (2019) suggested that these two instructional strategy dimensions reflect self-beliefs towards two purposes: communicative competency development and examination preparation. Such an interpretation aligns with findings from the interviews, as interviewees discussed a perceived dichotomy between beliefs about teaching for communication and teaching for examinations. For example, Taka suggested that teachers see communication and exam preparation as completely different things, while Yuri, Riho and Saki encountered resistance from colleagues to the integration of communicative activities (see Thompson & Dooley, 2019b). Indeed, while these two dimensions were weak to moderately correlated ($r = 0.36$, $p < 0.01$), EFA findings provide some support for Sakui's (2004) contention that JTEs see themselves as 'wearing two pairs of shoes' in trying to encourage communication and prepare students for exams (Nishino & Watanabe, 2008). A number of studies (Butler, 2011; Kikuchi, 2006; Nishino & Watanabe, 2008) have suggested a divergence between beliefs about learning for communication versus learning for exams. For example, in a study of four teachers, Underwood (2013) found that the participants saw CLT and exam preparation as competing pressures. Meanwhile, in a study of 14 teachers, Sakui (2004) noted a dichotomy in perceptions about CLT and entrance exams and found that teachers prioritised entrance exam preparation as 'serious' study. Variables that may influence these self-beliefs are further explored in Chapter 8.

The EFA results also indicated an underlying collective dimension of efficacy for JTEs. *Teamwork* is focused on a specific area of collective activity related to capability for communication and collaboration within teaching teams, in other words, efficacy beliefs for collaborative practice. This dimension appears to capture the overlap between two dimensions (*Working with Colleagues, Team Efficacy*) identified from thematic analysis of interview data. Respondents highlighted the need for effective collective collaboration in responding to curriculum change, and interview findings indicated that individual efficacy was influenced by perceptions of collective capability. This dimension of teacher efficacy is further discussed in Chapter 9.

Finally, the EFA results indicated a self-regulatory dimension of teacher efficacy for JTEs. Although reliability analyses indicated acceptable internal consistency of the sub-scales (see Thompson & Woodman, 2019), the factor *Managing Workload* was only represented by two items, leading the authors to suggest that this factor is relatively weak and requires further investigation. Given that measures of central tendency (see Table 6.1) indicated that teachers were least efficacious towards these two tasks; that other research (O'Donnell, 2005; Underwood, 2012; Yorimitsu et al., 2014) has suggested that non-teaching duties create significant stress for JTEs; and that interview findings showed that coping with the challenge of workload management was, perhaps, the most difficult challenge for JTEs, it seems clear that this domain of teacher efficacy requires future research.

Correlational analyses suggested that when teachers faced extra duties, such as being in charge of an afterschool 'club' activity (e.g. tennis, basketball), JTEs were more likely to have weaker efficacy towards this dimension. On the other hand, when the teaching context was 'easier', such as at schools with a higher *hensachi* (a standardised academic ranking metric that indicates academic level, see Saitoh & Newfields, 2010), efficacy was likely to be stronger.

These results can be interpreted using the framework of efficacy assessment presented in Chapter 2, as contextual factors that appear to influence task difficulty for managing self-regulation (easier teaching environment versus greater number of duties) appear to influence efficacy. Studies have suggested that discipline (Chang, 2009) is associated with teacher stress, while teachers at schools with better support systems and coping resources (e.g. psychologists, resource specialists) have been shown to have stronger teacher efficacy beliefs and be less likely to experience burnout (Betoret, 2006). Accordingly, the influence of school level and of extra duties may be that they contribute towards stress (e.g. discipline and motivation at higher-level schools) and workload (e.g. extra outside teaching duties), leading to variation in perceptions of regulatory capability.

This result indicates that teacher developmental opportunities (both pre-service and in-service) may need to focus more on providing teachers with skills and strategies for workload balance and control, rather than on the traditional approach towards providing teachers with strategies for coping with stressors such as discipline (Shimazu *et al.*, 2003). Future training experiences could focus on task-focused strategies for time management (e.g. Chang, 2009), emotional control techniques for stress management (e.g. Kyriacou, 2001), as well as developing socio-emotional competencies (see MacIntyre *et al.*, 2019).

Overall, it seems clear that the *Workload Management* dimension of language teacher efficacy requires further investigation. Heavy workload and irregular hours appear to be stressors common to language teachers in a variety of contexts (see MacIntyre *et al.*, 2019), and given that teacher attrition is a common concern both within Japan (Shimazu *et al.*, 2003; Yorimitsu *et al.*, 2014) and in the wider educational field (e.g. see Göker, 2012; Kyriacou, 2001; Swanson, 2010b), future studies could investigate this dimension in different contexts in order to identify if this domain can be (1) transferred to the wider language teacher field and (2) expanded by adding items that correspond to other tasks related to self-regulatory workload management.

6.4 Variation in Dimensions of Language Teacher Efficacy

Findings provide further support for an expanded view of language teacher efficacy, indicating various domains of activity over which teachers have control. The five dimensions identified via EFA cover perceived language capability, teaching duties and efficacy towards achieving pedagogic outcomes (*Communicative Teaching*, *Using English*, *Teamwork*, *Student Achievement*), as well as beliefs about workload balance (*Managing Workload*) and collaboration (*Teamwork*). This structure aligns most closely with the dimensions of teacher efficacy from Skaalvik and Skaalvik's (2007) study of Norwegian teachers, which included three dimensions related to teaching (Instruction, Maintain Discipline, Motivate Students), one individual non-teaching dimension (Cope with Change) and one collective dimension (Perceived Collective Teacher Efficacy). As Thompson and Woodman (2019) explained, there were strong correlations between factors. The strongest relationship was between perceived L2 capability (i.e. *Using English*) and efficacy towards *Communicative Teaching* ($r = 0.60$). Given that CLT involves significant use of the L2 by the teacher, this result is not surprising and it aligns with other studies (e.g. Nishino's [2012] study of JTEs), which found positive relationships between CLT self-efficacy and perceived L2 capability.

Findings also provide some support for the contention that the underlying dimensions of teacher efficacy beliefs reflect cultural and contextual beliefs about teaching. As discussed previously, there appears to be some dichotomy between beliefs towards pedagogy and instruction for Japanese high school language teachers. Thus, as Thompson and Woodman (2019) explained, JTE-TES factor loadings do not appear to reflect beliefs towards specific domains of classroom activity, such as instructional strategies or classroom management, but rather a distinction between instructional strategies and management for encouraging communication, versus pedagogic beliefs towards the development of student knowledge for examination preparation. This finding is supported by interview results, as participants discussed the tension for JTEs in trying to respond to exam preparation and competency development (Thompson & Dooley, 2019b). Overall, it appears that JTE instructional efficacy reflects beliefs towards different teaching purposes.

To illustrate and extend the discussion provided by Thompson and Woodman (2019), Table 6.2 provides an example of how EFA dimensions differ from domains of challenge identified from interview analysis. As explained in Chapter 5, JTE-TES items were developed for each of the eight domains of challenge identified from the thematic analysis of interview data. This procedure involved the adaptation and creation of items from existing scales, such as Tschannen-Moran and Woolfolk Hoy's (2001) TSES and Nishino's (2009, 2012) perceived teacher efficacy items, which were mapped over the domains. Table 6.2 shows three items, which were developed to reflect (CLT) instructional strategy, classroom management and L2 usage challenges.

Examination of the EFA item loadings illustrates how the dimensions of JTE efficacy appear to be influenced by teaching purpose. For example, Item 8 from the JTE-TES '*How confident are you that you can manage the classroom adequately when students are doing pair work or group work?*' was mapped on the Classroom Management domain as it primarily related to the facilitation and guidance of the class group. However, this item loaded on the *Communicative Teaching* JTE dimension, probably because of the association – for JTEs – of pair work with 'communicative' activities, rather than as a classroom management technique that may be used at different times. It loaded with Item 6 '*How confident are you that you can provide student-centred lessons?*' and Item 9 (see Table 6.2) '*How confident are you that you can provide activities in which your students can enjoy communicating in English?*' Research (Nishino, 2008; Sakui, 2004, 2007) has indicated that JTEs consider pair and group work to be associated with CLT implementation, as a focus on the encouragement of interaction also requires teachers to experiment

Table 6.2 JTE-TES items informed by the TSES

JTE-TES item	Domain of challenge	JTE dimension
(5) Adequately identifying and correcting student mistakes.	English for Teaching	Student achievement
(8) Managing the classroom adequately when students are doing pair work or group work.	Classroom Management	Communicative teaching
(9) Providing activities in which your students can enjoy communicating in English?	Instructional Strategies	Communicative teaching

with classroom management techniques beyond teacher-fronted pen-and-paper study. For example, in a study of 12 JTEs, Sakui (2004: 158) suggested that teachers displayed a 'lack of confidence' towards CLT due to their perceptions of the difficulty in implementing student-centred classroom activities. As a result, these tasks appear to group according to the teaching purpose of communicative activity implementation.

Another example is Item 5 from the JTE-TES '*How confident are you that you can adequately identify and correct your students' mistakes?*' which was developed to reflect one challenge of the 'show knowledge' theme from the English for Teaching domain (see Thompson & Dooley, 2019b). This item loaded with Item 14 '*How confident are you that you can help students to increase their English proficiency?*' and Item 15 '*How confident are you that you can help students to develop skills to pass university entrance tests?*' on the *Student Achievement* dimension rather than on *Using English* (i.e. with other tasks that require demonstration of language skill) or *Communicative Teaching* (i.e. with other instructional strategy items). This may be due to the importance of grammatical accuracy for providing students with direction to succeed in examinations. Overall, the EFA loadings suggest that the underlying latent dimensions of JTE instructional efficacy are related to two purposes: (1) beliefs about capability to teach in a communicative manner, and (2) perceptions of teaching efficacy for examination preparation and the development of student language knowledge.

6.5 Chapter Summary

In summary, JTE language teacher efficacy dimensions appear to have transferable and context-specific features. Findings suggest latent dimensions of teacher efficacy beliefs towards teaching and non-teaching tasks, including collective and individual efficacy beliefs. Results indicate that a number of dimensions of language teacher efficacy are transferable, such as perceived capability towards the L2 and workload management.

However, there also appears to be some contextual influence on the dimensions of language teacher efficacy. Results provide some support for the contention that efficacy beliefs for teachers in East Asian Confucian contexts (Ho & Hau, 2004; Tsui & Kennedy, 2009) reflect cultural and contextual values and beliefs about learning and teaching. Specifically, findings suggest that dimensions of teacher efficacy towards instruction in the JTE context reflect beliefs about different teaching purposes. Findings also indicate that teacher efficacy beliefs appear to reflect underlying beliefs (as suggested by Wyatt, 2014). As noted by Taka in the exploratory interviews, these underlying teacher beliefs appear to view communication and knowledge as different, 'competing' aspects of competence, which may be related to historical (Gorsuch, 1998) and cultural beliefs (Law, 1995) about teaching (e.g. the choice of grammar-translation for exam preparation).

This finding has implications for JTE development, as programmes may be needed to help teachers integrate these 'competing' aspects into broader models of language competence and teaching practice. For example, programmes could demonstrate how grammatical and vocabulary activities can be integrated with more 'communicative' teaching activities (e.g. Thompson & Yanagita, 2017); provide structured programmes to help develop specific areas of pedagogic knowledge, such as towards group work (e.g. Wyatt, 2010a); and raise these issues with teachers as part of teacher training programmes in order to highlight underlying beliefs towards language teaching (see Borg, 2001, 2011).

Furthermore, such developmental activities may also be important for professional development in the broader language teaching community (especially the East-Asian context), where there is often a conflict between studying English for examinations versus studying English for communication (e.g. Hatipoglu, 2016; Orafi & Borg, 2009; Prapaisit de Segovia & Hardison, 2008; Yung, 2015). By examining dimensions of teacher efficacy in a variety of language teaching settings, and the key tasks within these dimensions, more knowledge can be generated about the extent to which certain domains (e.g. L2 self-efficacy) are generally transferable, while others are dependent on context.

This book now moves towards discussion of specific dimensions of language teacher efficacy. The following chapters explore LTE beliefs towards L2 capability (Chapter 7), L2 instruction (Chapter 8) and collective capability (Chapter 9).

7 Language Teacher L2 Efficacy and L2 Usage

It is not surprising that language teachers are more likely to have stronger teacher efficacy beliefs if they believe themselves to be more proficient at using their second language (L2). Subject expertise is an important source of knowledge informing teacher beliefs, as are their beliefs about pedagogy (Shulman, 1986). For language teachers, this means that knowledge and awareness (Andrews, 2003) about the language they are teaching – whether they speak it as a first language (L1) or an L2 – may be an important source of efficacy information. Nevertheless, few studies have shown a link between positive self-beliefs of L2 capability and actual L2 usage. Furthermore, it is now being recognised that much of the language used by teachers during teaching has a specific pedagogic purpose separate from general proficiency (Freeman *et al.*, 2015; Johnson, 1995). Thus, the relationship between teacher L2 capability and teacher L2 usage may not be as direct nor as intuitive as it seems.

This chapter discusses the role of the L2 (i.e. the language being taught) as a domain of teaching challenge and a dimension of efficacy, and then introduces findings from the current study concerning the relationship between L2 efficacy and L2 proficiency. The chapter then explores the relationship between teacher efficacy and the use of English as a teaching language, before concluding with a discussion about factors that appear to influence teacher L2 efficacy.

A wide range of studies have shown that non-native teachers' beliefs (Li, 1998; Nishino & Watanabe, 2008) and self-confidence to teach via English (Choi, 2015; Glasgow, 2014; Kim, 2008) are likely to be influenced by their perceptions of language ability. A number of teacher efficacy studies have shown a positive relationship between perceived language proficiency and teacher efficacy (e.g. Chacon, 2005; Eslami & Fatahi, 2008; Yilmaz, 2011), with differences noted between teachers who are L1 or L2 users. For example, in a study of 12 teachers of French at the university level, Mills and Allen (2008) found that those who spoke French as a native language (i.e. L1 speakers) were more likely to have stronger efficacy beliefs than those who used it as an L2.

It seems clear that language teacher efficacy is positively influenced by greater perceived proficiency. In one of the first language teacher efficacy studies, Chacon (2005) identified language proficiency as a factor strongly related to the self-efficacy for teaching beliefs of Venezuelan English as a foreign language (EFL) teachers. This finding was replicated by Yilmaz (2011) in a similar study carried out in Turkey using a self-developed questionnaire based on the Teacher Sense of Efficacy Survey (TSES) (Tschannen-Moran & Woolfolk Hoy, 2001). The study found statistically significant correlations between teachers' efficacy beliefs and reported language proficiency, and Yilmaz (2011: 99) explained that 'the more proficient the EFL teachers perceived themselves to be across the four basic skills the more efficacious they felt'. A number of studies have confirmed this relationship in various countries and across various teaching contexts, such as Iran (Eslami & Fatahi, 2008), Korea (Choi & Lee, 2016; Hiver, 2013) and China (Chen & Goh, 2011). Other studies have discussed the importance of language ability as a source of efficacy beliefs (Phan & Locke, 2015; Zonoubi *et al.*, 2017), indicating that efforts to improve teacher L2 proficiency will have a positive influence on other efficacy belief dimensions.

In summary, research findings have supported the natural intuition that L2 knowledge influences efficacy beliefs, and while results from the current study indicate that (perceived) English proficiency is positively associated with stronger teacher efficacy beliefs, results also suggest that neither L2 ability nor L2 efficacy directly predicts L2 usage.

7.1 Perceived L2 Capability as a Dimension of Language Teacher Efficacy

Before discussing the *influence* of L2 ability, this chapter starts by discussing perceived L2 capability as a dimension of language teacher efficacy. The current study is one of few (e.g. Nishino, 2012; Swanson, 2010a) to examine perceived language proficiency as a dimension of teacher efficacy, that is, beliefs about perceived capability to bring about student learning via actions that involve the use of English. The integration of perceived language capability as a type of efficacy has been discussed by other researchers, such as Hiver (2013: 218), who in a study of English teachers in Korea, identified 'language self-efficacy' as a key driver of teacher motivation towards professional development. Findings from interviews with seven in-service teachers suggested that self-efficacy doubts (see Wheatley, 2002) were beneficial, as the teachers' insecurities about English spurred them to continue to improve their ability.

Interview and exploratory factor analysis findings from the current study (presented in Chapter 6) indicated that language teacher efficacy has a 'content' dimension, where proficiency is not only a factor that influences efficacy beliefs, but it is also related to a domain of activity in which teachers exercise control. Exploratory factor analysis identified five factors of teacher efficacy from the Japanese Teacher of English Teacher Efficacy Scale (JTE-TES) survey, one of which was called *Using English*, as it centred on tasks that involve the use of English for communication with students and other teachers (Thompson & Woodman, 2019). This result emphasises the role of the L2 in action. Teachers not only call on language resources as knowledge that they impart to students, but they also demonstrate that knowledge *via* the L2 as users, analysts and teachers (Edge, 1988) in social contexts (Tudor, 2001).

Findings from the exploratory interviews with the six experts also indicated that teacher–student and teacher–teacher language use are key challenges for Japanese high school teachers of English (JTEs). A number of participants (Maki, Yuri, Riho, Saki) discussed the difficulty of using the L2 with students and non-Japanese assistant language teachers (ALTs). Team teaching (and the associated preparation) is not only a feature of JTE activity; other countries also make use of local and non-local teachers in English classes (e.g. Hong Kong, South Korea, see Carless, 2006; Carless & Walker, 2006). As a result, this may be an important area for investigation in the wider field. Participants indicated that for some teachers, this arrangement could cause anxiety, mainly due to the social embarrassment of being seen to make mistakes in front of colleagues. For example, Saki mentioned that her school had a new ALT but that other 'English teachers ask me' to talk to him, as 'it seems they don't feel so comfortable when they talk to him'. In other words, it appears that for some teachers, the negative affect associated with social language usage would influence perceptions of *Using English* efficacy.

In another example, Taka suggested that once teachers use English, interlocutors could easily judge their ability, leading to anxiety if they perceived themselves to have insufficient expertise. He explained that 'compared with, for instance, Japanese or social sciences, once English teachers start speaking English, it's obvious to everybody – including the students – how high your level is'. In his interview, Taka suggested that teachers have pride, and that negative emotional affect influences language use, as teachers who were less confident about their capability to *use* English would be more likely to focus on grammar and translation – areas of knowledge transmission where they could show their expertise. His response was reminiscent of comments made by Korean teachers in Hiver's (2013) study, where teachers perceived themselves – or perceived others to see them – as experts. One participant in the Hiver (2013: 218) study explained that their students expected them to 'know everything about English', while another revealed that 'I always pretend to be an expert' even though they are still 'a learner'.

Another interview finding concerned the difficulty of maintaining ability. Even though the participants were clear about the importance of

English *use* as an aspect of their role, they also suggested that a hidden problem for many teachers is finding time to retain language competence. In other words, self-beliefs of capability may be negatively impacted if teachers perceived their language knowledge to be decreasing. Furthermore, as Ken explained, if teachers perceive themselves to be losing skill, they may not be able to take advantage of the daily opportunities to interact with students and other teachers. In other words, efficacy self-doubts may lead to a negative cycle with reduced L2 usage.

The use of the L2 by teachers has been commonly noted as a key challenge in the wider field of language teacher cognition research. A number of studies within Japan (Nishino, 2008; Nishino & Watanabe, 2008; Sakui, 2004) and overseas (Chen & Goh, 2011; Li, 1998) have shown that English language use is a significant challenge for L2-speaking EFL teachers. For example, Nishino and Watanabe (2008: 134) argued that the use of English in class with students may be a particular challenge for Japanese teachers, where their 'authority might be tarnished if they make mistakes in front of their students'. In another study, Glasgow (2014) noted that some teachers, who perceived their pronunciation to be poor, showed anxiety about making mistakes in front of students, and as a result, had low confidence. Overall, these findings indicate that perceived capability to use the L2 (i.e. L2 self-efficacy) is influenced by the task demands (e.g. using the L2 in a social setting). Furthermore, these findings are supported by Nishino's (2012) study of teacher beliefs, which showed that efficacy towards the use of communicative teaching strategies was mediated by L2 self-efficacy.

Teacher choices about practice appear to be influenced by their beliefs or perceptions of skill (Borg, 2001, 2003, 2006), and individuals are likely to avoid tasks in which they do not perceive themselves to be competent (Pajares, 1996); thus perceived L2 efficacy appears to be an important dimension of language teacher efficacy. Furthermore, given that the challenge of L2 language use has been demonstrated both within the specific field of language teacher efficacy research (Chen & Goh, 2011; Hiver, 2013; Swanson, 2010a) and in the wider teacher cognition field (Katz, 2017; Li, 1998; Nishino, 2012), it appears that perceived L2 capability (represented by the dimension *Using English* in the current study) may be a transferable dimension of language teacher efficacy.

This study also extends the results of the Swanson (2010a) and Nishino (2009, 2012) studies, by developing knowledge about specific tasks (i.e. areas of control) where L2 efficacy operates. Swanson (2010a) and Nishino (2009) both assessed capability at the domain level and did not focus on contextualised use of language. However, it is now generally recognised that teacher language use is specialised (Richards, 2017), and that the language use requirements of conducting lessons in English and working as language teachers require purposeful training and skills (Freeman *et al.*, 2015). The *Using English* dimension is represented by four items that reflect two key areas of L2 teacher language use: the use of English with (1) ALTs (i.e. other teachers) and (2) students. Results suggest that JTEs face challenges related to collegial and professional talk (having a conversation versus planning a lesson) with colleagues, alongside different challenges for communicating with students (e.g. giving instructions). Accordingly, these items could be adapted for use in future studies that investigate L2 efficacy, both within Japan and in other international contexts.

Perceived L2 capability may not only influence instructional decisions, but it may also have a significant impact on student beliefs and learner self-efficacy towards English. For example, Kawashima (2013) found that exposing students to non-native varieties of English (i.e. use of English in class by the L2-speaking teacher) helped them to develop positive attitudes towards such varieties and influenced student 'self-confidence'. Given that English is now a lingua franca used for international communication (McKinley & Thompson, 2018), these findings suggest that teacher development activities may need to challenge teachers to address their beliefs about their role. In other words, L2-speaking teachers not only impart knowledge, but they may also serve as important vicarious role models for students; their use of the L2 may be a vital model to demonstrate how meaning is negotiated by L2 speakers.

In summary, it seems clear that an important dimension of language teacher efficacy concerns the self-beliefs of teachers about their perceived capability to use the L2 as part of the educational process in the pursuit of student learning. Thus, language ability is not only a factor that influences teacher efficacy – but perceptions of L2 capability also appear to contribute a *dimension* of language teacher efficacy.

7.2 Teacher Efficacy Beliefs and English Proficiency

In the exploratory interviews, English proficiency was also commonly suggested to be a strong influence on teacher efficacy beliefs, with a number of participants (Maki, Saki, Ken) discussing their own difficulties and how it influenced their beliefs. Research has consistently demonstrated a positive relationship between language teacher efficacy and perceived L2 proficiency (Chacon, 2005; Eslami & Fatahi, 2008; Yilmaz, 2011), and all participants indicated that they had experienced or observed the influence of L2 proficiency perceptions on beliefs and action. For example, both Ken and Saki discussed examples involving interactions with non-Japanese ALTs; they expressed confidence in their L2 capability and accordingly felt efficacious towards communication and team teaching. However, they also discussed examples of observing colleagues who avoided the use of English with students and colleagues, due to perceptions of poor English ability.

In the survey stage of the study, the relationship between teacher efficacy and L2 proficiency was explored. Respondents were asked to report past achievement levels obtained for the 'Eiken' test (officially the *Jitsuyo Eigo Gino Kentei* or Test in Practical English Proficiency), and at the suggestion of Yuri, who had not taken any proficiency tests for more than 15 years, their perceived current Eiken level. As discussed in Chapter 4, Japanese high school teachers have significant knowledge about the test due to its popularity with high school students. Furthermore, although English teachers are not required to take the Eiken test, the Ministry of Education, Culture, Sports, Science and Technology (MEXT) sets a benchmark level for English instructors of 'Pre-grade 1', which is equivalent to the CEFR B2 level (see Eiken Foundation of Japan, 2016a). Accordingly, dichotomous variables were created for teachers who reported reaching, or perceived themselves to currently reach, this benchmark.

A total of 63 respondents (51%) reported achieving the MEXT benchmark of Eiken level 'Pre-grade 1' or higher, a finding similar to previous MEXT (2011a) surveys. A higher number of respondents (100, 77.7%) reported their perceived current level to be at or above the benchmark 'Pre-grade 1' level. Correlations between perceived current competence and past test scores were positive, but relatively weak ($r = 0.29, p < 0.01$). A total of 55% of respondents reported the same value for past score achievement and current perceived level, while 38% reported a higher perceived current level, and 7% reported a lower perceived current level. This result suggests that some teachers perceive their English skill to be decreasing – even as they are teaching English – a finding that aligned with an important result from the exploratory interviews, as a number of participants revealed that *maintaining* their English ability was a key challenge.

Correlational (see Table 7.1) and multiple regression analyses (see Table 7.2) showed that perceived current ability *generally* had a stronger

Table 7.1 Correlations between English proficiency and JTE-TES factors

Dimension	Past scores obtained		Perceived proficiency		Use of English
	Reported Eiken score r	Reported Eiken >benchmark Point-biserial	Perceived Eiken level r	Perceived Eiken >benchmark Point-biserial	Reported use of English as % of instruction r
UE	0.38**	0.33**	0.48**	0.52**	0.36**
CT	0.31**	0.26**	0.22**	0.26**	0.53**
TW	0.18	0.16	0.25**	0.36**	0.29**
SA	0.19*	0.13	0.30**	0.23*	0.19*
MW	0.16	0.12	0.17	0.11	0.15

Note: UE = Using English; CT = Communicative Teaching; TW = Teamwork; SA = Student Achievement; MW = Managing Workload; * indicates significance at $p < 0.05$; ** indicates $p < 0.01$.

(and more predictive) relationship with teacher efficacy belief dimensions than actual past proficiency scores achieved. Perceived current Eiken level was positively correlated to *Using English*, *Communicative Teaching*, *Teamwork* and *Student Achievement*. The strength of the relationship was highest for *Using English*, but significant for each of the other three teaching-related dimensions of the JTE-TES. For self-reported Eiken level (i.e. scores from past test results), significant positive relationships were noted between Eiken scores and beliefs towards the same four dimensions.

Overall, findings are consistent with other studies that have investigated the relationship between teacher efficacy beliefs and English proficiency (Chacon, 2005; Eslami & Fatahi, 2008; Yilmaz, 2011). It appears that English proficiency and perceived proficiency are key factors related to JTE efficacy beliefs, as they may inform the skills that teachers perceive to be available to them in assessing their capability for tasks that involve the use of English. Perceived current competence, rather than past performance, generally had a stronger relationship with efficacy beliefs. Such a result aligns with the model of teacher efficacy assessment introduced in Chapter 2 (and others, such as Tschannen-Moran *et al.*, 1998), in that perceptions of current ability are influenced by past performance *and* other factors such as perceptions of proficiency development (or atrophy).

Findings also suggest that when English usage is a part of the task (e.g. *Using English*, *Student Achievement*), there is a stronger relationship between perceived skill and teacher efficacy beliefs. When language proficiency is not a part of the task and does not influence task difficulty (e.g. *Managing Workload*), there is no significant relationship. Furthermore, results showed a stronger relationship between teachers' self-assessment of language proficiency and dimensions of teacher efficacy beliefs when proficiency is a greater contributor to the task (i.e. *Using English*).

While these findings are intuitive, they have clear implications for efficacy development, and how training may influence practice. They suggest that development activities can influence teacher efficacy beliefs by helping teachers to improve and maintain their English skills, and via activities that support teachers to perceive themselves as successful (e.g. mastery experiences that may lead to attributions of successful use of English). For example, by approaching L2 teacher English as a specific purpose, activities such as peer microteaching or role-play could be used to stimulate language and efficacy development. By linking language study to important domains of activity (e.g. teaching, communication with students and teachers), teachers may be able to improve the skill appraised (i.e. L2 ability) and draw on attributions of past cognitive mastery, that is, gain additional efficacy-forming benefits.

7.3 Use of English as a Teaching Language

Respondents also reported the percentage of classroom instruction they carried out in English. For the sample of teachers in the current study, English was used, on average, 52% of the time as the teaching language in class. However, there was a wide variation in the distribution ($SD = 27.92$), with one respondent reporting their use of English as only 1% while three respondents reported using English 100% of the time. As can be seen in Table 7.1, there were significant relationships between the four teaching-related efficacy dimensions and greater use of English in class. The strongest relationship was between the use of English and *Communicative Teaching* ($r = 0.53$, $p < 0.01$). This finding is somewhat surprising, as the strongest relationship was not between the use of English and *Using English*, but rather with the *Communicative Teaching* instructional efficacy dimension. However, given that L2 usage by the teacher is seen as a key aspect of communicative language teaching (CLT) approaches, by encouraging the negotiation of meaning as part of the learning process (Richards, 2006), the positive relationship between *Communicative Teaching* and the use of English is unsurprising.

Also, interestingly, both past Eiken scores achieved ($r = 0.16$, $p = $ n.s) and perceptions of current Eiken ($r = 0.05$, $p = $ n.s) proficiency levels were *not* significantly correlated with the use of English in class. Thus, in the current study, it seems that the relationship between teacher competency and teacher behaviour is more complex than 'more proficiency = more usage'. Analysis of the correlations between the use of English in class and other demographic variables provides some explanation for this somewhat counter-intuitive finding. The use of English in class by teachers had a strong positive correlation with personal teaching experiences related to CLT, such as greater in-service experience conducting CLT in lessons ($r = 0.61$, $p < 0.01$), indicating again the relationship between L2 usage and communicative approaches towards instruction. However, correlational analyses also highlighted the potential impact of contextual factors. A strong positive relationship was noted between use of English and having a teaching position at a school with a special designation ($r = 0.51$, $p < 0.01$). Other significant contextual variables were working in a school with a higher academic level ($r = 0.30$, $p < 0.01$) and working in a public school ($rpb = 0.27$, $p < 0.01$). Participants (Maki, Taka, Ken, Saki, Yuri) discussed such contexts during the exploratory interviews, revealing that teaching would be easier at higher-level schools with special designations. In fact, three participants had experience at schools with and without special designations, and discussed a number of contextual factors (such as support) that made teaching easier at such schools. Interviewees also suggested that higher academic level schools may be likely to value English instruction and have stronger student motivation (Taka,

Ken), while public schools may be more likely to follow MEXT guidelines towards the new national curriculum (Maki, Ken).

Accordingly, findings indicated that contextual factors may be an important factor influencing the use of English by teachers, a result with support in the research literature (e.g. Nishino, 2012; Underwood, 2012; Wiens *et al.*, 2018). For example, in a study of the beliefs of four JTEs, Underwood (2013) noted that all participants had high English proficiency. However, observation results showed that only one teacher used English to a significant extent in class. Underwood (2013: 294) suggested that there were institutional and contextual factors which constrained 'even highly fluent teachers' capacity or willingness to use English'. Thus, while teachers may have L2 competency, they may not actually *use* English in class due to contextual factors. Similar results were found by Wiens *et al.* (2018) in a study of English teachers in Niger, where the use of the L2 as a teaching language was not associated with past training experiences or teacher comfort, but mostly due to differences between teaching contexts.

There may be an indirect relationship between L2 proficiency, teacher efficacy and the use of English as a medium of instruction. In a study of 167 L2-speaking secondary school English teachers in South Korea, Choi and Lee (2016) used sequential multiple regression analysis (with interaction) to predict teacher use of English. They found a synergistic relationship between teacher self-efficacy and perceived L2 proficiency, in which each became a significant predictor of English usage above a threshold level. The authors explained that the impact of self-efficacy was conditional on teachers perceiving their L2 proficiency to be above the level that they (i.e. the individual teacher) identified as a minimum standard. In other words, unless teachers perceived themselves to have a level of perceived L2 capability above a certain point, teacher self-efficacy did not predict use of English. Equally, the impact of perceived proficiency as a predictor depended on a similar minimum threshold of self-efficacy. The authors suggested that once teachers reached the threshold levels, a synergistic relationship developed, where 'an increase in English proficiency magnified self-efficacy's impact on English use, which in turn may magnify English proficiency's impact' (Choi & Lee, 2016: 60). Teachers could not take advantage of this relationship unless they perceived themselves to have reached the minimum level of L2 proficiency. As the authors explained, such teachers 'are highly likely to find it difficult to increase their English use in their classrooms, even with very high levels of self-efficacy'(Choi & Lee, 2016: 59). Thus, teachers may need language proficiency training in order to reach the threshold levels, after which the synergistic relationship could take effect. Overall, the study indicated that the influence of perceived English proficiency might be moderated by other factors, such as teacher self-efficacy beliefs. It provides another means for considering the counter-intuitive non-significant relationship between L2 proficiency and reported use of English for the JTEs in this research. It suggests that proficiency may influence the use of English indirectly, or may be moderated by teacher efficacy beliefs.

7.3.1 Predictors of JTE English usage

A forward multiple regression analysis was carried out to examine the predictors of the use of English by JTEs. It identified a significant association between *Communicative Teaching*, in-service experience conducting CLT, working in a school with a special designation and use of English in class ($F(3, 124) = 40.08$, $p < 0.001$, $R^2 = 0.42$).

As shown in Figure 7.1, the individual predictors of use of English were in-service CLT experience ($\beta = 0.290$, $t = 3.06$, $p = 0.003$), working in a school with a special designation ($\beta = 0.280$, $t = 3.56$, $p = 0.001$) and the efficacy dimension *Communicative Teaching* ($\beta = 0.218$, $t = 2.28$, $p = 0.019$). The interaction between personal (experience with CLT), contextual (school designation) and efficacy beliefs (*Communicative Teaching*) as predictors of behaviour was in alignment with social cognitive theory and the model of teacher efficacy assessment presented in Chapter 2. In other words, self-efficacy beliefs, alongside other personal and contextual factors, appear to influence teaching behaviour.

Analysis of zero-order correlations (as suggested by Nathans *et al.*, 2012) showed that perceived L2 proficiency had weak, but significant positive relationships with *Communicative Teaching* ($r = 0.22$, $p < 0.01$) and in-service CLT experience ($r = 0.19$, $p < 0.05$). Accordingly, findings

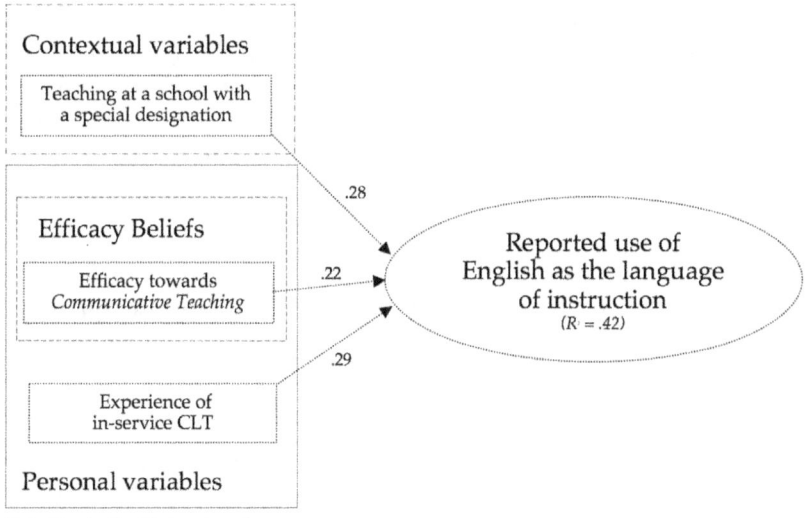

Note: Standardized beta values shown

Figure 7.1 Predictors of the use of English as the language of instruction

may be interpreted by seeing L2 proficiency as an indirect contributor towards the use of English in class, as L2 skill is likely to be assessed during the assessment of *Communicative Teaching* efficacy. In fact, as shown in Chapter 8, perceived current Eiken level is a predictor of this dimension.

Results also indicate that contextual factors play an important role; therefore, development initiatives, such as efforts to improve (perceived) L2 proficiency, may not be effective unless they also attend to the situations where teachers carry out instruction. Tschannen-Moran and McMaster (2009) explained that experience from teachers' *actual* contexts is important for providing skills that they can draw on in the assessment of their teacher efficacy beliefs, and in order to take advantage of the possible synergy between teacher efficacy beliefs and perceived L2 proficiency, it may be important to also attend to the development of efficacy via contextualised practice. That is, implementing training initiatives that provide teachers with skills and experiences using the L2 in their context, including support and feedback to help make such experiences enactive mastery experiences (e.g. see Thompson & Yanagita, 2017). As a result, teachers working in contexts that encourage the use of English (such as those working in schools with special designations) may be expected to have stronger efficacy towards the use of English as a language of instruction.

It appears clear that for the JTE context, efforts to improve teacher English proficiency may be important for helping teachers to develop skills that they can draw on in the assessment of their efficacy beliefs and use when teaching. However, context also appears to influence the assessment of efficacy beliefs. Thus, steps to improve teacher proficiency and implement greater use of English as part of the *Course of Study* may require different strategies, because efforts to encourage greater use of English in class will also need to address contextual factors that influence teachers' efficacy beliefs and intentions (Underwood, 2013). For example, teachers may need different strategies for working with student groups that have lower motivation or ability – interview participants suggested very different strategies were needed when teaching at a highly ranked versus lower-ranked school.

7.4 Factors that Influence Efficacy towards the Use of English

This chapter now returns to the dimension of L2 teacher self-efficacy (represented by *Using English* in the current study) and explores factors that may influence the strength of efficacy towards this domain of activity. As shown in Table 7.1, significant positive relationships were identified between the dimension *Using English*, proficiency and perceived current proficiency. A forward multiple regression analysis was carried out to identify factors that may predict stronger efficacy towards *Using*

Table 7.2 Summary of regression analysis for variables predicting Using English

Variable	B	SE B	β
In-service experience with CLT	0.14	0.02	0.37**
Perceived proficiency meets MEXT benchmark	0.47	0.07	0.42**
Experience living or studying abroad	0.40	0.12	0.21**
Experience studying via CLT as a student	0.17	0.06	0.17**

Note: $n = 127$; $R^2 = 0.57$; adjusted $R^2 = 0.55$; * indicates significance at $p < 0.05$; ** indicates $p < 0.01$; Excluded variables: Eiken meets benchmark; use of English in class; full-time teaching position; working in a school with a special designation; years of teaching experience; pre-service experience using CLT.

English (the dependent variable), using 10 predictors identified from correlational analyses related to teaching experience, L2 ability, CLT experience and contextual factors related to position or type of school. Table 7.2 shows that four variables explained a significant proportion of the variance in the factor *Using English* ($F(4, 122) = 40.07$, $p < 0.001$, $R^2 = 0.57$). The individual predictors were four personal factors: in-service experience with CLT (i.e. observing or conducting CLT); perceiving oneself to have achieved the MEXT Eiken benchmark proficiency of Pre-grade 1 or higher; having the experience of living or studying abroad; and having studied via CLT as a student.

Findings have been mixed when the relationship between language teacher efficacy and years of teaching experience has been investigated. Some studies have identified a positive relationship (Ghonsooly & Ghanizadeh, 2013), while others did not (Baleghizadeh & Goldouz, 2016; Chacon, 2005). Results from this study indicate a weak positive relationship between years of teaching experience and the dimension *Using English* ($r = 0.21$, $p < 0.05$); however, this factor is not a predictor of this dimension. Rather, multiple regression analysis findings suggest that specific experiences using English (rather than teaching experience overall) are more predictive as potential sources of efficacy information.

Standardised beta weights indicate that in-service experience with CLT is a strong predictor of *Using English*. Examination of zero-order correlations helps explain how this variable may influence teacher efficacy beliefs for *Using English*. Firstly, it has the strongest bivariate correlation with *Using English* ($r = 0.56$, $p < 0.01$), and is strongly correlated with a number of other potential predictive variables, such as greater use of English in class ($r = 0.62$, $p < 0.01$), pre-service experience with CLT ($r = 0.24$, $p < 0.01$) and working in a school with a special designation ($r = 0.48$, $p < 0.01$). The forward regression technique looks for predictors that explain additional variance, which may mean that these variables are sources of efficacy information, but are not included in the model, as they do not significantly add to the amount of variance explained when included alongside this variable. For example, when in-service CLT experience is removed from the list of predictors, teacher use of English in class becomes a significant predictor of *Using English*, indicating a reciprocal relationship between behaviour and efficacy beliefs.

Results from this study highlighted a positive and predictive relationship between experience living or studying abroad and the dimension *Using English*. Results have also been mixed concerning the relationship between experience abroad and teacher efficacy. For example, in a study of teacher efficacy beliefs, Chacon (2005) found that 'study abroad' did not have a significant relationship with teacher efficacy dimensions. On the other hand, Choi and Lee (2016) found a weak, but significant relationship between time abroad and general teacher efficacy beliefs. In both studies, adapted TSES instruments were used to assess efficacy beliefs for student engagement, classroom management and instructional strategies. Thus, the studies focused on a limited number of teacher efficacy belief dimensions. However, findings from this study suggest that study abroad experience may positively influence teacher efficacy beliefs when the skills derived from that experience are related to the teaching task. For example, this variable is also a significant predictor of stronger *Communicative Teaching* beliefs; however, it is not significantly correlated with *Student Achievement*. Thus, it appears that study abroad experiences may provide a range of opportunities for teachers from which they may derive mastery experiences, such as attributions of successful use of English. However, time abroad may be less likely to involve experiences that help teachers to develop skills that they can employ in assisting students with the development of skills to pass university entrance tests (i.e. *Student Achievement*).

Research has commonly found positive relationships between study abroad participation and perceptions of language proficiency development (Ball, 2000; Martinsen *et al.*, 2011; Meara, 1994). For example, studies have shown that participants report improvements in their language proficiency via experience speaking in the L2 (Meara, 1994), developments in their proficiency and other aspects of knowledge such as cultural understanding (Ball, 2000), have stronger 'confidence' for using the foreign language (Ball, 2000; Martinsen *et al.*, 2011) and stronger self-efficacy following study abroad programmes (Tanaka & Ellis, 2003). Study abroad experiences may provide a range of opportunities for teachers, such as mastery experiences from successful use of English in different contexts; greater linguistic and pragmatic knowledge; and opportunities to develop communicative strategies. Therefore, experience abroad is likely to influence individuals' perceptions of their competence for tasks that involve the use of English.

This finding may suggest that language teacher education programmes should encourage teachers to spend time abroad. However, analysis of correlations with other demographic variables indicates that teachers who had spent time abroad were also more likely to have experienced studying via CLT as students ($r = 0.25$, $p < 0.01$) and have carried out CLT during pre-service teacher training ($r = 0.31$, $p < 0.01$). Thus, although it seems that this experience may be a source of efficacy information to investigate, it is also unclear *how* this variable may influence teacher efficacy beliefs. Thus, future studies could examine the *way* in which time abroad influences teacher efficacy beliefs.

Finally, it may also be important to consider the individual contribution of perceived L2 ability. The Choi and Lee (2016) study of Korean secondary school teachers also identified similar relationships, and after controlling for the study abroad variable, noted that perceived proficiency was a significant predictor of the use of English, working in tandem with teacher self-efficacy beliefs. Furthermore, other studies (e.g. Zonoubi *et al.*, 2017) have shown how teachers' perceive high language ability as essential for efficacy, where efficacy beliefs strengthen after perceiving language development. Findings from analysis of the exploratory interviews and survey data have indicated that perceptions of L2 efficacy also influence teacher efficacy beliefs, thus efforts to develop teacher proficiency are likely to have an effect on language teacher efficacy and behaviour.

7.5 Chapter Summary

Numerous studies (e.g. Butler, 2004; Freeman *et al.*, 2015; Nakata, 2010) have noted the importance of teacher language proficiency for teaching English. The current study develops understanding about the relationship between efficacy beliefs and teacher language proficiency by showing how specific tasks related to the use of English comprise a dimension of language teacher efficacy. It builds on previous work (e.g. 'L2 self-confidence' in Nishino, 2009, 2012) by developing a set of items with stronger alignment to self-efficacy theory to represent language teacher efficacy beliefs towards L2 usage. Although this domain was named *Using English* in the current study, more generally, *teacher L2 self-efficacy* can be defined as perceived capability to use the L2 as part of the educational process in the pursuit of student learning.

Survey findings highlight the strong relationship between L2 proficiency and language teacher efficacy; four dimensions of the JTE-TES had significant positive correlations with perceived and reported proficiency. Therefore, it appears clear that English proficiency is a key skill associated with teacher efficacy and is crucial for informing the skills that teachers call on. Furthermore, results align with models of efficacy assessment (such as the model introduced in Chapter 2, and others, such as Gist & Mitchell, 1992; Tschannen-Moran *et al.*, 1998), in that perceptions of current ability (i.e. perceived L2 capability) are a stronger predictor of efficacy in comparison to past achievements (i.e. actual proficiency test scores). The assessment of efficacy beliefs is proposed to involve an assessment of the 'resources' available to the individual, while being informed by attributions of past personal and vicarious experiences, social persuasion and physical responses. Correlational and multiple regression findings indicate that personal experiences related to teaching and overseas study may be key sources of efficacy information. Findings also suggest that perceived L2 proficiency makes an independent contribution to L2 self-efficacy by contributing to available skills.

Crucially, this study found no significant relationship between language ability and use of English in class. Although the instructional efficacy dimension *Communicative Teaching* predicted JTE English usage, further study is needed of the relationship between teacher L2 proficiency, L2 self-efficacy and use of the L2 in class.

Some additional findings may be important for teacher development. During the exploratory interviews, experts suggested that many teachers may perceive atrophy in their English proficiency. Survey results supported this contention, with a significant percentage of teachers reporting their perceived current L2 proficiency to be below past test achievements. As perceived competence has been shown to influence willingness to communicate (Yashima *et al.*, 2004) and language teacher efficacy beliefs appear to have a synergistic relationship requiring a threshold level of proficiency (Choi & Lee, 2016), this result has implications for teacher development. It suggests that efforts are needed to help teachers revise, review and *maintain* their L2 proficiency. Due to the predictive relationship between experience studying via CLT and L2 self-efficacy, such efforts may have additional efficacy benefits if lessons – for teachers – are carried out using English as the language of instruction. This potential efficacy-forming action could be investigated and used beyond Japan in other countries such as Korea, China and Vietnam – countries where the relationship between teacher efficacy and L2 proficiency has been noted, and where efforts are underway to encourage teachers to use the L2 as a teaching language (Chen & Goh, 2011; Choi, 2015; Glasgow, 2014; Katz, 2017).

8 Efficacy for Language Instruction

It is widely accepted that teacher beliefs significantly influence instructional decisions (Borg, 2003, 2006; Pajares, 1992). Teachers with a stronger sense of efficacy have been shown to be more creative (Horng *et al.*, 2005) and open to change (Ghaith & Yaghi, 1997; Guskey, 1988; Skaalvik & Skaalvik, 2007), with greater student achievement occurring in their classrooms (Bolshakova *et al.*, 2011; Chang, 2015; Goddard *et al.*, 2000). Accordingly, it seems clear that perceptions of teaching capability may be an important aspect of language teacher practice. This chapter discusses language teacher efficacy beliefs regarding second language (L2) instruction and introduces findings from this study of Japanese high school teachers of English (JTEs). The chapter starts by discussing the dimensionality of teacher efficacy beliefs with respect to instruction, before introducing the two dimensions of instructional efficacy identified in the current study. The chapter then explores the relationship between instructional efficacy and demographic factors that may act as potential sources of efficacy information.

Efficacy towards L2 instruction has usually been discussed with respect to teaching change and teacher development, including studies concerned with the implementation of communicative language teaching (CLT) (Thompson & Yanagita, 2017), adaptation to different learners (Wyatt, 2013b) and the development of strategies for using group work effectively in class (Wyatt, 2010a). A number of studies have discussed the development of instructional efficacy via professional development initiatives (e.g. Atay, 2007; Cabaroglu, 2014; Zonoubi *et al.*, 2017), with some researchers suggesting that teacher efficacy beliefs are influenced by underlying beliefs about learning and teaching (Wyatt, 2014). Research has provided some support for this assertion. For example, a study of Japanese high school teachers (Nishino, 2009, 2012) found that positive beliefs about CLT were mediated by CLT self-efficacy beliefs. Studies have also noted a relationship between low teacher efficacy and perceptions of weak pedagogic (Chen & Goh, 2011) and content knowledge (Nguyen & Ngo, 2017). It has been shown that teacher self-perceptions of knowledge may lead to them avoiding certain areas of instruction, such as grammar (Borg, 2001), while a substantial amount of research has indicated that teachers' pedagogic knowledge influences teaching practice (Andrews, 2003; Shulman, 1986). Overall, it seems clear that teacher beliefs influence teacher action, and the extant language teacher efficacy research (e.g. Nishino, 2012) has indicated that efficacy beliefs may mediate this relationship.

8.1 Two Dimensions of L2 Instructional Efficacy for the JTE Context

The dimensionality of teacher efficacy beliefs towards instruction and other areas of practice has been a common research focus, with a number of studies using exploratory or confirmatory factor analysis to examine the latent dimensions of teacher efficacy beliefs (Cheung, 2006; Swanson, 2010b; Tsui & Kennedy, 2009). Differences have been noted in the factor structure of the Teacher Sense of Efficacy Scale (TSES) when carried out with teachers in the United States (e.g. Swanson, 2010a; Tschannen-Moran & Woolfolk Hoy, 2001) versus Asian contexts (e.g. Cheung, 2006; Tsui & Kennedy, 2009). The TSES is commonly considered to comprise three dimensions named Instructional Strategies, Student Engagement and Classroom Management. However, in a study of teachers in Hong Kong, Tsui and Kennedy (2009) carried out exploratory factor analysis (EFA), identifying a two-factor model as most appropriate. In the Tsui and Kennedy study, most 'Student Engagement' items loaded with the 'Instructional Strategies' items on the *same* factor, which they called 'Efficacy for Teaching and Support'. The result was interpreted from a cultural perspective, with the authors arguing that instruction and engagement are significantly integrated for teachers in Hong Kong. As a 'Chinese-Confucian heritage society' (Tsui & Kennedy, 2009: 256), engagement was interpreted to be integrated with instruction due to values of professional responsibility. In other words, the authors suggested that for teachers in Hong Kong, guidance not only comprised of instructional decisions, but also included strategies to encourage learner motivation. Similar findings have been noted in other studies (Ho & Hau, 2004), indicating that efficacy towards instruction may be contextually and culturally derived. Thus, instructional efficacy dimensions may be generalised across contexts; equally, the specific tasks and activities that comprise the dimension (or dimensions) of instructional efficacy may be country or culture specific.

Interview findings suggested that the three dimensions of the TSES were appropriate for the Japanese context, in support of research (e.g. Ruan *et al.*, 2015) with Japanese teachers in studies of general teacher efficacy, where satisfactory loadings have been obtained for the three dimensions. However, as Wyatt (2014) has suggested, the adaptation of existing scales may miss key challenges for the population of interest, and interview and EFA findings also indicated that JTE instructional efficacy reflected beliefs towards two different instructional purposes. While each of the interview participants discussed similar contextual difficulties across schools, such as workload and administrative duties, as well as common practices for materials design and instruction (e.g. collaborating in small teams to prepare materials for different classes and cohorts, working with assistant language teachers [ALTs]), a crucial point of difference *between* schools concerned the level of the school and the purpose of instruction. For example, during his interview, Taka was asked about key teacher challenges within the classroom, to which he replied, 'it depends on the school'. Interview participants indicated that there would be significant variability between lowly ranked and highly ranked schools, due to the students they attracted and the goals of those students. In other words, while many of the procedures and cultural features of schools appeared relatively constant, differences among students were generally seen to be a reflection of the level and purpose of the school. Specifically, participants discussed the extent to which schools focused on university entrance examination preparation (or not) within English lessons. For this reason, Saki suggested that attendance to the *individual* needs of each student was not necessarily a common feature of the schools she had worked at, rather that teachers should attend to the relative importance of university entrance examinations for the student *group*. For the interview participants, teaching practice and purpose would reflect the level of the school, as content-specific instruction was contextually dependent – despite other common contextual (e.g. teacher collaboration, workload management) challenges across schools.

In their summary of the interview data, Thompson and Dooley (2019b) explained that participants often discussed instruction with respect to two outcomes: (1) the development of communicative competency and (2) the development of student knowledge about language for university entrance examinations. Such a finding has been commonly noted in studies of JTEs (e.g. Gorsuch, 2001; Nishino & Watanabe, 2008; Sakui, 2004), where a dichotomous view of teaching instruction has been a consistent theme of language teacher cognition research. Interestingly, the interview participants wanted to reject this divergent view, but also at times noted that due to time constraints (and others, such as materials), they would emphasise knowledge development ahead of language practice. One example comes from Saki, who explained that it was very difficult to attend to both purposes at her examination-oriented school, while Maki revealed that examinations were her primary focus, where as a teacher she could 'add' communicative activities when appropriate. In accordance with other studies (Sakui, 2004), results indicated that teachers prioritised entrance exam preparation as 'serious' study. Overall, a consistent pattern from the interviews was a view of CLT and examination preparation as competing pressures.

This relationship was also identified by EFA of the responses to the Japanese Teacher of English Teacher Efficacy Scale (JTE-TES; see Thompson & Woodman, 2019), where results indicated two dimensions of efficacy related to instructional strategies: (1) *Communicative Teaching* comprised of three items concerned with self-beliefs towards instructional practices for encouraging student interaction and communication, while (2) *Student Achievement* reflected a dimension of teacher efficacy beliefs focused on perceived capability to influence the development of student language knowledge in the pursuit of future outcomes, specifically university entrance. CLT is a key challenge for JTEs; this domain of activity is represented by the dimension *Communicative Teaching*. The three items comprising this dimension included tasks noted as ongoing difficulties for Japanese teachers in the implementation of CLT (see Sakui, 2004), such as classroom management and facilitation (Sakui, 2007); using materials and encouraging communication (Sato & Kleinsasser, 1999; Taguchi, 2005); and encouraging student-centred learning (Butler, 2011; Humphries & Burns, 2015).

In summary, L2 instructional efficacy dimensions appear to be contextually dependent. While other studies (e.g. Tsui & Kennedy, 2009) have noted culture to inform underlying efficacy dimensions, the current study found that teaching purpose appears to influence efficacy belief dimensions. This finding may also indicate that underlying beliefs about language learning and teaching (Nishino, 2012; Wyatt, 2014) are reflected in teacher efficacy beliefs, given that research in Japan has consistently shown dichotomous views towards communicative competency and linguistic knowledge development. However, is this limited to Japan? A number of other countries across Asia have similar challenges (e.g. Chen & Goh, 2011; Li, 1998; Mak, 2011), with similar divergences in views towards CLT versus language knowledge development. Furthermore, research from the wider language teaching field (e.g. Basturkmen, 2012; İnceçay & İnceçay, 2009; Karimi & Nazari, 2017) has shown differences between teacher (and learner) beliefs and practices regarding the integration of CLT. Given that efficacy beliefs may mediate the impact of other beliefs and is assessed against contextual limitations, future studies could adapt JTE-TES items in order to examine whether L2 instructional efficacy reflects different purposes in the wider field.

8.2 Factors that Influence Efficacy towards L2 Instruction

Efficacy towards L2 instruction appears to develop when teachers have enactive mastery experiences (Phan & Locke, 2015; Thompson & Yanagita, 2017), receive positive social feedback (Moradkhani & Haghi, 2017) and perceive themselves to be prepared (Atay, 2007). A number of studies have examined the role of teaching experience as a potential source of teacher efficacy (Chacon, 2005; Ghonsooly & Ghanizadeh, 2013; Swanson, 2010a), and findings generally have indicated a positive relationship. On the other hand, a lack of teaching experience has been noted as a key concern for beginning language teachers (Mills, 2011), as such individuals may have had fewer efficacy-strengthening opportunities. It seems that reflection is a key process informing efficacy development (Wyatt, 2010a, 2010b, 2013b, 2015), as individuals conceptualise and experiment with practice. Not all experiences strengthen efficacy, and 'efficacy doubts' (Wheatley, 2002; Wyatt, 2013b) may also be important, as these may stimulate reflection and collaboration.

Teaching (Choi & Lee, 2016; Faez & Valeo, 2012; Ghonsooly & Ghanizadeh, 2013) and professional development (Atay, 2007; Cabaroglu, 2014; Zonoubi et al., 2017) experiences have been key factors associated with stronger language teacher efficacy. Studies have shown significant positive relationships between efficacy beliefs and pre-service (Atay, 2007; Göker, 2006) and in-service (Cabaroglu, 2014; Wyatt, 2010a, 2010b; Zonoubi et al., 2017) teacher development experiences. Specifically, practical experience appears to be a key source of teacher efficacy belief information. For example, in a study of novice English as a second language (ESL) teachers carried out in Canada, it was shown that the practicum and 'actual' teaching experiences were the primary source of efficacy beliefs, where participants' efficacy beliefs were weakest for teaching tasks they had not experienced or felt unprepared for by their practicum experience (Faez & Valeo, 2012). In a similar study, pre-service English as a foreign language (EFL) teachers in Turkey showed a significant increase in their efficacy towards instruction strategies after completing a practicum (Atay, 2007). The study suggested that teachers developed their self-awareness (i.e. teacher language awareness, see Andrews, 2003) during the practicum, and experienced teaching problems within their practice, indicating development by overcoming difficulties (Atay, 2007). In other words, teachers may not only develop skills, but also greater capacity to deal with the task demands of contextual difficulties (see Chapter 2: Section 2.6).

However, the Atay (2007) study also noted some factors that appeared to weaken teacher efficacy, such as contextual difficulties related to colleague cooperation and school practices regarding instruction. Studies from Japan have found similar issues (Sato & Kleinsasser, 2004; Thompson & Yanagita, 2017; Underwood, 2012), as collective beliefs towards existing practice appear to influence individuals' efficacy and teaching practice. This relationship is explored in greater depth in Chapter 9 with respect to a collaborative dimension of language teacher efficacy; however, it seems clear that contextual factors may be an important influence on teacher efficacy beliefs. For example, perceptions of support (Capa Aydin & Woolfolk Hoy, 2005), availability of resources (Chen & Goh,

2011; Tschannen-Moran & Woolfolk Hoy, 2007) and class size (Chen & Goh, 2011; Nguyen *et al.*, 2015) appear to be variables that influence teacher efficacy towards instruction.

Few language teacher efficacy studies have investigated the relationship between instructional efficacy beliefs and contextual variables such as school level or school designation, despite such factors being likely to inform perceptions of task difficulty. Studies from the general field have noted a relationship between 'academic emphasis' and stronger efficacy beliefs (Chong *et al.*, 2010; Pas *et al.*, 2012). For example, in a study from Singapore, a positive relationship was identified between the academic 'track' of the school and teacher self-efficacy beliefs (Chong *et al.*, 2010), indicating that school level may be a factor associated with stronger efficacy beliefs. Research has identified school type (e.g. public or private) to be a factor influencing the efficacy beliefs of EFL teachers. For example, teachers in private schools in Iran had significantly stronger efficacy, and expressed more positive statements about efficacy development, in comparison to teachers in public schools (Moradkhani & Haghi, 2017). A number of reasons were given to explain this finding, such as the (often) compulsory nature of English classes in public schools, greater motivation in private schools, poor resources and a lack of time. Furthermore, the authors found that teachers in private schools were more likely to perceive themselves to receive positive collegial support (Moradkhani & Haghi, 2017). Thus, the study indicated that contextual factors could not only weaken efficacy beliefs, but also provide opportunities for development.

8.3 Factors Associated with Communicative Teaching Efficacy

During the exploratory interviews, participants focused on the importance of experience with CLT, as opposed to overall experience, as an essential element informing teacher beliefs and behaviour. All participants suggested that developing *conceptual knowledge* of CLT was a key challenge, a finding observed in both international (Li, 1998; Littlewood, 2007) and Japanese (Sakui, 2004; Taguchi, 2005) studies of teacher beliefs, where teachers have commonly been noted to have an incomplete understanding of CLT as an approach to language teaching. Two participants (Yuri, Saki) discussed how they had developed their knowledge via professional development and in-service practice, overcoming misunderstandings about *implementation*, a secondary problem also often discussed in the research literature (e.g. Orafi & Borg, 2009; Prapaisit de Segovia & Hardison, 2008; Taguchi, 2005). In an example discussed by Thompson and Dooley (2019b), Yuri stated that her 'confidence' towards task-based learning grew from a professional development seminar, which helped her understand the reasons for encouraging communication (i.e. conceptual knowledge of CLT) and how to design 'good tasks' (i.e. implement CLT via task-based learning). In other words, she suggested that such experiences help teachers integrate the purpose of such activities into pedagogy, positively influencing efficacy beliefs.

Other participants (Riho, Ken) discussed problems with the teaching training system, which in their view limited the opportunities for efficacy development. Thompson and Dooley (2019b) introduce an example from Riho, who stated that many teachers are not adequately *prepared* to become English language teachers. She suggested that some teachers are not given opportunities to develop any understanding about what CLT entails, as many teachers do not study English language, but rather about English (e.g. history, literature). A further example comes from Ken, who suggested that his major in English *language* meant that he had studied via and about CLT methods, and as a result was more comfortable towards CLT implementation. He suggested that some of his colleagues preferred to focus on grammar translation as they had studied English as a subject (particularly English literature), and translation of texts was the means by which they had developed an interest in English – and therefore English teaching. He explained that his colleagues had learned in the 'traditional way' and 'are successful learners' so may reject CLT methods. Overall, interviewees argued that many of their colleagues were not prepared with experiences of learning via or about CLT, and that such teachers would be unlikely to teach in ways other than those they had experienced.

Overall, findings were consistent with research that has shown perceived mastery experiences to influence efficacy beliefs (Atay, 2007; Phan & Locke, 2015; Thompson & Yanagita, 2017), including the importance of pedagogic mastery experiences (Palmer, 2006) as a factor influencing the skills and knowledge available to teachers. Research has indicated stronger efficacy in teachers who perceive themselves to be 'prepared to handle a range of classroom management and instructional challenges' (Pas *et al.*, 2012: 142), and teacher training experiences were highlighted by participants as opportunities for developing such preparedness. Research has shown that teachers are likely to be influenced by the ways in which they learned as students (Feiman-Nemser, 2001; Lortie, 1975), and interview results indicated that JTEs use behaviours they have observed as students (i.e. vicarious modelling).

Correlational findings from the survey stage also indicated a relationship between student CLT experiences and teacher efficacy beliefs. As may be expected, the *Communicative Teaching* dimension had significant positive relationships with pre-service practice of CLT ($r = 0.22$, $p < 0.01$) and in-service experience conducting CLT lessons ($r = 0.66$, $p < 0.01$). However, in comparison to pre-service CLT experience, a stronger relationship was identified with student CLT experience ($r = 0.35$, $p < 0.01$), suggesting that the exposure to studying via CLT may be a stronger source of efficacy development. Indeed, as shown in Table 8.1, this

Table 8.1 Summary of regression analysis for variables predicting Communicative Teaching

Variable	B	SE B	β
In-service CLT experience	0.15	0.03	0.39**
Experience living or studying abroad	0.41	0.12	0.21**
Experience studying via CLT as a student	0.25	0.07	0.23**
Use of English in class	0.01	0.00	0.24**
Perceived Eiken meets MEXT benchmark	0.18	0.07	0.15*

Note: $n = 128$; $R^2 = 0.60$; adjusted $R^2 = 0.58$; * indicates significance at $p < 0.05$; ** indicates $p < 0.01$. Excluded variables: Eiken meets benchmark; full-time teaching position; homeroom teacher; working at a school with a special designation; member of a teaching association; time teaching with an ALT; pre-service CLT experience.

variable was identified as a predictor of *Communicative Teaching* efficacy. This result aligned with interview findings, as participants referred to their student learning experiences as key sources of efficacy-forming information.

A forward multiple regression analysis was carried out to identify factors that may predict stronger efficacy towards *Communicative Teaching* (the dependent variable), using 12 predictors identified from correlational analyses related to past and perceived L2 ability, pre-service and in-service CLT experience and contextual factors related to position or school (e.g. special designation). As shown in Table 8.1, five variables explained a significant proportion of the variance in the factor *Communicative Teaching* ($F(5, 122) = 36.13$, $p < 0.001$, $R^2 = 0.60$).

As discussed in Chapter 7: Section 7.2, positive relationships were identified between *Communicative Teaching* and L2 proficiency. However, in accordance with interview findings discussed previously, results from the regression analysis indicated that contextualised personal experiences (e.g. in-service CLT experience, experience learning via CLT as a student) were stronger predictors. Interview findings indicated that L2 proficiency informs the skills that teachers can call on when teaching; however, participants also discussed teacher L2 capability with respect to the context of usage. For example, Riho discussed the difficulty of using easier language when talking with students (see Thompson & Dooley, 2019b), while Maki talked about instructions and student direction, mentioning that it was dependent on the 'teacher's ability' to use English to guide students effectively. Studies are beginning to emphasise the specific nature of teacher L2 language usage (Freeman *et al.*, 2015; Katz, 2017), and results indicate that L2 proficiency may also inform L2 instructional efficacy indirectly, by contributing to the skills that individuals perceive to be available to them. With respect to teacher development, this finding indicates that contextualised practice (as suggested by Nishino, 2012; Thompson & Yanagita, 2017) may be an effective means of encouraging the development of specific purpose L2 capability for JTEs – what is recently being described as 'English-for-Teaching' (Freeman et al., 2015; Katz, 2017).

A number of contextual factors were identified to have positive bivariate correlations with *Communicative Teaching*, such as working at a school with a special designation ($r = 0.42$, $p < 0.01$) or working at an academically higher-ranked school ($r = 0.19$, $p < 0.05$). Other contextual variables positively correlated with stronger *Communicative Teaching* beliefs related to position (e.g. working full-time), while respondents with stronger *Communicative Teaching* efficacy beliefs were also more likely to report greater time teaching with non-Japanese ALTs ($r = 0.18$, $p < 0.01$). However, as shown in Table 8.1, no contextual variables made an independent contribution to the model. This may be due to the analysis technique used, as forward multiple regression identifies predictors that explain additional variance. For example, when the variable in-service experience with CLT was removed from the list of predictors, a model was generated that explained a lower proportion of variance, but included the contextual variable of working at a school with a special designation. This may mean that in-service CLT experience is likely to be influenced by context. Future studies could further explore these relationships using more sophisticated techniques, such as structural equation modelling.

With respect to behavioural change, results also suggest that in-service training opportunities, specifically in-service practicum opportunities, may be integral for developing L2 instructional efficacy. A number of approaches could be taken, such as action research (e.g. Cabaroglu, 2014; Thompson & Yanagita, 2017; Wyatt & Dikilitaş, 2015), integrated professional development training (Karimi, 2011) or introducing professional learning committees (Zonoubi et al., 2017). The common factor among such interventions appears to be the strong focus on the development of skills (e.g. pedagogic knowledge, L2 development) for dealing with *contextual* difficulties. While research has often shown dramatic shifts in the efficacy of relatively novice teachers (e.g. Thompson & Yanagita, 2017), some studies (e.g. Zonoubi et al., 2017) have shown that such interventions can influence the efficacy beliefs of experienced teachers. As self-efficacy beliefs have been argued to become stable over time (Bandura, 1997; Tschannen-Moran & Woolfolk Hoy, 2001), such changes to experienced teachers' efficacy indicate the value of in-service, contextualised, professional development as an important means of teacher belief and behaviour change.

Both reported use of English during class and perceived L2 proficiency were identified as predictors. Given the integrated role of the L2 as part of communicative approaches to language teaching (Richards, 2006), this relationship is not surprising. As also discussed in Chapter 7, a synergistic relationship has been identified between perceived L2 proficiency, teacher efficacy and the use of English as a teaching language (Choi &

Lee, 2016), as increases in perceived L2 proficiency appear to magnify the impact of teacher efficacy (and vice versa). Given the predictive relationship between teacher efficacy and the use of English, the relationship identified in the current study is intuitive, as greater use of the L2 in class provides efficacy-strengthening opportunities. Overall, this finding again suggests that contextualised usage provides more potential for efficacy development, thus returning to the question of how such interactions can be stimulated.

The final predictor of *Communicative Teaching* efficacy is time abroad. Findings have been variable about the potential influence of this factor as a likely source of teacher efficacy. In their study of L2-speaking secondary school English teachers in South Korea, Choi and Lee (2016) identified it as a personal factor positively associated with teacher efficacy beliefs. However, other studies have found no significant relationship between experience abroad and teacher self-efficacy (Chacon, 2005). Time abroad may aid in the development of (perceived) L2 proficiency (see Ball, 2000; Martinsen *et al.*, 2011; Meara, 1994), thus such experiences may also indirectly influence L2 efficacy beliefs by contributing to skills that individuals perceive to be available to them.

Given the relationship between student CLT experience and instructional efficacy, there may also be vicarious apprentice of learning effects (Lortie, 1975). For example, it may be that such individuals have spent time in countries where English is studied as an L2, and where teaching (and teacher training) emphasises CLT-oriented approaches (Bax, 2003). Thus, while findings from this study suggest that overseas experience is a useful predictor of both *Communicative Teaching* and *Using English* efficacy beliefs, more clarity is needed about *how* this variable may influence teacher efficacy beliefs, as studies have not always found overseas experience to be directly beneficial. For example, one study of in-service JTEs found that participation in an overseas professional development programme helped teachers to develop their pedagogic understanding of CLT and positively influenced their teaching practice, leading to stronger 'confidence' (Kurihara & Samimy, 2007). However, in another study, a novice JTE had significant difficulty implementing the ideas they had learned from participation in an overseas MA programme (Thompson & Yanagita, 2017). Future studies should attempt to confirm the relationship between L2 efficacy and overseas experience, and investigate *how* overseas experiences influence teacher beliefs. Such research is needed, as new policies from some local areas in Japan have made overseas study mandatory for English junior and senior high school teachers (*The Japan Times*, 2013).

Results provide support for findings from the literature (e.g. Nishino, 2012; Thompson & Yanagita, 2017; Tschannen-Moran & McMaster, 2009) that have emphasised the importance of 'real' experiences as sources of teacher self-efficacy belief information. Such experiences may also be vicarious. For example, from interviews with four teachers, Nishino (2012: 392) noted that the participants 'learned teaching techniques from their colleagues', and there appears to be a relationship between student learning experiences and L2 instructional efficacy. Findings suggest an apprenticeship of observation (Lortie, 1975) effect, where teacher efficacy beliefs and practices may be informed by perceptions of successful learning experiences.

Furthermore, as findings from this study have noted the potential influence of *student* learning experiences (i.e. cognitive mastery) on L2 instructional efficacy, efforts to improve teacher language proficiency may have positive indirect influences on instructional efficacy by learning *via* methodologies that are derived from a CLT approach, such as task-based language learning. Thus, programmes could provide teachers (particularly pre-service teachers) with opportunities to learn via different CLT methods, in order to stimulate proficiency development, and provide vicarious and pedagogic cognitive mastery experiences.

8.4 Predictors of Efficacy towards Student Achievement

The *Student Achievement* dimension focused on instructional beliefs towards the development of student knowledge, with a strong focus on accuracy and preparation for (grammar-focused) entrance examinations. A number of personal and contextual factors appear to be related to this domain of L2 instructional efficacy; these provide additional clarity about the variation across Japanese high schools, specifically with respect to the academic level of schools. Forward multiple regression analysis identified four variables that explained a significant proportion of the variance in the factor *Student Achievement* ($F(4, 122) = 13.90, p < 0.001, R^2 = 0.31$). The individual predictors were in-service CLT practice, years of teaching experience, school level and membership of the university counselling committee (see Table 8.2).

Although the predictive power of this model was relatively low (adjusted $R^2 = 0.31$), results highlight the influence of experience and context as factors that may influence L2 instructional efficacy beliefs. Firstly, findings indicated a positive relationship between teaching experience

Table 8.2 Summary of regression analysis for variables predicting Student Achievement

Variable	B	SE B	β
Years of teaching experience	0.15	0.04	0.33**
In-service CLT experience	0.10	0.03	0.26**
School level	0.24	0.08	0.23**
Member of the university counselling committee	0.09	0.04	0.18*

Note: $n = 127$; $R^2 = 0.31$; adjusted $R^2 = 0.29$; * indicates significance at $p < 0.05$; ** indicates $p < 0.01$. Excluded variables: perceived Eiken meets benchmark; Eiken meets benchmark; school type; use of English in class; pre-service experience with CLT and efficacy towards *Student Achievement* ($r = 0.37$, $p < 0.01$). Findings have been inconsistent when studies have examined language teacher efficacy beliefs and teaching experience; however, it is generally accepted that novice teacher efficacy beliefs are malleable (Woolfolk Hoy, 2000; Woolfolk Hoy & Spero, 2005), and thus may strengthen over time as greater experience provides more experiences of success and failure, from which teachers can develop effective knowledge and skills (Tschannen-Moran & McMaster, 2009; Tschannen-Moran & Woolfolk Hoy, 2007). In the Japanese context, teachers with greater experience are likely to have more opportunities to master university entrance preparation, and gain more developed knowledge about examinations. Thus, these results may indicate past mastery and *knowledge* about university examinations as sources of efficacy-forming information. Similarly, participants who reported serving on the 'university counselling committee' (an administrative role that involves advising students about university examinations) were more likely to have stronger *Student Achievement* efficacy ($r = 0.20$, $p < 0.05$), and this variable was identified as a predictor of this dimension (see Table 8.2). This may be due to teachers on such committees developing a greater understanding of what is required for successful university entrance. Such knowledge may then influence instructional decisions.

More experienced teachers may have had more opportunities for reflection, from which they may be able to develop better routines as experts working towards educational outcomes (Berliner, 1988). For example, such teachers may have a better understanding of the skills required for success in university entrance examinations and may have more refined strategies for identifying student errors and helping students build knowledge for language tests. Furthermore, such teachers may be more likely to also have broader knowledge about entrance examinations and procedures. The L2 instructional strategy dimension *Student Achievement* appears to be focused on linguistic knowledge, to which more experienced teachers in Japan may have a stronger orientation, as discussed by a number of participants (Taka, Saki, Ken, Maki, Riho) in the exploratory interviews and noted in the research literature (Takanashi, 2004). Also, many long-serving Japanese teachers *may not* have had enactive mastery experiences related to CLT study, observation or practice. For example, correlational results indicated that more experienced respondents were less likely to have had pre-service experience observing ($r = -0.18$, $p < 0.05$) or conducting ($r = -0.21$, $p < 0.05$) CLT lessons.

On the other hand, in-service teacher CLT practice was positively related to, and a predictor of *Student Achievement* efficacy. During the exploratory interviews, Taka suggested that teaching communicatively and teaching for entrance exams are not opposite aims, while Yuri is an example of a highly experienced teacher with strongly positive views about and efficacy towards CLT and strategies for university examination success. Although results from this and other studies (Nishino & Watanabe, 2008; Sakui, 2004; Underwood, 2013) have suggested a disconnect between teacher beliefs about CLT and university entrance examination preparation, it is also important to remember that research continues to show examples of teachers who are attempting to achieve both aims (Nishino, 2012; Thompson & Yanagita, 2017; Underwood, 2013), and that these two aims may not be dichotomous for all teachers. In fact, an important question for teacher development in Japan (and likely beyond) concerns how to build efficacy beliefs towards both dimensions of activity.

The final predictor of *Student Achievement* efficacy was school 'academic' level. Previous studies within and outside Japan (Moradkhani & Haghi, 2017; Nishino, 2009) have focused on school type (e.g. public versus private) as a variable influencing teacher beliefs. However, a key finding from the exploratory interviews concerned the possible influence of school academic level (*hensachi*) as a factor that may influence student motivation, teacher beliefs and teacher practice. A small number of teacher efficacy studies have noted a positive relationship between academic emphasis and stronger efficacy beliefs (Chong *et al.*, 2010; Pas *et al.*, 2012); however, this study may be the first to identify this relationship for language teachers.

Findings indicate a positive relationship between school level and efficacy towards both *Communicative Teaching* ($r = 0.20$, $p < 0.05$) and *Student Achievement* ($r = 0.29$, $p < 0.01$). Participants in the exploratory interviews also considered the impact of school level as positive (i.e. associated with stronger teacher efficacy beliefs). An example comes from Taka, who suggested that teaching English was easier at schools with higher academic rankings, due to higher student level. Another comes from Riho, who revealed that higher-ranked schools had better discipline, which provided teachers with a better environment for encouraging communicative activities. Meanwhile, Ken discussed how school level and teachers' perceptions of student level could lead to teacher rejection of CLT. He suggested that teachers from *lower*-ranked schools may reject techniques or ideas they observe in his classes during observations, because teachers judge their students to be too poor at English. Overall, interview results indicated that teaching is 'easier' at schools with a higher academic level, and this is likely to influence teacher beliefs and practice. For example, Nishino (2009, 2012) has shown that teachers' beliefs are influenced by their perceptions of their students' level, while other research has shown a relationship between teacher expectations and perceptions of student attributes and student achievement (Rubie-Davies, 2010; Rubie-Davies *et al.*, 2006).

Thus, results suggest that school level may have a positive influence on teacher efficacy beliefs by influencing teachers' perceptions of the difficulty of the task. However, other studies of JTEs have shown that teachers considered the academic level of their school when making instructional decisions, favouring examination preparation activities above CLT preparation (Underwood, 2013). In other words, school academic level may also negatively influence the *implementation* of communicative teaching. It may be that school level influences teachers' beliefs both positively (i.e. better students, better discipline) and negatively (i.e. need to maintain academic ranking by focusing on examinations rather than communication) in the Japanese context.

Although discipline (Sakui, 2007) and willingness to communicate (Yashima *et al.*, 2004) have been noted as variables influencing English teacher practice in Japan, these challenges are also common to teaching situations in other countries (Ho & Hau, 2004; Skaalvik & Skaalvik, 2007). Furthermore, learner self-efficacy and achievement in adolescents may be influenced by their learning environments and peers (Schunk & Meece, 2005), thus the academic level and purpose of schools (e.g. examination orientation) may be a variable for consideration in future language teacher efficacy studies.

8.5 Chapter Summary

This chapter has discussed the growing body of research focused on teacher efficacy beliefs towards language instruction. Results suggest that L2 instructional efficacy dimensions are contextually derived. While some domains (e.g. TSES dimensions) appear to be generalisable across countries, latent dimensions may also reflect country- or culture-specific factors. Although the two instructional strategy dimensions (*Communicative Teaching*, *Student Achievement*) identified in the current study reflect the Japanese context, findings may have implications for other countries and contexts across Asia that have difficulties balancing communicative development and entrance examination preparation (Hatipoglu, 2016; Ramezaney, 2014; Yung, 2015) or emphasise the use of English for teaching (Choi, 2015; Hamid *et al.*, 2013). The JTE-TES items could be adapted for use in such contexts in order to examine teacher beliefs towards communicative methods and knowledge development.

Previous learning and teaching experiences appear to be important sources of efficacy information. Research has shown that teachers are likely to be influenced by the ways in which they learned as students (Feiman-Nemser, 2001; Lortie, 1975), and an interesting finding from the current study concerns the impact of student learning experiences as a potential source of instructional efficacy information. Most studies in Japan have highlighted the negative influence of previous learning experiences (specifically the grammar translation methodology *yakudoku*) on teachers' beliefs and practice for language teaching (Humphries & Burns, 2015; Nishino, 2012; Underwood, 2013), while other studies (Nishino,

2012) have found no relationship between student learning experiences, teacher beliefs and teaching behaviour. However, both interview and survey findings identified this factor as a significant source of information that appears to influence teacher efficacy beliefs. As Riho mentioned during her interview, teachers should experience learning *via* a range of teaching techniques, in order to understand the value for learners. Overall, findings indicate that students' learning experiences – at home and abroad – may act as filters through which experiences are appraised (Watzke, 2007). Such experiences may contribute to efficacy directly, as vicarious modelling experiences, or may influence future pedagogy indirectly by contributing to the skills that teachers draw on (e.g. L2 proficiency) during instruction. The predictive nature of the relationship identified in the current study indicates a direct influence, and future studies could explore this relationship further.

Contextual factors may provide opportunities for efficacy development. In the current study, teachers who reported serving on the 'university counselling committee' were more likely to have stronger instructional efficacy towards the development of student knowledge. This contention should be tested and investigated further in future studies of JTE efficacy. For example, it may be that teachers with stronger efficacy beliefs volunteer for such committees, or that more experienced teachers are automatically placed on such committees.

Finally, school factors may need greater exploration. While school type (Moradkhani & Haghi, 2017) has been a feature considered in some language teacher efficacy studies, future research could consider the potential impact of school level. Interview findings suggest that teaching is easier at schools with a higher academic level. In other words, results from the current study suggest that this variable may influence perceptions of task difficulty (Tschannen-Moran *et al.*, 1998). However, other studies (Underwood, 2013) have suggested a negative relationship between such school contexts and communicative teaching practices. Given the contradictory nature of the small body of research that has discussed this variable, it seems that future research is necessary to explore the relationship between school level, teacher efficacy beliefs and pedagogic practice. Furthermore, differences have been identified between teachers' perceptions of efficacy development at different types of schools (Moradkhani & Haghi, 2017), indicating again that school context is a source of information influencing efficacy beliefs. Future studies, both within Japan and in the wider field, could investigate school level, school designations and local contextual factors with respect to teacher efficacy dimensions and development.

9 Efficacy Towards Collaborative Practice and Collective Action

Education is not an individual activity. Planning, text selection and materials design (De Oliveira & Richardson, 2001; Goddard *et al.*, 2004a; Skaalvik & Skaalvik, 2007) are examples of activities in which teacher collaboration and cooperation are necessary. Given that many teaching challenges are faced by teams, teacher beliefs about collective capability have become an increasingly important area of study, with perceived 'collective' teacher efficacy being positively associated with student achievement (Goddard, 2002; Goddard *et al.*, 2015; Tschannen-Moran & Barr, 2004), commitment (Klassen *et al.*, 2013; Ware & Kitsantas, 2011) and job satisfaction (Göker, 2012; Klassen *et al.*, 2010). Furthermore, the collective domain of activity may be broader for language teachers, many of whom co-teach as part of language education (Carless, 2006; Mahoney, 2004; Tajino & Tajino, 2000) or content and language integrated learning (CLIL) programmes (MacDonald *et al.*, 2012). Thus, teacher beliefs of capability towards areas of collective activity, and their relationship with performance, may be of strong importance for language teachers.

Social cognitive theory recognises that behaviour is influenced not only by beliefs about individual self-capability, but also by social factors and perceptions of group (e.g. team, faculty, school) capability. Schools are social institutions, and Bandura (1997: 248) has argued that the 'belief systems of the staff also create an organizational culture that can have vitalizing or demoralizing effects on the perceived efficacy of its members'. Due to triadic reciprocal causation, social experiences and school culture may strengthen or undermine teachers' sense of efficacy towards language teaching. One example of collective action concerns teacher collaboration, which has been shown to predict (Goddard *et al.*, 2015) and be mediated by school-level collective teacher efficacy (Moolenaar *et al.*, 2012). Greater collaboration appears to positively influence student achievement (Goddard *et al.*, 2007) and is noted as a feature of effective schools (Rosenholtz, 1985; Rosenholtz *et al.*, 1986).

Collaboration between teachers is also generally seen as positive for professional development (Avalos, 2011). For example, 'lesson study' is a means of development that started in Japan, which requires teachers to work together in the design of lessons, with observation, feedback and revision used to improve teaching (Chong & Kong, 2012; Fernandez, 2002; Puchner & Taylor, 2006). However, other research has noted that teacher collaboration may not always be positive (Little, 1990, 1993; Sato & Kleinsasser, 2004); it may lead to actions that preserve the status quo of teaching behaviour and instruction (Little, 1990; Sato & Kleinsasser, 2004; Underwood, 2012) rather than lead to actual change in practice. Research from a number of contexts (e.g. Hong Kong, see Boyle, 1997; Korea, see Shin, 2012; and Japan, see Thompson & Yanagita, 2017) has indicated that collaborative practice causes strain for language teachers, often due to teachers being forced to teach in ways contrary to what they prefer. As a result, such teachers may avoid cooperation, reducing the potential benefits for collective efficacy development. On the other hand, those with strong self-beliefs about the capability of their collegial group to *successfully* work together may be more likely to engage in collaborative practice and develop stronger collective efficacy.

This chapter discusses language teacher efficacy towards collaborative practice, focusing on the *Teamwork* efficacy dimension of the Japanese Teacher of English Teacher Efficacy Scale (JTE-TES). It starts by locating collaborative efficacy as a dimension of second language (L2) teacher efficacy that covers self-beliefs of personal and group capability. It then discusses the small body of research that has examined collective L2 teacher efficacy, including the collaborative (sub)domain. The chapter then introduces interview and survey findings to highlight the integrated nature of collaborative efficacy for Japanese high school teachers of English (JTEs) (i.e. incorporating beliefs of both personal and group capability), before exploring variables that may influence efficacy towards this domain.

9.1 Individual, Collective and Collaborative Teacher Efficacy

Schools are social organisations where much of the work carried out by teachers is interdependent. Bandura (1993) suggested that in their contribution to student achievement and development, efficacy beliefs operate in three ways: (1) student self-efficacy, which relates to the capability of individuals to regulate their own learning and master content; (2) personal teacher efficacy, which is concerned with the perceptions of capability that individual teachers have towards different areas of teaching control, such as instructional efficacy (i.e. *Communicative Teaching* and *Student Achievement*); and (3) collective efficacy, which represents beliefs about the capability of the school faculty to carry out teaching activities to positively influence student learning. In other words, teacher capability has 'an organizational dimension' (Goddard et al., 2004a: 4), which moves beyond the beliefs of teachers for individual action to include beliefs about the 'the performance capability of a social system as a whole' (Bandura, 1997: 469).

Efficacy towards collaboration has been investigated and considered at both the personal and collective level. In other words, collaborative efficacy may involve perceptions of *both* individual self-capability (i.e. personal self-efficacy to contribute towards collaborative activity) and 'group-level' capability, that is beliefs about colleague and faculty capability towards collective action (see Klassen, 2010: 342).

A significant amount of research has examined collaborative efficacy as a dimension of personal teacher efficacy. For example, within research of teacher efficacy towards the implementation of inclusive education practices (e.g. Malinen *et al.*, 2013a, 2013b; Sharma *et al.*, 2012), collaborative efficacy has primarily been considered as an individual self-belief of capability towards collaborative action. In their introduction of the Teacher Efficacy for Inclusive Practices (TEIP) Scale, Sharma *et al.* (2012: 16) argued that 'teachers competent in using effective teaching strategies, collaborating with others and managing disruptive behaviours would likely be more efficacious when teaching in an inclusive classroom'. In other words, research from such studies has primarily examined collaborative capability as a dimension of *personal* teacher efficacy alongside instructional and behavioural management efficacy. Such an approach to collaborative efficacy does not include any evaluation of group capability, with items using 'I am able to' (see Sharma *et al.*, 2012: 19) phrasing.

However, research has also indicated that collaboration constitutes one aspect of collective efficacy (Abedini *et al.*, 2018a, 2018b). This may be due to the change in orientation of collective efficacy research. As early studies and instruments did not necessarily have clear conceptual and definitional clarity (see Klassen *et al.*, 2011), the measurement of the construct has altered over time. Early studies (e.g. Bandura, 1993; Goddard & Goddard, 2001) aggregated the individual responses of teachers from each school and used these as a basis for comparison. In other words, collective efficacy was examined during this time by summing together each teacher's personal efficacy ratings. As greater attention was given to perceived collective teacher efficacy, scales with stronger theoretical clarity were developed (e.g. Tschannen-Moran & Barr, 2004) with items that had a group orientation and clarified the construct from 'shared beliefs' towards 'individual beliefs about collective capability'. More recent studies (e.g. Goddard *et al.*, 2015; Skaalvik & Skaalvik, 2007; Tschannen-Moran & Barr, 2004) now use collective self-representations such as 'we' in items, and collective efficacy is examined as *individual* perceptions of *collective* capability. Accordingly, definitional clarity of perceived collective teacher efficacy has evolved from 'the groups' shared belief in its conjoint capabilities to organise and execute courses of action required to produce given levels of attainments' (Bandura, 1997: 477) to a focus on individuals' 'perceptions of group-level attributes' (Klassen, 2010: 342).

Perceptions of group-level characteristics may involve individuals evaluating the extent to which their school or faculty can effectively carry out collective actions (i.e. group materials design, textbook selection) in the pursuit of student learning. As a result, perceptions of collaborative efficacy may contribute towards perceived collective efficacy. As will be discussed further in the following section, research from English as a foreign language (EFL) contexts (Abedini et al., 2018a, 2018b) has indicated that collaborative efficacy constitutes an underlying dimension of collective efficacy – that is, it can be considered as one aspect of collective efficacy. As a result, collaborative efficacy has been measured with items using 'How well can we' (Abedini et al., 2018a: 32) phrasing.

In summary, it appears that teacher efficacy beliefs towards collaboration cannot easily be demarcated into personal versus collective beliefs. While research has generally considered efficacy beliefs at the personal or collective level, findings from this study (see Chapter 6) indicate that collaborative efficacy appears to overlap these, incorporating both (1) beliefs about personal self-capability to effectively contribute towards collective activity; and (2) beliefs about group capability to effectively carry out collective actions in the pursuit of student learning.

9.2 Collective and Collaborative Efficacy in Language Teaching Contexts

Researchers have responded to calls (Klassen et al., 2011) for greater attention to collective teacher efficacy in language teaching contexts by investigating dimensions of collective L2 efficacy (Abedini et al., 2018a, 2018b); the development of school-level collective efficacy (Zonoubi et al., 2017); its relationship with job stress and satisfaction (Göker, 2012); and the relationship between collective efficacy and demographic factors such as years of teaching experience (Baleghizadeh & Goldouz, 2016). Other studies have investigated the relationship between personal and collective teacher efficacy for novice teachers (Zakeri et al., 2015), while some studies have carried out related work, such as examining the role of organisational factors (e.g. collective beliefs) on individuals' teacher efficacy (Shin, 2012; Thompson & Yanagita, 2017).

Within the relatively small body of work that has examined language teacher collective efficacy beliefs, studies have generally used existing scales (e.g. Baleghizadeh & Goldouz, 2016; Göker, 2012; Zakeri et al., 2015), although some studies (e.g. Abedini et al., 2018b; Zonoubi et al., 2017) have examined L2 collective efficacy using interviews and focus groups. For example, in a study of 10 Iranian EFL teachers, Zonoubi et al. (2017) used thematic analysis of interview data to explore the development of personal and collective teacher efficacy via participation in a professional learning community (PLC). Using pre and post-programme interviews, the authors identified a change in the language used by participants, finding that teachers used more collective self-representations (e.g. 'we') after participating in the development programme. The study noted positive differences in the individuals' perceptions about the competency of other teachers, and suggested that the PLC intervention provided participants with the opportunity to successfully work together and provide critical feedback, leading to stronger collective efficacy. Although the study did not specifically discuss 'collaborative efficacy', it seems that the participants in the study also developed stronger efficacy towards collaborative practice by completing the PLC programme. The authors explained that the programme enabled participants to perceive that their teaching 'team' became more effective at materials development and curriculum planning. Each of these tasks involves collaborative interpersonal interactions between teaching staff, and due to their perceived success, participants' perceptions of school-level collective efficacy also appeared to strengthen. This suggests that stronger perceptions of collaborative efficacy among teachers contributed to stronger school-level (i.e. higher level) collective efficacy.

Such an interpretation has support from other studies, as research has now shifted to examining the underlying dimensions of collective teacher efficacy. In a study of 30 EFL teachers from different education contexts (i.e. high school through university) using analysis of interview and focus group data, Abedini *et al.* (2018b) found that collaboration constituted one underlying domain of collective efficacy. Study participants discussed the importance of collegial communication, cooperation and feedback as key activities that contributed to self-beliefs of group capability and accordingly influenced institutional success. In a separate study, Abedini *et al.* (2018a) developed an EFL-specific collective efficacy scale, using exploratory (EFA) and confirmatory factor analysis (CFA) to examine underlying latent factors of the scale. The authors identified four dimensions of L2 collective efficacy, which they named (1) Efficacy in collaboration with colleagues; (2) Efficacy in decision-making; (3) Efficacy in instruction; and (4) Disciplinary and coping efficacy. Taken together, these findings suggest that L2 collective efficacy has a collaborative domain, including the capability to 'work collaboratively to achieve educational goals' (Abedini *et al.*, 2018a: 14). This domain is explored further below.

9.3 Efficacy towards Collaborative Practice

The current study explored the teacher efficacy beliefs of JTEs via interviews with six participants in the exploratory interviews, and via analysis (EFA, multiple linear regression) of survey data. Interview participants were selected purposefully due to their expertise as teachers, consultants or trainers. Similar to the Zonoubi *et al.* (2017) study, the group of participants also included novice teachers, in order to provide voices with a range of experiences (Beecham *et al.*, 2005; Hyrkäs *et al.*, 2003). Results from the exploratory interviews indicated a close and interconnected relationship between individual and collective challenges, as individual teacher efficacy beliefs appear to be influenced by perceptions of staff (and specifically teaching team) capability. Furthermore, individual and collective challenges appeared to be linked by perceptions of collaborative efficacy.

As introduced by Thompson and Dooley (2019b), and summarised in Chapter 6, interview findings identified eight dimensions of teacher challenge, including two that involved a collective element: (1) *Working with Others* involved beliefs about both personal and collective capability towards collaboration; and (2) *Team Efficacy*, which focused on areas of collective action, such as implementing new curricular guidelines. These findings extend understanding about tasks where beliefs about collective capability may be represented, such as team teaching, collaborative materials design, textbook selection, responding to national curriculum change and in novice teacher support.

A key finding from the interviews concerned the challenge of working as part of a team. The interview questions asked respondents to discuss their (1) key activities; challenges (2) within and (3) beyond the classroom; including (4) key factors that would influence their 'confidence'. Collaboration was discussed with respect to each of these four questions as most respondents discussed the necessity of collaboration as part of the teaching and materials design procedures at their schools; the difficulty of working effectively with non-Japanese assistant language teachers (ALTs) inside and outside class; the challenge of collaborative communication and materials design between JTEs; and the impact of such experiences on their perceptions of personal, group (i.e. for their materials design team) and school (i.e. collective) efficacy.

These findings may reflect the use of 'lesson study' for professional development in the local Japanese context, and the importance of cooperation for materials design and assessment between *gakunen kyoin* (i.e. instructors teaching the same subject) at high schools in Japan. However, collaborative practice is a feature of many language teaching contexts and the challenge of team teaching is not only limited to Japan but is also used across Asia (Carless, 2006; MacDonald *et al.*, 2012; Mahoney, 2004). Indeed, collaborative efficacy has been identified as a dimension of teacher efficacy in studies from the wider (e.g. Norway, see Skaalvik & Skaalvik, 2007) and language teaching (e.g. Iran, see Abedini *et al.*, 2018a, 2018b) fields. As a result, these results may highlight a key aspect of language teacher practice, as effective collaborative action and the associated efficacy beliefs of teachers appear to be an important dimension of efficacy for future study. Little is known about collaborative efficacy and what factors may influence teacher self-beliefs of capability towards this area.

In the analysis of interview findings and the design of JTE-TES items, challenges related to collective action were divided following Goddard *et al.*'s (2000: 3) distinction, in which efficacy beliefs may be about 'individual or group capability'. The dimension *Working with Others* focused on beliefs about individual capability towards collaborative action, such as personal capability to effectively communicate and share ideas with other teaching members. For example, a number of participants (e.g. Riho, Saki) explained that they did not want to share their ideas with others, expressing weak personal capability efficacy towards collaborative practice. In other words, beliefs towards collaborative practice were (firstly) viewed as a dimension of personal efficacy. On the other hand, the *Team Efficacy* domain was associated with the use of collective self-identifications (Brewer & Gardner, 1996) such as 'we' by participants when they discussed tasks and challenges faced by the teaching team, department or school as a group. An example comes from Ken, who suggested that his school was not capable of successfully responding to the new national curriculum. He revealed, 'we cannot keep the same level of the class', mainly due to members who would not use the materials designed by the teaching team for each class. In other words, this challenge primarily represented an evaluation of group-level attributes.

However, findings also indicated some overlap between *Working with Others* and *Team Efficacy* due to the interpersonal nature of collaboration and its influence on perceptions of collective capability. Ken went on to indicate that his perception of weak collective capability was due to his actions and those of his teaching team (i.e. their collaborative practice) as they could not effectively communicate and collaborate to respond to the collective challenge of curriculum change.

Furthermore, participants indicated that their personal teaching efficacy was influenced by their perceptions of collaborative (i.e. among the teaching team) and collective (i.e. school-level) efficacy. Interview results suggested that collaborative interactions often required teachers to *change* their practice and follow the 'unwritten rules' of the school (Nagamine, 2007: 214), leading to weaker perceptions of collaborative and collective capability, as well as doubts (see Wheatley, 2005) about individual capability. Thompson and Dooley (2019b) introduced an example from Saki, who discussed an example of collaborative materials design in which she perceived her ideas to be ignored and rejected by her senior colleagues. This led her to lose 'confidence' in her capability to contribute towards collective materials design and moved her to question her personal efficacy. She suggested that her personal teacher efficacy remained weak until she moved to a new school, where she experienced a more positive environment, leading to stronger perceptions of collaborative (i.e. interpersonal) and collective (i.e. school-level) efficacy that positively influenced her individual (i.e. personal) efficacy towards instruction.

Exploratory factor analysis of survey data (see Thompson & Woodman, 2019) identified an integrated dimension of L2 efficacy related to collaboration. The three items comprising this factor were:

(1) *How confident are you about your team/departments' capability to communicate ideas effectively?*
(2) *How confident are you about your team/departments' capability to develop teaching materials, syllabus and assessments collaboratively?*
(3) *How confident are you about your capability to share teaching ideas and materials with colleagues?*

The dimension was named *Teamwork*, and appears to represent a domain of teacher efficacy that links perceptions of collective (i.e. capability of a teaching team to communicate and develop materials) and individual (i.e. personal capability to share materials and collaborate) capability. It is similar to the collaborative dimension of efficacy identified by Skaalvik and Skaalvik (2007) in their study of Norwegian teachers; however, the JTE-TES items ask respondents to assess perceptions of both individual (Item 3 above) and group capability (Items 1 and 2 above), which differentiates it from the Skaalvik and Skaalvik (2007) scale, in which collaborative efficacy was primarily assessed as a personal efficacy dimension.

In summary, analysis of interview and survey findings indicated that L2 teacher efficacy has a collaborative dimension, focused on group communication and materials design. Interview findings also indicated that this domain links individual and collective efficacy. Given that collective efficacy appears to influence personal efficacy (Goddard *et al.*, 2004a; Kurt *et al.*, 2011; Viel-Ruma *et al.*, 2010), this finding was consistent with the research literature, as results indicated that perceptions of individual (i.e. personal) capability were informed by perceptions of the organisational (i.e. collective) and team (interpersonal) capability. In other words, personal efficacy appeared to be influenced by 'the functioning of the team' (Skaalvik & Skaalvik, 2007: 613).

Although the task of collaborative practice is necessarily interdependent – regardless of teaching context – the collective nature of Japanese culture and emphasis on group approval and action may strengthen the importance of collaborative interactions on perceptions of individual capability. As Thompson and Dooley (2019b) have explained, individuals may align their personal beliefs about their own capability with their beliefs about the collective capability of their group as they attempt to adjust to the expectations of their teams (Morling *et al.*, 2002). In other words, 'normative pressure', a type of social persuasion that involves individuals taking on group expectations as they are socialised to the faculty (see Goddard et al., 2004a), may play a role in the development of efficacy for JTEs. This is further explored in Chapter 10, as findings indicated that teachers strongly focused on social persuasion and attributions of interpersonal group experiences as sources of efficacy belief-forming information.

9.4 Predictors of Efficacy towards Collaborative Practice

A forward multiple regression analysis was carried out to predict the JTE-TES collaborative *Teamwork* efficacy dimension (dependent variable). Table 9.1 shows that three variables were identified to predict 34% of the proportion of the variance in the factor *Teamwork* ($F(3, 124) = 19.6$, $p < 0.001$, $R^2 = 0.32$). The individual predictors were in-service CLT experience, the average age of the teaching team and perceived L2 capability. Although the predictive power of this model was relatively low ($R^2 = 0.32$), this result highlights the potential impact of contextual factors – specifically towards the make-up of the teaching team – as an influence on collective teacher efficacy beliefs.

As noted in the expert interviews, teachers often collaborate for syllabus and lesson preparation, and these findings suggest that teachers with more in-service CLT experience are more likely to be confident in sharing ideas and contributing towards collaborative materials design. Furthermore, as teachers with greater in-service CLT experience were more likely to be members of a professional development organisation (e.g. teaching associations), and reported spending more time teaching with non-Japanese ALTs, it may be that such teachers have more opportunities to experience and learn about collaborative teaching and materials design. In other words, such experiences may provide direct efficacy development information via mastery experiences (i.e. personal practice), vicarious modelling (e.g. observation of others) and social persuasion (e.g. feedback from observers).

However, these correlational findings could also be interpreted in an alternate way. It may be that teachers with stronger collaborative efficacy choose to carry out CLT activities and participate in professional development activities. Given the reciprocal nature of behaviour

Table 9.1 Summary of regression analysis for variables predicting Teamwork

Variable	B	SE B	β
In-service CLT experience	0.47	.08	0.45**
Average age of teaching team	−0.36	.12	−0.22**
Perceived Eiken meets MEXT benchmark	0.48	0.20	0.19**

Note: $n = 128$; $R^2 = 0.32$; adjusted $R^2 = 0.31$; * indicates significance at $p < 0.05$; ** indicates $p < 0.01$. Excluded variables: Eiken meets benchmark; use of English in class; experience abroad; teaching at a school with a special designation; pre-service CLT experience; experience studying via CLT; school level.

and efficacy beliefs, it may be that teachers with stronger efficacy make a greater effort to involve their non-Japanese ALTs in class (often via CLT activities), from which collaborative efficacy and practice is stimulated. Such patterns have been noted in the research literature, as JTEs and ALTs have reported that effective, collaborative team teaching requires greater time in preparation and planning, as each participant must overcome communicative challenges and negotiate their role (Carless, 2006; Moote, 2003). When teachers perceive that this effort leads to success in teaching (e.g. greater participation by students) or provides other benefits (e.g. stimulates L2 development for the L2-speaking teacher), they may be more likely to continue to engage in collaborative action (see Carless & Walker, 2006). Accordingly, this reciprocal process may strengthen efficacy and influence practice. Future studies could use longitudinal designs to investigate the causality of these variables and identify other key factors that stimulate collaborative efficacy.

It seems clear that when (perceived) L2 proficiency informs the task (e.g. via needed skills), there is a positive and predictive relationship between language teacher efficacy and perceived proficiency (see Chacon, 2005; Yilmaz, 2011). The collaborative dimension of L2 teacher efficacy may be directly and indirectly influenced by perceptions of L2 proficiency. Teachers with stronger (perceived) L2 ability may assess themselves to be more capable to communicate with other teachers via the L2 (i.e. a task that involves a direct assessment of L2 ability), and engage in materials development that requires demonstration of L2 knowledge (i.e. a task that indirectly involves an assessment of L2 ability). Such challenges were noted in the exploratory interviews, as participants mentioned the social nature of L2 teaching – colleagues and students can assess the language competence of teachers. Simply put, individuals are likely to feel more confident about activities for which they perceive themselves to have more competence (Pajares, 1996). As a result, teachers who perceive themselves to have higher English proficiency may be more likely to engage in collaborative usage of the L2 and to share their ideas for judgement by other professionals.

The third variable that made a significant contribution as a predictor of *Teamwork* is the contextual variable concerned with average age of respondents' teaching teams, for which there was a *negative* relationship. In other words, younger teams are associated with stronger *Teamwork* efficacy beliefs, while JTEs working within relatively older teams are likely to have weaker beliefs towards this dimension of efficacy. This result may suggest that younger teachers and younger teams are more familiar with sharing work and collaborative teaching. It may also suggest that more experienced teams are resistant to collaborative work, as suggested by Cook (2009) and Underwood (2012), which makes the collaborative task more difficult. Given that age and years of teaching experience appear to be essentially collinear for the JTEs in this sample

($r = 0.92$, $p < 0.01$), it may also suggest cultural differences by generation. For example, research of attitudes towards democratic values and political orientation has suggested a gap in attitudes of Japanese people towards 'authoritarian' leadership, as younger people are more likely to accept different opinions in comparison to their older peers (Dalton & Shin, 2014).

Interview findings expand on this result, indicating that traditional practices and cultural values influence teacher perceptions of collaborative efficacy. Interview participants suggested that established (older) teachers often influenced novice (younger) teachers with pressure *against* change and innovation. This appeared to be systemic, rather than due to interpersonal differences, as participants reported that evaluation systems often relied on teachers demonstrating that they had been acculturated to existing practices, rather than encouraged to innovate (Cook, 2009; Sato & Kleinsasser, 2004; Underwood, 2012). In an example discussed by Thompson and Dooley (2019b), Riho explained that during her teaching practicum, she received negative teaching evaluations because she attempted to implement communicative activities in her English lessons. She suggested that there was little actual collaboration; rather that teachers would be 'beaten' down and forced to follow common school instructional procedures, as 'you have to follow what other teachers are doing'. Other respondents (Ken, Maki, Saki, Taka) discussed similar examples, suggesting that events (e.g. group meetings) in which collaborative practice could take place had involved negative experiences. As discussed previously, Saki reported a complete loss of confidence towards collaborative action after perceiving her ideas to be rejected during a materials design meeting.

In accordance with social cognitive theory (Bandura, 1997), these results indicate that social perceptions influence teachers' perceived efficacy. It may be that team dynamics (e.g. average age) influences efficacy beliefs directly via (negative) emotional arousal. One interpretation is that during their analysis of experience, individuals consider the relative difficulty of collaborative effort with older teachers, leading to stronger perceptions of task difficulty and weaker perceived capability to collaborate. This has some support from the interview findings, as younger participants expressed difficulty about communicating and expressing their ideas to more senior colleagues. Specifically, Saki mentioned that there are cultural norms, encoded in language, which she should follow in the way she addresses and responds to senior colleagues. Furthermore, cultural values towards communication may also influence perceptions of difficulty towards collaborative action. For example, meetings in Japan are not often a forum for expressing new ideas; rather decisions are often made beforehand and participants may not express their preferences clearly (Kitao & Kitao, 1985). Such requirements may influence perceptions of collaborative efficacy due to greater task difficulty and complexity. This difficulty has been noted in countries with cultural and teaching similarity (e.g. Korea, see Shin, 2012), thus these relationships may be of interest to researchers in the broader language education field, particularly Asian contexts.

Interestingly, Yuri (an older, highly experienced JTE) discussed this challenge from a different perspective, mentioning the difficulty of carrying out collaborative planning with younger non-Japanese ALTs, who did not have experience working with Japanese students, nor the ability to share their ideas via Japanese. This finding highlights an area for future studies to explore, as collaborative efficacy may be dependent on a range of factors. Research could examine this dimension under different task conditions, including via the L2, with older colleagues and with non-local colleagues. Other factors may also influence efficacy beliefs towards collaborative practice. It may be that younger teachers disagree with existing practice (Thompson & Yanagita, 2017) and wish to implement change (Shin, 2012), which leads to weaker efficacy towards collaborative practice.

9.5 Towards Stronger Efficacy for Collective Action

Given that social factors appear to influence collaborative, collective and personal teacher efficacy, findings from the current study and wider literature indicate that a key concern for schools should be the development of an environment that encourages collective efficacy development.

Interview findings indicated that leadership was a key element associated with stronger perceptions of collective efficacy. In alignment with the research literature (e.g. Goddard *et al.*, 2015; Kurt *et al.*, 2011; Ross & Gray, 2006), participants specifically discussed a causal link between principal support, school leadership, collaborative activity and stronger perceived collective capability. For example, when talking about her past experience in a very effective programme that had achieved significant curricula developments, Yuri suggested that it was due, in large part, to the culture that her principal created. She suggested that schools need strong leadership to break down resistance against change and move positively towards innovation, revealing that in her experience older 'teachers don't share their ideas and don't want to share their ideas'. She mentioned that there had been teacher resistance and that some teachers had followed 'unwillingly'; therefore, 'without that kind of super strong leader', behavioural change by teaching teams was unlikely. She explained that as a result of the principal's efforts, she perceived her team to develop strong collective capability. Similar to participants in the Abedini *et al.* (2018b) study, Yuri suggested that communication and collaboration were a key aspect informing her perceptions of collective efficacy.

Another example came from Taka, a consultant to a number of high schools. He picked up on a similar issue, suggesting that risk aversion influences teaching groups against innovation. Taka explained that strong leadership was important for achieving group consensus (see Hofstede & Soeters, 2002) as this cohesiveness shared the potential burden of responsibility for failure across the faculty. In other words, he suggested that principals themselves could influence the systemic procedures of schools that work against innovation by taking responsibility for dealing with outside stakeholders. These examples support Bandura's (1997: 501) contention that leadership can 'unite the community for common cause'.

Results from the exploratory interviews (Taka, Yuri, Maki, Saki) also revealed that 'successful' collaborative efforts often involved the use of outside consultants. Outside assistance may be effective in breaking the established social culture within the team (i.e. that works against change and collaboration), due to respect for such individuals as leaders or respected outsiders. Findings from this study indicate that such actions may be required for certain schools to overcome social cultures that emphasise acculturation, rather than innovation via collaborative efforts.

There is support from the literature for these findings. For example, previous studies in Asia (Cheng, 1994: 309) have shown that effective principal leadership encourages 'adaptivity' and 'flexibility' and helps build a 'shared educational mission', while previous studies in Japan have shown that outside support has encouraged collaboration (Sato & Takahashi, 2008). Furthermore, in a study of more than 3000 teachers, Ross and Gray (2006) found collective teacher efficacy was mediated by transformational leadership (an approach that emphasises shared vision), which had both direct and indirect effects on teacher commitment.

Regarding the contextual difficulties related to collaboration in the JTE teaching situation, studies from other fields (e.g. manufacturing, see Olivella *et al.*, 2008) have suggested that effective teamwork in the Japanese context involves a change in the functions of leadership, with a greater focus on support and facilitation (i.e. towards a transformative mindset). Therefore, local developmental efforts may need to focus on leadership training for senior teachers and principals by applying empirical evidence from other areas (e.g. manufacturing) to education.

It appears that collective efficacy can be strengthened via professional development activities, specifically those which have a collaborative focus (Zonoubi *et al.*, 2017). Furthermore, effective collaboration appears to be important for teacher development (Rosenholtz *et al.*, 1986), and collaborative problem-solving has been suggested as the key ingredient for school, rather than individual change (Hawley & Valli, 1999). Recent research (Abedini *et al.*, 2018a, 2018b) and results from this study have indicated that collaborative efficacy may be an underlying dimension of school-level collective efficacy. As a result, the encouragement of greater interdependency, and stronger *positive* social networks between teachers may lead to stronger collective efficacy and, accordingly, better student achievement (Moolenaar *et al.*, 2012).

9.6 Chapter Summary

Collective efficacy beliefs have been suggested as key beliefs for investigating schools (Goddard *et al.*, 2004a) because teachers do not only work alone (Skaalvik & Skaalvik, 2007). Discussion in this chapter has been limited to one aspect of collective efficacy regarding capability to collaborate effectively with colleagues in the pursuit of student L2 development. It has argued that this dimension also includes beliefs of self-capability, due to the interpersonal nature of collaborative action.

These beliefs may have vital importance for language teachers, as much L2 teaching activity involves collaborative effort (Carless, 2006; MacDonald *et al.*, 2012; Underwood, 2012). This chapter has discussed the different tasks within the collaborative domain, including communication, materials development, team teaching and feedback. It has examined personal (e.g. L2 ability) and contextual (e.g. team dynamics) variables that may directly and/or indirectly influence these self-beliefs.

Interview findings from the current study identified beliefs about collaborative and collective capability, indicating that these cognitions influence participants' personal teacher efficacy beliefs and teaching behaviours. EFA of JTE-TES questionnaire data revealed an integrated dimension of teacher efficacy concerned with teachers' perceptions of capability towards collaboration. Findings extend knowledge by showing areas of collective challenge for the JTE context and respond to Klassen *et al.*'s (2011) call for more research in international contexts. As noted by Thompson and Dooley (2019b), these results also challenge the assumption (see Huff & Kelley, 2005) that Japan's collectivist nature makes group work easier. In fact, findings suggest that communication difficulties (Popov *et al.*, 2012) and attitudes towards collaboration may negatively impact teachers' collective efficacy beliefs.

Collaboration involves risk and 'encourages teachers to move beyond reliance on their own memories and experiences with schooling and toward engagement with others' (Goddard *et al.*, 2007: 892). International studies have shown that teacher collaboration helps communities of practice to develop that help encourage self-efficacy for teaching (Takahashi, 2011) where a key mediating influence appears to be school leadership (Goddard *et al.*, 2015; Hallinger & Heck, 2010; Ross & Gray, 2006). Leadership may have an indirect influence by developing an environment where teachers perceive stronger support and collaborate effectively, within a social network that emphasises shared expectations of action (Sampson *et al.*, 1999).

There is growing evidence that collective efficacy influences personal teacher efficacy (Goddard *et al.*, 2004a; Kurt *et al.*, 2011; Viel-Ruma *et al.*, 2010), as individual perceptions of capability are likely to be informed by perceptions of the capability of the organisations to which they belong and operate within. There may also be a synergistic reciprocal relationship between collective and individual efficacy (Goddard & Goddard, 2001; Kurz & Knight, 2004), particularly for novice teachers (Zakeri *et al.*, 2015), as perceptions of individual capability may strengthen (or weaken) based on perceived collective efficacy and vice versa. Findings from this study have indicated that teachers with low personal teacher efficacy may develop and strengthen their perceived personal capability when they perceive strong organisational support, trust with their colleagues and effective leadership, factors which also positively influence perceptions of faculty capability (Kurt *et al.*, 2011; Lee *et al.*, 2011).

Finally, results may also have implications for curricular change, as teachers who have a voice in the curriculum design process may display stronger ownership towards innovation (Englert *et al.*, 1993). As significant changes to teaching practice are being introduced to a number of contexts across Asia (Baldauf *et al.*, 2011; Butler, 2011; Hamid *et al.*, 2013), results may also have implications for other contexts with similar cultural backgrounds and difficulties regarding collaborative practice (e.g. Korea, see Shin, 2012). Future research should investigate the way that teaching teams operate and identify best practices for encouraging effective collaboration and collaborative efficacy. Studies could examine the extent to which teams are facilitative (Olivella *et al.*, 2008), and examine contextual variables identified in this study related to team dynamics in order to develop knowledge about how such factors may contribute to L2 collaborative teacher efficacy beliefs.

10 Language Teacher Efficacy Belief Development

One focus of language teacher efficacy (LTE) research is understanding the reciprocal relationships between teachers' self-beliefs of capability, their behaviour and the teaching contexts they work within. Efficacy beliefs have been demonstrated to mediate (Nishino, 2012) or moderate (Choi & Lee, 2016) second language (L2) teaching behaviours, and a significant body of research from the wider field has demonstrated that efficacy beliefs predict student achievement (Caprara *et al.*, 2006; Goddard *et al.*, 2000; Marjolein & Helma, 2016). Efficacious teachers are more likely to expend greater effort and have stronger commitment to teaching (Chesnut & Burley, 2015; Ware & Kitsantas, 2007). Furthermore, teachers with low efficacy are more likely to leave the language teaching profession (Swanson, 2010b). Thus, it seems clear that one goal for teacher educators should be the strengthening of LTE. As a result, a key area for attention by teacher efficacy researchers surrounds the development process of self-efficacy for teaching beliefs. More knowledge is needed about the sources of efficacy information and the integration of such sources (Morris *et al.*, 2016). As there is some evidence that cultural factors may influence the way in which individuals focus on different sources of information (Klassen *et al.*, 2011; Phan & Locke, 2015), there is also a need for studies to examine the development of LTE beliefs in a variety of cultural contexts, in order to better understand the factors that may strengthen such beliefs for individuals (and groups) across the wide range of teaching situations that encompass language teaching practice.

This chapter discusses the small body of research that has examined the four sources of information proposed to influence LTE beliefs. The chapter then draws on interview and survey data to discuss the importance of past experiences, such as communicative language teaching (CLT) learning experiences. It then examines the role of social persuasion in the Japanese high school teacher of English (JTE) context, including how feedback and perceptions of school culture lead to change and development in personal (e.g. towards instruction) and collaborative (e.g. towards collective materials design) efficacy. The chapter concludes with discussion about the development of efficacy sources over time. Although some of the findings in this chapter (e.g. social persuasion as a key source of JTE efficacy) have been presented by Thompson and Dooley (2019b) elsewhere, their discussion is expanded on in this chapter with new examples and an examination of the relationship between LTE efficacy sources and knowledge.

10.1 Sources of Language Teacher Efficacy

As explained in Chapters 2 and 3, teacher efficacy beliefs are posited to develop via cognitive processing of information from four primary means: personal mastery experiences, vicarious modelling, verbal persuasion and physiological and affective states. These sources of information do not influence efficacy beliefs in an automatic fashion, but rather are proposed to influence teacher efficacy via attributions of success or failure, and via reflective thought (Bandura, 1997). In other words, efficacy beliefs are assessed by a cognitive process that draws on and weights information from a number of sources. Self-concept and other beliefs about language learning (and teaching) are likely to influence the weighting of factors and the extent to which individuals attend to different sources, and some research has shown that efficacy beliefs mediate the influence of other beliefs (Nishino, 2012). Generally, studies have suggested that personal mastery experiences are the strongest source of information influencing efficacy beliefs (Atay, 2007; Karimi, 2011; Zonoubi *et al.*, 2017), and a number of studies (e.g. Wyatt, 2010a, 2010b, 2015) have re-emphasised the importance of reflection as part of the process of teacher efficacy development, highlighting the procedure by which information from personal teaching (i.e. enactive mastery) or modelling (i.e. vicarious) experiences are integrated via reflection as individuals develop their pedagogic knowledge and self-beliefs about capability. For example, Cabaroglu (2014) investigated the impact of action research (AR) on teacher self-efficacy, and suggested that the cyclical AR process stimulates reflection. The author argued that AR provides individuals with opportunities to consider specific problems within their classes (e.g. student participation), and devise strategies for dealing with them. The study also emphasised the importance of vicarious experiences, as participants observed mentors and appeared to use these performances to consider their own teaching behaviour, from which they developed stronger personal efficacy towards instruction.

Research has identified social persuasion to be a key source of information considered by language teachers, with some studies (e.g. Moradkhani & Haghi, 2017; Phan & Locke, 2015) identifying this source to have the strongest impact on teachers. There is some evidence that this source of efficacy information may be more strongly attended to in Asian contexts, due to cultural factors that emphasise collective interdependence and induce individuals to attend to the group ahead of themselves.

In a study carried out in Vietnam, Phan and Locke (2015) used thematic analysis of interviews with eight EFL teachers, and identified all four sources of efficacy information as influences on the individuals' efficacy beliefs. However, the authors explained that teachers attended to 'other-oriented' (i.e. social persuasion) rather than 'self-oriented' (i.e. personal mastery) evaluation when considering their efficacy. Interestingly, the study also noted that participants were influenced by a perceived *lack* of feedback. In other words, some individuals appeared to be negatively influenced by the social setting, in which group meetings focused on knowledge transfer and did not provide teachers with opportunities to learn about how their performance was viewed by the institution management – an element that appeared to negatively influence their efficacy beliefs. Participants in the study also suggested that the school culture did not value professional development, and did not provide opportunities to contribute to institutional decision-making.

There is some discussion about how the source social persuasion (originally 'verbal persuasion', see Bandura, 1977) has been interpreted to include various social factors related to school support (Morris *et al.*, 2016). For example, some studies (e.g. Capa Aydin & Woolfolk Hoy, 2005) have interpreted 'perceived support' as an example of social persuasion. However, such an interpretation appears to be beyond the original conceptual representation of this source, which is theorised to involve *evaluative* feedback. As a result, rather than only limiting this source to specific verbal feedback that is clearly evaluative, some researchers (e.g. Moradkhani & Haghi, 2017; Phan & Locke, 2015; Wyatt, 2015) have expanded the definition of this source by including any information received from others that teachers interpret as feedback or use to 'reflect, conceptualize or plan' (Wyatt, 2015: 16).

This expanded definition is useful, as teachers appear to infer evaluation via the 'messages' that they perceive themselves to receive. For example, in a study of 10 high school teachers in Singapore, Chong and Kong (2012: 276) found that participants considered feedback messages – without any specific evaluative language – such as 'a slight frown' from a colleague in a meeting, or from their ideas being 'acknowledged' by colleagues. Thus, it may be appropriate to also consider the extent to which teachers perceive advice, support or non-verbal feedback from others to be an influence on their efficacy beliefs. This interpretation was used in the analysis of interview data presented in this chapter. Another example comes from Phan and Locke (2015), who introduced the situation in which a teacher received flowers from her students. This was interpreted as positive evaluative feedback and considered as a form of social persuasion in the study. Interestingly, such a situation does not easily align with Wyatt's (2015) suggested term of 'interactive experience' to replace 'social persuasion', and for that reason this chapter uses the expanded definition of social persuasion, rather than adapting a new term.

Physiological affect also influences teacher efficacy beliefs. Research from the wider field has consistently shown negative relationships between anxiety about teaching and teacher self-efficacy (Gresham, 2008; Hoffman, 2010; Swars *et al.*, 2006). In studies of language teachers, there is support for this relationship, as research has demonstrated positive relationships between emotional intelligence (EI) and teacher efficacy (Koçoğlu, 2011; Moafian & Ghanizadeh, 2009). It appears that teachers with stronger efficacy expectations may be more likely to overcome negative affect (e.g. anxiety); efficacy beliefs appear to mediate the influence of stressors on engagement (Skaalvik & Skaalvik, 2016) and job satisfaction (Skaalvik & Skaalvik, 2010). Analysis of teacher interviews has identified positive emotions about teaching as a potential source of efficacy (Phan & Locke, 2015), while other research has noted that participants gained 'a feeling of pleasure from teaching' after completing a programme designed to strengthen efficacy, indicating a relationship between change in affective responses and efficacy development (Zonoubi *et al.*, 2017).

However, it should be noted that the influence of this source has usually been discussed with respect to other sources. In other words, research has generally shown that this and other sources of efficacy information often appear to act in concert with each other. To illustrate, a number of studies have documented positive change in teacher efficacy (Karimi, 2011; Zonoubi *et al.*, 2017), in which professional development opportunities have allowed each of the sources to simultaneously influence teacher efficacy beliefs. For example, Zonoubi *et al.* (2017) explored the efficacy development of 10 EFL teachers who participated in a professional learning community (PLC), finding that all four sources of efficacy development acted on the participants. The research showed that participants interpreted their development to be based on personal teaching experiences (i.e. mastery), via observation of colleagues (i.e. vicarious), from feedback from others (i.e. social persuasion) and due to increases in the pleasure that they took from teaching (i.e. physiological response). Similarly, Karimi (2011) showed a significant positive change in pedagogic efficacy for teachers who participated in a comprehensive professional development programme, which involved a practicum, feedback, observation, collaborative group study and mentoring. Given that different individuals may weight different sources of information in different ways, one implication from these studies is that effective professional development programmes should provide individuals with opportunities for all sources of efficacy development information to act.

As discussed in Chapter 2, some researchers (e.g. Palmer, 2006) have considered mastery experiences in three ways: (1) enactive mastery, which is derived from a *teaching* experience perceived to be successful; (2) cognitive content mastery, which is associated with a successful *content learning* experience (e.g. perceiving oneself to have mastered some aspect of the L2 due to a learning experience); and (3) cognitive pedagogical mastery, which is concerned with *learning experiences* that helped individuals to perceive mastery of *teaching strategies*. Within the smaller field of language teacher research, some studies (e.g. Phan & Locke, 2015) have used these three different aspects of mastery to interpret findings. The Phan and Locke study introduced examples related to teacher perceptions of L2 mastery (a positive influence) versus a lack of pedagogic knowledge about how to deal with classroom situations, such as working with less motivated students (a negative influence). The authors noted that teachers who expressed low efficacy towards some teaching activities attributed this to a lack of training on how to deal with such situations. The three-way interpretation of mastery introduced by Palmer (2006) is useful for considering the potential impact of learning experiences as sources of efficacy information; however, it is also important to remember that knowledge is derived from experience (see Morris *et al.*, 2016). Therefore, when participants expressed a lack of 'knowledge and skills' (Phan & Locke, 2015: 78), it was not immediately clear that this can be attributed to a lack of cognitive pedagogical mastery (i.e. unsuccessful learning) or just a lack of knowledge (e.g. no exposure to the strategy). Conceivably, one could also learn about skills without it being a mastery experience. Indeed, for some teachers, experimentation may be required for conceptual knowledge to clarify (Thompson & Yanagita, 2017).

The teachers in the Phan and Locke (2015) study suggested that observation and mentorship would be effective means for helping them to develop such knowledge, indicating that the pedagogic knowledge appraised during efficacy assessment is derived via personal or vicarious experiences. Furthermore, efficacy beliefs do not operate effectively when individuals have insufficient knowledge for the task. Therefore, traditional approaches to knowledge transfer (e.g. reading about teaching strategies or attending seminars) may also be likely to contribute towards efficacy beliefs when individuals perceive themselves to *not* have sufficient knowledge to perform the activity. The sticky point here concerns whether individuals perceive their efficacy to be derived from successful *past learning experiences* (i.e. a direct source of efficacy, in accordance with the definitions offered by Palmer, 2006) or just due to a *lack of knowledge* (i.e. a lack in the skills that are appraised during efficacy assessment). The difference here concerns the source of the information versus the skill being appraised. For example, pedagogic knowledge (i.e. what is appraised) may be derived via different means (i.e. various efficacy sources); therefore, one difficulty for researchers concerns how they interpret findings about knowledge and whether the focus is on the appraisal of skills (e.g. pedagogic knowledge) or the source of the developmental information (e.g. cognitive mastery via learning, teaching or other experiences).

10.2 Personal Experience as a Source of Efficacy Information

Generally, research in the developing field of language teaching efficacy has shown personal mastery experiences to be the strongest source of information influencing efficacy beliefs (Atay, 2007; Karimi, 2011; Zonoubi *et al.*, 2017). Multiple regression findings from the current study have also consistently shown a strong and predictive relationship between past in-service experiences and efficacy beliefs related to the use of the L2 (Chapter 7), instructional strategies (Chapter 8) and collaborative practice (Chapter 9).

Respondents to the online survey reported the extent of their experience participating in pre-service and in-service training related to (1) the development of *knowledge* about CLT (e.g. attending seminars about CLT); (2) their *opportunities* to observe CLT (e.g. modelling by others); and (3) their experience of conducting lessons that integrated a CLT approach. An exploratory factor analysis identified five dimensions of JTE efficacy related to the use of English with students and other teachers (*Using English*); instructional strategies towards interaction (*Communicative Teaching*) and the development of student language knowledge (*Student Achievement*); perceived collective capability towards collaborative practice (*Teamwork*); and regulatory capability for workload (*Managing Workload*). As shown in Table 10.1, when CLT experience was more likely to contribute information towards the dimension, stronger correlations were observed. For example, participants who reported greater experience with CLT were more likely to have stronger *Communicative Teaching* (L2 instructional efficacy) beliefs. As can also be seen, at both the pre-service and in-service level, stronger correlations were observed between efficacy dimensions and direct personal experiences (i.e. potential mastery experiences) in comparison to observation (i.e. potential vicarious experiences) and learning experiences (i.e. potential cognitive mastery experiences that provide knowledge). Furthermore,

Table 10.1 Correlation matrix: JTE-TES dimensions and experience with CLT

	Using English	Communicative Teaching	Student Achievement	Teamwork	Managing Workload
CLT as a student	0.26*	0.35*	0.07	0.23*	0.11
PS studying about CLT	0.17	0.14	0.02	0.09	0.10
PS observing CLT	0.10	0.20*	0.00	0.04	0.05
PS conducting CLT	0.15	0.22*	0.02	0.06	0.05
IS learning about CLT	0.34**	0.51**	0.16	0.21**	0.18*
IS observing CLT	0.46**	0.58**	0.25*	0.33**	0.21*
IS conducting CLT	0.56**	0.70**	0.32**	0.49**	0.28**

Note: PS = pre-service; IS = in-service; * indicates significance at $p < 0.05$; ** indicates $p < 0.01$.

in-service experiences had a stronger and more predictive relationship in comparison to pre-service experiences.

It should be noted that the wording of items did not specifically ask participants to report whether such experiences were attended to or considered to be factors that influenced efficacy, thus these results only highlight *potential* sources of efficacy information. Nevertheless, taken together, these findings indicate that potential cognitive mastery experiences (i.e. learning experiences) may act as sources of efficacy information; however, *personal teaching* (i.e. conducting CLT) and *contextualised* (i.e. in-service) experiences with the task appear to be stronger sources of efficacy information. Thus, teachers who perceived themselves to have had more opportunities to *learn about* CLT may be likely to have stronger efficacy beliefs in comparison to teachers with less knowledge. However, those who reported more personal experience with in-service CLT implementation were more likely to have stronger efficacy beliefs.

Interview findings support such a view, as personal teaching experiences appeared to be stronger sources of efficacy information in comparison to vicarious experiences or knowledge derived from study. Thompson and Dooley (2019b) explained that past personal practice was a strong source of efficacy for participants with respect to collaborative practice and L2 instructional efficacy. An example not discussed in their summary comes from Saki, who explained that she was 'confident' in her capability to introduce CLT activities due to her past experience of using such activities with students. She suggested that she knew *about* CLT from her graduate studies, but that her 'confidence became stronger' after her practical experience of implementation and the response she observed in students. This example highlights the integrated nature of sources; participants often discussed the impact of multiple sources (i.e. mastery, vicarious, social, affective) when reflecting on development in their efficacy. The integrated nature of source information is further discussed in Section 10.4.

Student experience learning via CLT was identified to have a positive and predictive relationship with L2 self-efficacy (*Using English*) and CLT teaching (*Communicative Teaching*) efficacy (for correlations, see Table 10.1). Interview participants discussed the impact of past learning experiences. Learning *via* CLT appeared to contribute towards efficacy directly, often via vicarious modelling of teaching behaviour. Additionally, this source appeared to act indirectly, via the development of L2 skills that individuals could draw on in their teaching practice. Such experiences also appear to include overseas study, another variable identified as a predictor of *Using English* (i.e. L2 self-efficacy) and *Communicative Teaching* (i.e. CLT efficacy).

As noted by Thompson and Dooley (2019b), Ken explained in his interview that he and his colleagues teach in the same way that they learned English. As a learner, Ken had studied via CLT approaches, specifically task-based and project-based learning methodologies. He suggested that such experiences were an important part of his confidence, as going through that experience gave him an understanding of what CLT is, and how to implement it. It appears that these learning experiences provided a model that could be reflected on later in life when Ken became a teacher. Furthermore, Ken explained that due to these learning experiences, he had chances to actually use English, indicating that a variety of opportunities for cognitive mastery may have influenced his perceived capability to use the L2 effectively in different circumstances.

A further example (not discussed by Thompson & Dooley, 2019b) comes from Taka, who explained that learning English via English was a crucial opportunity for L2 instructional development. Taka had experienced studying abroad and learning via English. As a consultant who works in teacher development, he suggested that the 'the biggest' influence on teacher reluctance to teach via English was that 'they have never learned English in English'. For that reason, he emphasised the role of interaction via English in teacher training programmes, as the way 'in which they learn' would be an important factor on future teaching practice. He suggested that learning experiences provided opportunities for individuals to develop teaching strategies. Similar discussions arose during the interviews with Riho and Saki, both of whom had also experienced studying abroad; each suggested that these past learning experiences had contributed to their confidence towards the implementation of CLT.

Interview results also suggested that *maintaining* language ability is a key challenge for JTEs. As perceived ability has been shown to influence cognitive engagement (Greene & Miller, 1996), perceptions of declining competence may lead to less cognitive engagement, weaker efficacy beliefs and less effort for tasks that involve the use of English. Therefore, efforts may be needed to provide *ongoing* professional development for teachers, with specific strategies for helping teachers to maintain a positive 'attainment trajectory' (Bandura, 1997). This highlights the potential vicarious impact of teacher L2 development programmes to simultaneously address both perceived L2 capability and efficacy towards L2 pedagogy. In other words, teacher development programmes could focus on L2 proficiency development via CLT methodologies that involve significant use of the L2 by the teacher and the students. Such efforts may provide experiences that directly and indirectly influence multiple dimensions of LTE, by acting as modelling experiences (i.e. a potential direct influence on *Using English* and *Communicative Teaching*) while also contributing to cognitive mastery (i.e. perceived L2 proficiency), a common challenge for language teachers.

10.3 The Social Nature of Teacher Practice

Social persuasion is concerned with evaluative feedback from significant stakeholders, such as students, colleagues and parents (Morris *et al.*, 2016). However, as discussed in Section 10.1, this chapter extends the definition of social persuasion to include any information from others that individuals interpret as messages about their professional capability (Wyatt, 2015: 16), including non-verbal messages (Chong & Kong, 2012; Phan & Locke, 2015).

As Thompson and Woodman (2019) note, there was a strong and positive relationship between efficacy dimensions, including self-beliefs about individual efficacy (e.g. *Using English*, *Communicative Teaching*) and those concerned with beliefs about capability towards tasks involving collaborative collective action (i.e. *Teamwork*). This result indicates that teachers who perceive stronger collective efficacy for collaboration are also likely to have stronger efficacy towards other domains of efficacy (and vice versa). Furthermore, multiple regression findings showed that individuals who worked with older teaching teams were less likely to have stronger efficacy beliefs towards the *Teamwork* dimension. In other words, teacher efficacy towards collaborative practice appears to be influenced by the dynamics of the teaching team; the older the team, the less likely it is that individuals will have stronger perceived capability towards collaborative materials design and planning. Given the nature of efficacy beliefs within triadic reciprocal causation and the social nature of teacher practice, a number of researchers have suggested that perceptions of collective efficacy influence individual teacher efficacy beliefs (Goddard *et al.*, 2004a; Kurt *et al.*, 2011; Viel-Ruma *et al.*, 2010). Thus, one interpretation of these findings is that individual JTEs' perceived personal teaching capability is informed by their perceptions of the capability of their teaching teams (i.e. those with whom they have interpersonal, collaborative relationships) and the wider organisation (i.e. school-level efficacy).

This interpretation has support from the interview findings (see Thompson & Dooley, 2019b), as each of the six participants spent considerable time discussing the various ways in which social factors and collegial interactions influenced their efficacy in a positive (Taka, Yuri, Saki, Maki) and negative (Taka, Riho, Saki, Ken, Maki) manner. Specific instances of social feedback from colleagues were discussed by almost all participants (Taka, Yuri, Ken, Saki, Riho), while the importance of mentorship (Saki, Yuri, Taka) and the influence of school culture (Taka, Maki, Riho, Ken, Saki) were also brought up as key influences on individual practice and perceptions of capability. Klassen *et al.* (2011) contended that the collectivist nature of East Asian countries, such as Japan, would lead individuals to value and weight in-group experiences to a higher degree, and there is some support from the interview findings for this assertion. Two examples from Riho and Saki specifically focused on the influence of social feedback (both direct and indirect) on their individual practice. Despite strong perceived individual capability based on enactive (Riho) and cognitive (Saki) mastery experiences, both teachers explained that they aligned their pedagogic practice with the form of instruction 'required' (Saki) by the school, often due to a sense of powerlessness (Goddard *et al.*, 2000) in the face of social pressure or perceived rejection, leading to doubts (Wheatley, 2002) about their personal efficacy.

In his interview, Taka discussed his experience observing social pressure within schools, in which teachers who were *not* teachers of English could influence English teachers about the appropriate means for entrance preparation, often due to their position as senior members or 'homeroom' teachers (i.e. those responsible for the pastoral care of a cohort of students). Discussing this issue, Thompson and Dooley (2019b) introduced an example from Riho, who talked about her experiences as a trainee teacher. She suggested that indirect (e.g. school culture) and direct (e.g. evaluation) feedback would lead novice teachers to give up, and over time, to reinterpret their beliefs and behaviour to align with the existing practice of the school. She had followed a common path for trainee teachers in Japan and had returned to the high school where she had studied (Lamie, 1998; Yonesaka, 1999). She suggested that as a 'young' teacher, 'you kind of have to follow what other teachers are doing' and talked about the pressure she felt from her colleagues to focus on examination preparation rather than implementing the practices she had learned about during her teaching training. She received negative evaluations during her teacher observations – especially from teachers of other subjects with no training in language teaching – because her focus was to attend to both examination preparation and communicative development. She suggested that this was not considered to be important by the teachers who evaluated her work. She argued that while many young teachers 'tend to be more open minded and more focused on communicative aspects', social pressure and *direct* feedback would induce such teachers to conform to existing practice. Overall, she indicated that as a novice teacher, she felt powerless against the social force of the school culture.

A second example of a participant attending to *perceived* social feedback comes from Saki, a novice teacher with four years of experience (also discussed by Thompson & Dooley, 2019b). During her interview, she focused on one experience of collaborative practice with a teaching team (from her previous school) where the team was preparing for a lesson on debate. Saki explained how the (general) silence of the group towards her suggestion left her confused (i.e. an affective response), which she interpreted as rejection. She explained that she lost her confidence to participate and contribute towards collective materials development after that experience. Skaalvik and Skaalvik (2007: 613) have suggested that individual teacher self-efficacy may be reliant on 'the functioning of the team', and this example shows how junior teachers, in particular, may pay close attention to the feedback (or lack of feedback, see Phan & Locke, 2015) that they perceive from their colleagues. Interestingly, Saki appeared to have had cognitive pedagogic mastery experiences of CLT from her graduate studies, yet demonstrated strong attendance to other-oriented feedback and, furthermore, attended to the message she *perceived* from the overall group (i.e. negative towards her idea) rather than, as Thompson and Dooley (2019b) note, the positive verbal feedback she received from one colleague.

Phan and Locke (2015) suggested that Vietnamese EFL teachers weighted information from others more strongly, due to cultural values that emphasise collectivism. In their summary of the exploratory interview data, Thompson and Dooley (2019b) suggested that participants strongly attended to both direct (Riho) and perceived (Saki) negative feedback from senior teachers. Silence was considered by Saki and interpreted to be rejection. Such reactions may be due to the influence of cultural values in Japan that emphasise interdependence (Kitayama *et al.*, 1997), the need for group approval (Kitao & Kitao, 1985; Yamaguchi, 1994), where individuals are likely to adjust their practice to the group when they perceive themselves to be misaligned (Morling *et al.*, 2002). For example, following the unsuccessful attempt to contribute to materials development, Saki indicated that she ceased sharing her ideas with her older peers. Due to cultural obligations of respect, she explained that she simply followed their decisions and did as she was asked.

The alignment of behaviour by less senior members of an organisation has been suggested to reflect a collectivist orientation that emphasises the needs of the in-group (Yamaguchi, 1994), as 'social pressure' or 'group think' (Sato & Kleinsasser, 2004; Underwood, 2012) may influence teacher beliefs and practice. Such pressure is not limited to the Japanese context; it has been discussed in countries with similar cultural attributes, such as Korea (Moodie, 2016; Shin, 2012), where the socialisation of teachers may lead them away from the techniques they learn during pre-service training in favour of practices preferred by senior colleagues within the school.

Overall, it seems that colleague feedback may be an important source of efficacy beliefs. Results indicate that normative pressure (Goddard *et al.*, 2000) and school culture (Sato & Kleinsasser, 2004; Shin, 2012; Underwood, 2012) play a significant role in the socialisation process. Analysis of interview data shows that participants often tended to focus more on direct or perceived feedback from others (i.e. social persuasion), above personal mastery, as a source of their teacher efficacy beliefs. Accordingly, findings provide some support for the contention that social persuasion is a strong source of efficacy in East and Southeast Asian contexts (Klassen *et al.*, 2011; Phan & Locke, 2015), perhaps due to cultural attributes that may influence the weighting of information towards in-group experiences and attendance to the social environment. However, as the current study had a limited number of interview participants, it seems that more cross-cultural research is needed to better understand the ways in which individuals consider different sources of information across various contexts.

It should also be noted that the influence of social factors was not only negative. As Thompson and Dooley (2019b) note, a majority of participants (Maki, Taka, Yuri, Saki) also discussed examples of positive social feedback, and its influence on the school environment, collective beliefs and individual confidence. Interview participants discussed how the cultural values of adjustment and alignment (Morling *et al.*, 2002) can be harnessed by schools (and specifically principals) in the development of stronger collective efficacy beliefs, with a number of participants (Yuri, Taka, Maki, Saki) emphasising the importance of school leadership and colleague support as a key factor associated with a positive teaching climate. Two of the more senior participants (Yuri, Taka) explained that principal leadership was crucial for developing a culture that emphasised collaboration and trust. Taka suggested that without effective leadership, teaching teams would display risk aversion to change and reliance on existing practice, while Yuri discussed an enactive mastery experience related to successful curriculum change, attributing the success of the project to the 'strong leadership' of the principal.

An example not discussed by Thompson and Dooley comes from Saki, who had recently moved to a school where she perceived *strong* colleague support for collaborative practice, a positive culture and a collective focus on both examination preparation and student communicative competency development. As a result, she appeared to be overcoming the efficacy doubts (Wheatley, 2002) about her capability to contribute towards collaborative materials design that had arisen during her time at her previous school. She stated, 'this year and last year for me was totally different', as her new colleagues *encouraged* her to share and contribute to collective materials design. This highlights the contextual nature of self-efficacy belief assessment, as Saki expressed very weak collaborative and instructional efficacy when discussing her past school, yet stronger (and positive) efficacy when considering her new school.

Given the cultural focus on seniority and respect for authority in the JTE teaching context, it seems that leadership and colleague support are key ingredients for creating an environment where L2 teacher efficacy developmental sources can act in a positive manner. Research has suggested that leadership can empower teachers (Goddard & Goddard, 2001), and it appears to have a mediating influence on collective and personal teaching efficacy (Kurt *et al.*, 2011; Kurz & Knight, 2004). Findings from the current study indicate that without effective leadership at the faculty and team level, social factors may act in a negative fashion. Future studies could examine the relationship between leadership, collective efficacy and personal efficacy in a variety of language teaching contexts, in order to investigate the potential causal effect of leadership on teacher beliefs and practice. Given that the strength of these forces may be culturally derived, studies could also examine the relationship in cross-cultural contexts.

10.4 Efficacy Development Over Time

In their summary of the interview findings, Thompson and Dooley (2019b) broke down the different efficacy sources in accordance with self-efficacy theory, identifying personal mastery, vicarious modelling and social persuasion as the three main sources of efficacy for the participants. However, they did not highlight the integrated nature of the various sources and the way in which efficacy developed over time. Certain experiences appeared to contribute towards knowledge and acted as initial models (i.e. cognitive mastery or vicarious experiences). These led to changes in practice, after which teachers reflected on their behaviour, perceived such experiences to involve enactive mastery and accordingly developed stronger efficacy.

An example comes from Yuri, who discussed her in-service practice of CLT over 20 years. She suggested that her confidence for CLT implementation was due to her understanding of how to develop and facilitate task-based learning with her students. She explained that this focus originally came from her experience of participating in a training programme that specifically focused on task-based language teaching. She revealed, 'I learned the difference between "task" and "exercise"' and suggested that this seminar contributed to her knowledge about CLT, which gave her 'confidence' to try to integrate interactive exercises in her classes. She perceived such activities to be successful, and subsequently developed strong efficacy towards the integration of CLT – to the point where she gave special lessons to students in order to meet the needs of both examination preparation and competency development. As a result, Yuri expressed satisfaction (i.e. positive affective response) about her teaching.

Yuri also discussed the vicarious impact of mentors, suggesting that teachers learn by observing others, and explained that when other teachers talked about her classes as 'noisy', it was due to their lack of knowledge. Overall, she demonstrated strong efficacy towards both examination preparation and competency development, and she reported expending extra effort in the pursuit of each outcome. She appeared to draw on various sources of efficacy (enactive mastery, vicarious experiences, cognitive pedagogic mastery), and it seemed that her teacher efficacy beliefs were *strengthened* via personal practice and perceptions of mastery. However, the initial in-service behaviour was traced back to her perceiving herself to have sufficient skills and knowledge to try to implement such a teaching action. This knowledge came from a seminar, and although it was somewhat unclear whether this involved both vicarious and cognitive pedagogical mastery elements, the initial change in her teaching appeared to be reliant on knowledge. Her further behavioural change and efficacy development was then strengthened via personal experimentation, further modelling and positive affect. Although most of these examples from Yuri were included – separately – by Thompson and Dooley (2019b) in their discussion of the interview data, the process of her efficacy development over time is an additional key finding; it highlights the impact of various sources of efficacy-forming information.

Furthermore, this finding indicates that teachers may need a benchmark level of know-how about CLT (or other instructional strategies) in order to initiate change. Such an interpretation aligns with self-efficacy theory, as efficacy beliefs are reliant on knowledge (Bandura, 1997). Above this level (i.e. when teachers have enough understanding to form heuristics about their capability to successfully complete the task), efficacy beliefs may be able to operate synergistically with knowledge in a similar manner to the relationship between efficacy and L2 ability identified in other studies (Choi & Lee, 2016).

Such an interpretation also aligns with findings from the research literature. In a study on the implementation of CLT by one JTE, Thompson and Yanagita (2017) found that the experience of in-service experimentation led to stronger efficacy. The teacher in the study perceived herself to become more capable of using information about CLT implementation that she had learned during her teacher training, by observing student behaviour, adjusting her practice and perceiving improvements in student communicative capability. In another study of Vietnamese EFL teachers (Phan & Locke, 2015), participants appeared to draw on their personal teaching experiences, particularly their observations of the response of their students to different teaching behaviours. However, in the Phan and Locke study, the participants also appeared to perceive themselves to be lacking in pedagogic knowledge, which limited their development. Overall, teachers cannot implement strategies they do not know about, thus knowledge is crucial. However, knowledge alone is not sufficient (Bandura, 1997), and personal experience also appears to be vital for strengthening efficacy – even if this process involves doubts (Thompson & Yanagita, 2017; Wyatt, 2013b) as individuals experiment with their teaching practice.

10.5 Chapter Summary

The development of L2 teacher efficacy remains a key area for future research. The small body of work in the field of LTE has generally shown that each of the theorised sources contributes towards efficacy development. Survey and interview findings from the current study indicated that personal, in-service mastery experiences were a strong source of efficacy-forming information. Results also suggest that individuals with a greater number of learning experiences (i.e. potential opportunities for cognitive pedagogic mastery) are likely to have stronger efficacy beliefs. Interview findings indicated that a certain threshold level of cognitive mastery may be required for individuals to attempt behavioural change, after which personal enactive mastery experiences appear to play a stronger role for strengthening efficacy. In other words, efficacy beliefs do not appear to operate effectively without sufficient knowledge, and it seems that different sources of efficacy may operate simultaneously and in concert.

Results also suggest that experiential activities (e.g. actual practice) have a stronger and more predictive relationship as potential sources of teacher efficacy beliefs. Teachers appear to prefer training that involves opportunities for mastery and vicarious modelling (Phan & Locke, 2015), while programmes that have shown significant changes in teacher efficacy have had opportunities for each of the sources to act on participants (Karimi, 2011). Therefore, it seems that professional development programmes should attempt to provide opportunities for each of the four sources to operate, including a focus on reflection. Future studies could further examine the relationship between knowledge and efficacy in order to identify whether efficacy beliefs become more predictive of behaviour when teachers have sufficient knowledge to form appropriate (enough) heuristics about their personal and collective competence.

Findings from the current study (and others, e.g. Phan & Locke, 2015) have also indicated that different sources may be attended to more strongly in different contexts. Interview participants appeared to strongly attend to direct and indirect social feedback as a source of efficacy information, perhaps due to the strong influence of cultural values that emphasise adjustment and alignment with the group. Interview findings also highlighted the strong attendance of novice teachers to direct and indirect feedback; these appear to be received as evaluations of competency that then exhibit influence on efficacy (and practice). Accordingly, there are also some implications for teacher development. Studies have shown that social support reduces stress (Yorimitsu et al., 2014) and teacher burnout (Kahn et al., 2006), while some research has suggested that Japan has higher levels of teacher burnout than other countries (Maslach et al., 2001). Accordingly, the role of in-service mentors appears vital. Senior teachers may need training opportunities that help them to develop effective strategies for providing effective efficacy-forming feedback to colleagues.

While discussion of these findings has focused on the Japanese context, school culture has been identified as a crucial element informing efficacy in the wider language teaching field (e.g. Eslami & Fatahi, 2008; Göker, 2006, 2012; Shin, 2012). Thus, future LTE studies should further explore the potential impact of school climate and social persuasion. It seems that efficacy development may be reliant on organisation support and agency, colleague trust and effective leadership (Demir, 2008; Kurt et al., 2011; Lee et al., 2011). Therefore, future studies could examine these variables in different language teaching contexts.

Finally, results have also highlighted two potential sources of efficacy information for further study. Survey participants who reported greater experience (1) studying via CLT or (2) studying abroad (i.e. potential cognitive content mastery) were more likely to have stronger efficacy beliefs. Interview results indicated that these sources may act vicariously and as opportunities for cognitive mastery. Given that other studies have noted the positive relationship between efficacy and time abroad (Choi & Lee, 2016), it seems that more research is needed to examine the relationship between these variables, teacher efficacy beliefs and teacher practice. Specifically, future studies could investigate *how* such experiences influence the attributions that individuals develop about their competence, and in what ways they act as vicarious (i.e. modelling) or cognitive mastery experiences.

11 Where Next for LTE Research?

Most language teacher research, to date, has been carried out in West Asian contexts (such as in Turkey and Iran, e.g. Cabaroglu, 2014; Moradkhani & Haghi, 2017; Zonoubi *et al.*, 2017). However, as a belief construct with a strong history of research in the wider field of education and psychology, self-efficacy for language teaching beliefs is now receiving more attention in diverse language teaching contexts, such as Vietnam (Nguyen *et al.*, 2015; Nguyen & Ngo, 2017; Phan & Locke, 2015), Korea (Choi & Lee, 2016; Hiver, 2013; Shin, 2012) and Oman (Wyatt, 2010a, 2010b, 2013b). Few studies have examined teacher efficacy beliefs in Japan in accordance with a social cognitive theoretical framework, and the research presented in this book is one of the first studies of Japanese high school English language teacher efficacy (LTE). Accordingly, it contributes to the needed expansion of LTE research.

This book was written to introduce readers to LTE, explore the key dimensions of LTE and examine the personal and contextual factors that may influence these beliefs. It has discussed how teacher efficacy research has developed as a type of self-efficacy within the theoretical framework of social cognitive theory (Chapter 2), introduced readers to the growing field of LTE (Chapter 3) and discussed approaches for investigating LTE beliefs – including the research design of the current study (Chapter 4) and how efficacy scales can be developed with the input of local participants (Chapter 5). The book has explored the dimensionality of LTE (Chapter 6) and focused on three LTE domains: perceived second language (L2) capability (Chapter 7), L2 instructional efficacy (Chapter 8) and collaborative efficacy (Chapter 9). It has also discussed the development of LTE beliefs (Chapter 10). This chapter brings things together by highlighting key findings and pointing out how results from this study can be further developed in future LTE research.

Although the research presented in this book has focused on the compulsory high school English teaching situation in Japan, many of the challenges discussed in this book may be transferable to other contexts. For example, this book has explored self-beliefs of instructional capability towards entrance examination success; such tests remain important in a variety of language teaching contexts (e.g. Turkey, Iran, China, see Hatipoglu, 2016; Ramezaney, 2014; Yung, 2015). This book has also explored efficacy towards communicative L2 instruction. Research has consistently shown that teachers have continued to have difficulty in developing learner communicative competency and implementing communicative language teaching (CLT) across East Asia (e.g. Butler, 2011; Chung & Cheng, 2009; Hiep, 2007), Western Asia and the Middle East (e.g. Dastgahian *et al.*, 2018; İnceçay & İnceçay, 2009) and Africa (e.g. Orafi & Borg, 2009; Wiens *et al.*, 2018). Furthermore, as has been argued in this book, some dimensions of challenge, such as teacher L2 self-efficacy (i.e. perceived capability to use the L2 effectively with students and other teachers), appear to be clearly generalisable to the wider LTE field.

11.1 Key Findings

This book has highlighted the multidimensional nature of LTE. Bringing together findings from exploratory factor analysis of survey data (see Thompson & Woodman, 2019) and thematic analysis of participant interviews (see Thompson & Dooley, 2019b), this book has discussed potentially transferable dimensions of LTE related to L2 usage, instructional strategies, collaborative practice and workload regulation. However, within these domains, the specific tasks may reflect the continuing educational, social and cultural challenges of the local contexts. For example, instructional efficacy dimensions in Japan appear to highlight the divide between self-beliefs of capability about teaching to encourage communication (*Communicative Teaching*) versus preparing students for entrance examinations (*Student Achievement*).

Previously unpublished correlational and multiple regression analyses were also presented, as this book examined the relationship between LTE efficacy and personal and contextual demographic variables. This book has explored the relationship between effort and perceived capability for implementing the 2013 *Course of Study* for foreign languages (i.e. high school English curriculum guidelines for Japan). Findings reflect general trends from the research literature. Similar to a number of other studies (e.g. Enochs *et al.*, 1995; Mulholland & Wallace, 2001; Woolfolk Hoy & Davis, 2006), teachers who expressed stronger efficacy for implementation of the new curriculum were more likely to self-report spending greater time on preparation and grading. Thus, efficacious Japanese high school teachers of English (JTEs) may be more likely to persist and show commitment to the implementation of the new curriculum guidelines.

This book also explored the relationship between efficacy, L2 ability and the use of English in class. Research has shown that teachers with stronger L2 capability are more likely to use the L2 with students and other teachers. For example, Choi and Lee (2016) found that teacher efficacy beliefs appeared to work synergistically with perceived L2 proficiency as predictors of teacher L2 use in class. In the current study, however, it appears that L2 competence is indirectly related to the use of the L2 by teachers. No significant direct relationship was identified between perceived L2 competency and the use of English in class. Rather, efficacy beliefs towards *Communicative Teaching*, alongside greater reported in-service CLT experience and having a position at a school with a special designation (i.e. a teaching context that encourages the use of English) were found to predict a significant percentage of the variance of the use of English by teachers. This finding not only supports the contention that efficacy beliefs predict practice, but also questions the direct link between teacher L2 proficiency and teaching behaviour.

Multiple regression analyses were carried out to investigate the relationship between efficacy belief dimensions and personal and contextual variables that may act as sources of efficacy information (i.e. variables that may influence the strength of individuals' perceived capability towards different dimensions) with respect to three key domains of teacher action: (1) perceived capability to use the L2 with students and other teachers (Chapter 7); (2) L2 instructional efficacy (Chapter 8); and collective LTE (Chapter 9). Figure 11.1 provides a summary of the relationship between Japanese Teacher of English Teacher Efficacy Scale (JTE-TES) dimensions and predictor variables, based on multiple regression findings. Interview findings were also used to enhance the significance of the survey results. Overall, findings indicated that different personal and contextual variables were related to, and predictive of,

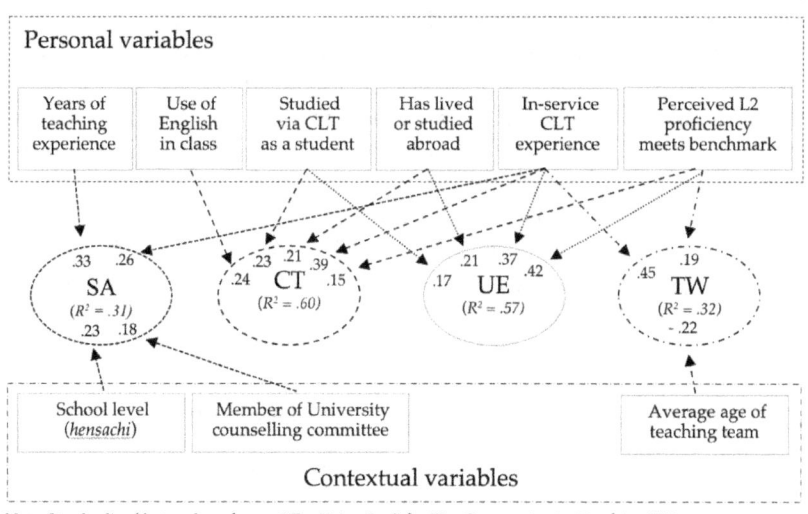

Note: Standardized beta values shown; UE = Using English, CT = Communicative Teaching, TW = Teamwork, SA = Student Achievement, MW = Managing Workload

Figure 11.1 Predictors of JTE-TES dimensions

different dimensions of teacher efficacy beliefs, indicating that various sources of information influence specific dimensions of teacher efficacy.

Self-efficacy judgements reflect perceptions of competence for successful task completion. As discussed in Chapter 2: Section 2.5, efficacy beliefs appear to involve a dynamic assessment of the skills an individual perceives to be available to them (e.g. knowledge about how to use a teaching strategy) against the difficulty of implementation (e.g. with lesser motivated students) within the context (e.g. action is valued by the school). These beliefs are strengthened when individuals perceive themselves to have developed greater skills (e.g. more knowledge about how to implement strategies) or can better deal with the demands of the task (e.g. perceive themselves to be better equipped to help lesser motivated students) and are working within contexts that encourage such teaching behaviours (e.g. a school culture positive towards the integration of more communicative methods).

Results indicate that when personal or contextual variables do not influence the skills informing task success or perceptions of task difficulty, there is no significant relationship. Thus, L2 ability was not found to have a relationship with the self-regulatory efficacy dimension *Managing Workload*, as L2 ability neither contributes towards the skills required for successful time management nor influences the perceived difficulty of the task.

On the other hand, findings suggest a close relationship between efficacy beliefs and experience with the task, or experiences that may indirectly inform the perceptions of skill available to individuals. It is generally accepted that previous experiences influence teacher efficacy beliefs (Bong & Skaalvik, 2003; Tschannen-Moran & McMaster, 2009; Wyatt, 2014) by contributing to the skills that teachers can draw on in their assessment of their efficacy beliefs for tasks. For example, individuals with more in-service experience teaching via CLT methods (i.e. with the task), studying via CLT (i.e. experiencing the task) and with the use of English in class (i.e. a key skill that is incorporated within the task) were more likely to have stronger teacher efficacy beliefs for *Communicative Teaching*. Likewise, individuals who had lived or studied abroad may have developed skills (e.g. language competence) or had experiences (e.g. vicarious influences) that they can draw on when assessing their teacher efficacy beliefs towards *Communicative Teaching* and *Using English*.

11.2 Where Next: Suggestions for Future Research

These findings highlight a range of areas for future study. Indeed, throughout this book, a number of questions have been raised that researchers could further investigate. Table 11.1 outlines some suggestions for future research; the parentheses included in the following paragraphs refer the reader back to each suggestion in the table.

Table 11.1 Suggestions for future research

(1)	Use or adapt JTE-TES *Using English* items to investigate teacher L2 self-efficacy.
(2)	Extend understanding of tasks within the teacher L2 self-efficacy domain.
(3)	Further explore dimensions of L2 instructional efficacy.
(4)	Extend knowledge of tasks within the L2 instructional efficacy domain.
(5)	Explore further dimensions of language teacher efficacy.
(6)	Develop understanding about the collective language teacher efficacy domain.
(7)	Investigate the relationship between personal, collaborative and collective LTE beliefs.
(8)	Develop further knowledge about JTE efficacy.
(9)	Investigate the relationship between LTE beliefs and language teacher behaviour.
(10)	Examine the relationship between non-teaching duties and LTE beliefs.
(11)	Adapt and test the *Managing Workload* dimension in different contexts.
(12)	Examine how individuals select, weight and assess various efficacy sources.
(13)	Extend understanding about additional sources of efficacy-forming information.
(14)	Employ more diverse methods for investigating efficacy development.
(15)	How does LTE efficacy develop for pre-service, novice and experienced teachers?
(16)	Explore the relationship between pedagogic knowledge and LTE beliefs.
(17)	How does efficacy development occur for experienced teachers?
(18)	Develop and test an efficacy source scale.
(19)	Examine the influence of different interventions on teacher efficacy development.
(20)	What influences collective language teacher efficacy development?
(21)	Do student learning experiences provide efficacy sources of forming information?
(22)	In what ways do student learning experiences influence LTE beliefs?
(23)	To what extent does teacher efficacy change under different task conditions?
(24)	Examine the social features of teaching contexts and their influence on LTE beliefs.
(25)	How do different sources of efficacy information act in different cultural settings?
(26)	Explore LTE beliefs, student efficacy and student achievement.

11.2.1 Dimensions of language teacher efficacy

There appears to be some transferability in the domains of control over which teachers exert action; there is similarity in the dimensions of L2 efficacy identified in this and other studies. It seems that teacher L2 self-efficacy is a generalisable dimension of LTE, thus (1) the four items comprising the *Using English* dimension of the JTE-TES could be used alongside other JTE-TES dimensions, or with other scales (e.g. the Teacher Sense of Efficacy Scale [TSES]), to investigate language teacher-specific domains of efficacy beliefs. Future studies could extend this dimension by (2) identifying other key tasks within this domain.

As discussed above, other key challenges in the JTE environment also appear transferable to the wider language teaching field, such as instructional challenges related to CLT implementation (Aloreibi & Carey,

2017; Hayes, 2018; Wiens *et al.*, 2018) and entrance examination instruction (Hatipoglu, 2016; Ramezaney, 2014); collaboration in curriculum design and implementation (Dastgahian *et al.*, 2018; Moafian & Ghanizadeh, 2009); and self-regulatory pressures on language teachers (Ghanizadeh & Jahedizadeh, 2016; Ghonsooly & Ghanizadeh, 2013). Accordingly, JTE-TES items and dimensions related to instruction, collaboration and workload management could be adapted for use in future studies. For example, instructional efficacy in the JTE context appears to be either CLT or examination focused. Future studies could explore whether (3) such a division can be identified in other teaching contexts, both within (e.g. junior high school, technical college, university) and beyond Japan.

Further exploration is also needed of (4) additional key tasks and (5) dimensions for language teachers. For example, in Norway it appears that a key domain of teacher efficacy involves perceived capability to respond to the needs of different students (Skaalvik & Skaalvik, 2007). Interview findings from this study also indicated that efficacy towards student motivation is a key domain of L2 teacher efficacy. Future research could further explore the overlapping areas of teacher challenge and identify context-specific domains of efficacy for different teaching groups.

Little is known about L2 collective teacher efficacy, and future studies could (6) investigate collective LTE efficacy and examine (7) how it relates to the individual and collaborative domains identified in the current study. Furthermore, interview findings indicated that perceptions of collective capability influenced perceptions of individual efficacy. Future research could explore the interrelationships between different dimensions of individual and collective efficacy, using structural equation modelling (SEM) or path analysis modelling techniques.

One limitation of this and other (e.g. Nishino, 2012) teacher efficacy studies is the number of participants who were surveyed in the study. It is becoming more difficult to gather data from large samples, thus (8) further examination of JTE efficacy is also needed. The JTE-TES could also be used or adapted alongside other scales, such as Nishino's (2009, 2012) teacher belief items, in order to examine the relationship between teacher efficacy and other self-beliefs against teacher practice. Indeed, the link between efficacy beliefs and teacher practice requires further investigation; although this study and other research (Choi & Lee, 2016; Nishino, 2012) has shown a predictive link between teacher efficacy beliefs and reported practice, this (9) relationship needs further exploration across the wider language teaching field.

Interview findings and analysis of survey results indicated that non-teaching duties, time pressure and workload management are key challenges for JTEs, in support of a number of other studies within Japan (O'Donnell, 2005; Underwood, 2012, 2013) and beyond (e.g. Ghanizadeh & Jahedizadeh, 2016; Ghonsooly & Ghanizadeh, 2013; MacIntyre *et al.*, 2019). Teacher beliefs were weakest for the two tasks comprising the regulatory efficacy dimension *Managing Workload*, while interview results showed that a number of participants (e.g. Ken, Maki, Yuri) perceived non-teaching duties to influence the time and resources that they had available for teaching, grading and preparation. As has been noted in other studies (e.g. Berger *et al.*, 2005), such perceptions may inhibit teachers from engaging in the types of professional development required to successfully implement new teaching approaches, such as the curricular changes required of revisions to the *Course of Study* in Japan. Thus, it seems clear that the relationship between (10) efficacy beliefs and non-teaching duties needs further attention. The JTE-TES dimension *Managing Workload* is a relatively weak factor, only represented by two items, which appears to provide a measure of regulatory efficacy for language teachers. Future studies could (11) add items to this dimension and use confirmatory factor analysis to investigate the model fit of the JTE-TES (or certain dimensions of the scale) in various contexts.

11.2.2 Language teacher efficacy development

Findings indicated that past learning and teaching experiences are associated with teacher efficacy beliefs, which suggests that different individuals drew on different sources of efficacy-forming information. Although patterns can be identified about the influence of certain sources across populations (e.g. the positive influence of professional development, see Karimi, 2011), the cognitive process of efficacy assessment also involves the integration and the weighting of different information. This appears to vary considerably across individuals as they use personal 'heuristics' (Bandura, 1997: 19) that, hopefully, function effectively *enough* to judge self-capability from the various forms of information that provide evaluative feedback.

Thus, the ways in which past experiences influence efficacy directly (e.g. as mastery or vicarious experiences) and/or indirectly (e.g. by contributing to skills informing the task) require further exploration. Future studies should examine *how* such experiences influence teacher efficacy beliefs, specifically (12) in what ways are efficacy sources drawn on or considered by individuals during their assessment of LTE beliefs? and (13) what factors (e.g. beliefs about language learning and teaching) influence the weighting of information for different individuals?

More (14) diversity in research methods may be needed to further understand the cognitive processing of individuals. Think-aloud (or talk-aloud) methods (see Van Someren *et al.*, 1994) may be useful for examining such processes, and have been suggested by researchers from the wider (Morris *et al.*, 2016) and L2 (Rastegar & Memarpour, 2009) teacher efficacy fields. Although some research has investigated the development of teacher efficacy beliefs over time (Wyatt, 2010a, 2010b, 2013b), more longitudinal studies are required to help understand how efficacy sources are considered and reflected on, leading to potential change and reassessment of teacher efficacy.

The heuristic guides that individuals use are likely to change as new information is learned, and in fact, may be incorrect. Bandura (1997) has argued that efficacy beliefs may be misjudged by individuals due to incorrect assessments of performance, such as perceiving a class to be successful when it was not; or due to incomplete understanding of the task, such as conceptual misunderstandings of the various skills required to implement a communicative teaching approach (for discussion of other factors that may influence efficacy misjudgement, see Bandura, 1997).

Thus, one distinction that may be important for consideration concerns whether efficacy is considered during the skills development stage (e.g. pre-service teachers) versus whether efficacy is examined for teachers with established skills (Bandura, 1986, 1997). In other words, (15) the relative professional position of participants may be important, particularly for pre-service and novice teachers in comparison to established in-service teachers; those going through the skills development stage may be more likely to misjudge their efficacy. Findings from this study indicated that efficacy belief and behaviour change were reliant on individuals perceiving themselves to have sufficient knowledge to implement CLT, while other research has shown that a benchmark level of L2 proficiency is required for efficacy beliefs to operate (see Choi & Lee, 2016). Future studies should (16) examine the relationship between pedagogic knowledge (see Gatbonton, 1999), LTE beliefs and practice for both experienced and novice teachers.

Such a distinction may also be important for interpreting findings from the research literature. Firstly, a significant number of studies (e.g. Hiver, 2013; Moradkhani *et al.*, 2017; Wyatt, 2010a) have noted efficacy 'doubts' (Wheatley, 2002), particularly for novice teachers or those developing new skills. Such anxiety may be beneficial, as 'self-doubt creates the impetus for acquiring knowledge and skills' (Bandura, 1997: 76). In other words, doubt may be an important and positive influence on teacher efficacy *if* it drives motivation to improve. Mentoring and collaborative professional development appear to be valuable in such instances, as the support of more experienced or trusted others may be useful for overcoming self-doubts (Thompson & Yanagita, 2017). However, if doubts remain over time (Wyatt, 2010a), particularly once individuals perceive themselves to have the necessary skills, such affective processes may negatively impact teacher efficacy beliefs and may require different types of interventions. Thus, it is also important to consider (17) how various sources of information may work in different ways on individuals at different stages in their careers. It has been argued that efficacy beliefs become stable over time (Pajares, 2002; Tschannen-Moran & Woolfolk Hoy, 2001; Tschannen-Moran *et al.*, 1998) and few studies (e.g. Karimi, 2011) have discussed how significant efficacy change can be achieved with experienced teachers, who may be less likely to have malleable efficacy beliefs.

As Klassen *et al.* (2011) and others (e.g. Morris *et al.*, 2016; Wyatt, 2014) have noted, a key area for research involves (18) the development of a reliable scale for examining the influence of the theorised efficacy sources (i.e. mastery experiences, vicarious modelling, social persuasion, affective response). Thus far, studies that have developed scales (e.g. Poulou, 2007) have not been able to isolate the different sources using psychometric analyses. As a result, future LTE studies could contribute towards knowledge development by examining whether efficacy sources do act according to efficacy theory, can be grouped in other ways or need to be extended.

Future studies could continue the line of research started by Karimi (2011), who considered the effect of different types of professional development on teacher efficacy beliefs. In the Karimi study, a group of teachers experienced an integrated professional development programme that involved various efficacy-forming opportunities (e.g. mastery, vicarious), and displayed stronger efficacy at the end of the programme in comparison to a control group. Such studies could consider the (19) influence of different interventions using experimental methods, in order to identify which models have a stronger impact. If teachers are going through the process of knowledge development, efficacy beliefs may be likely to naturally strengthen over time as they gain experience (Bandura, 1997; Tschannen-Moran & Woolfolk Hoy, 2001). Thus, it seems natural that these individuals will consequently develop stronger efficacy beliefs from professional development, as has been consistently shown in the research literature (e.g. Atay, 2007; Wyatt, 2010b; Zonoubi *et al.*, 2017). Accordingly, a key concern for researchers revolves around identifying the types of interventions that are likely to have a *stronger* impact on the development of teacher efficacy beliefs. Few studies, thus far, have examined the influence of different *types* of development programmes on the efficacy of language teachers from the same population, within the same study.

Finally, (20) how can collective L2 efficacy beliefs be strengthened? Research (e.g. Zonoubi *et al.*, 2017) has shown that collaborative professional development efforts may lead to stronger perceptions of personal and collective efficacy. Future studies could investigate factors that aid in the development of efficacy in this domain.

11.2.3 Sources of efficacy-forming information

Findings from this study indicate that student learning experiences contribute efficacy-forming information. Past student learning experiences – both at home and abroad – appear to act as sources of efficacy-forming information. This may be an important area for future studies to explore, as teacher cognition research has also suggested that teachers draw heavily on past learning experiences (Borg, 2003, 2006). Such experiences may contribute to efficacy directly (i.e. as vicarious experiences) or indirectly by contributing to skills (e.g. L2 proficiency). Such experiences may also influence beliefs about language learning, that is influence the cognitive processing during efficacy assessment, as a 'filter' that values or weights certain approaches above others (see Watzke, 2007). Although a relationship between overseas experience and LTE has been noted in other studies (Choi & Lee, 2016), more research is needed to (21) identify whether such a relationship is transferable across different teaching contexts; investigate which domains of L2 teacher efficacy such experiences may influence; and (22) examine how such experiences contribute to teacher efficacy. Such studies may be particularly needed in Japan, as some districts have made study abroad a required activity for language teachers (*The Japan Times*, 2013).

It also seems clear that contextual variables are influential in the assessment of LTE beliefs. This study investigated the dimensionality and strength of teacher efficacy beliefs for different tasks. Future studies could (23) investigate the strength of individuals' teacher efficacy beliefs for the same task under different conditions (i.e. towards levels of task difficulty). By using the contextual variables identified in the current study (such as school level, administrative assignments, school with a special designation) and others (such as class size), studies could also investigate the relative influence of different contextual variables on LTE teacher efficacy in different teaching situations. Furthermore, differences have been identified between teachers' perceptions of efficacy development at different types of schools (Moradkhani & Haghi, 2017); context also appears to be a source of information that influences efficacy expectations. Future studies, both within Japan and in the wider field, could investigate school type, level, designation and other local contextual factors with respect to teacher efficacy assessment and development.

This study has raised questions about the influence of social factors on LTE beliefs. It has identified one dimension of collaborative efficacy (named *Teamwork*) and explored the influence of group dynamics on LTE beliefs. Interview findings have indicated leadership as a variable that influences perceptions of collaborative and collective efficacy, while regression analysis identified teaching team member age as a factor that negatively impacted on perceptions of collaborative efficacy. Future studies could further examine (24) the social features of the teaching context and investigate in what ways these may influence LTE beliefs.

Greater understanding is needed about the influence of different efficacy sources in various cultural contexts. Findings from the exploratory interviews suggested that social persuasion is strongly attended to by JTEs and may be a crucial source of information for novice teachers. Results have suggested that cultural forces may influence the ways in which teacher efficacy develops and the weighting of different sources of information. Thus, future studies could (25) investigate the ways in which teacher efficacy beliefs are assessed in cross-cultural language teaching settings.

11.2.4 Language teacher efficacy, student efficacy and student performance

Finally, future studies should (26) investigate teacher efficacy beliefs for language teaching with respect to student efficacy and achievement, areas where more teacher efficacy research is required (Klassen *et al.*, 2011). Past studies have shown that teacher efficacy beliefs were significant in predicting successful teaching and learning in other contexts (Ashton & Webb, 1986; Bandura, 1993; Goddard *et al.*, 2000), while there is some evidence of a relationship between teacher and student efficacy (Bolshakova *et al.*, 2011; Chang, 2015). It is important for future research to show what, if any, relationship exists between LTE efficacy beliefs and student language growth and communicative development.

Within such research, the influence of other factors can also be examined.

Findings from the current study have indicated a positive relationship between teaching experience and *Student Achievement* efficacy, thus future studies could examine whether students taught by more experienced teachers perform better on entrance examinations and/or other measures of language competency. Also, student self-efficacy and achievement (particularly in adolescents) appear to be influenced by the learning environment, and by their peers (Schunk & Meece, 2005), thus the academic level and purpose of schools (e.g. examination orientation) may be a variable for consideration in future studies of the relationship between LTE beliefs, student efficacy and student performance.

11.3 Final Summary

LTE is multidimensional and appears to be a key mediator of teacher practice. It seems clear that teachers' perceptions of capability for teaching are significantly related to their practice, prior experiences and the contexts in which they work. JTE teacher efficacy beliefs reflect context-specific dimensions of teaching and non-teaching challenges. Findings suggest that personal past experiences may contribute to the skills that individuals draw on when assessing their perceived competence, where greater experience with the task (or experience with skills that inform the task) is associated with stronger efficacy beliefs for that task. Accordingly, variables such as English proficiency, years of teaching experience and the use of English as a language of instruction appear to influence different dimensions of teacher efficacy beliefs.

While the results from this study reflect the Japanese context, and are limited by the constraints of the study (such as the sample size and research design, see Chapter 4: Section 4.4 for discussion), results indicate language teaching specific domains related to perceived proficiency and L2 instruction. It also seems that there is a collaborative domain of L2 teacher efficacy, which may contribute towards a wider collective dimension. Furthermore, findings indicate that perceptions of collaborative and collective teacher efficacy may influence personal teacher efficacy, thus future studies should examine the relationship between personal, collaborative and collective LTE beliefs.

Efforts to increase language teachers' language proficiency and teacher knowledge are important; these act as affordances that individuals can reflect on in the assessment of their beliefs for teaching tasks and provide teachers with more experiences from which to develop greater perceived competence. However, a key finding from the current study concerned the relationship between language proficiency and the reported use of English as a language of instruction, where no significant relationship was identified. Results identified perceived L2 proficiency as a predictor of CLT efficacy, which in turn was a predictor of use of English in class. Results align with self-efficacy theory, in that efficacy beliefs appear to mediate the relationship between personal factors (such as L2 skill) and behaviour. Findings also highlight the importance of teaching context. Accordingly, while attempts to provide teachers with skill development are important, opportunities for *contextual* practice appear to be crucial, given the nature of teacher efficacy beliefs as context-specific perceptions of capability assessed against environmental conditions. Professional development efforts may need to focus on providing greater opportunities for language teachers to experiment in their individual teaching contexts, that is, at their schools, in their classrooms, with their students.

It seems clear that LTE development occurs when professional development opportunities provide individuals with an environment in which teachers can experiment and learn from each other (Atay, 2007; Karimi, 2011; Moradkhani et al., 2017; Zonoubi et al., 2017); however, little is known about how efficacy sources are actually drawn on by individuals. Furthermore, although it seems clear that efficacious teachers put in more effort and show greater commitment, few studies have shown a relationship between LTE beliefs and student achievement. Future studies should examine the sources of LTE, and the relationship between LTE efficacy and student achievement.

Teacher efficacy has a long history of research within the wider field of education and psychology; however, this belief construct has barely been scratched for language teaching contexts. Given the robustness of teacher efficacy as a means of understanding how teachers' self-beliefs about capability can mediate the ways in which they exercise control of student learning, the developing field of LTE provides many opportunities, not only for researchers, but also for contributing towards language teacher development.

References

Abedini, F., Bagheri, M.S. and Sadighi, F. (2018a) Exploring Iranian collective teacher efficacy beliefs in different ELT settings through developing a context-specific English language teacher collective efficacy scale. *Cogent Education* 5 (1), 1–33.

Abedini, F., Bagheri, M.S., Sadighi, F. and Yarmohammadi, L. (2018b) The constituent elements of collective teacher efficacy beliefs and their contributing factors in different ELT educational contexts: A qualitative study. *Cogent Social Sciences* 4, 1500768.

Abednia, A. (2012) Teachers' professional identity: Contributions of a critical EFL teacher education course in Iran. *Teaching and Teacher Education* 28 (5), 706–717.

Akbari, R. and Tavassoli, K. (2014) Developing an ELT context-specific teacher efficacy instrument. *RELC Journal* 45 (1), 27–50.

Aloreibi, A. and Carey, M.D. (2017) English language teaching in Libya after Gaddafi. In R. Kirkpatrick (ed.) *English Language Education Policy in the Middle East and North Africa* (pp. 93–114). Cham: Springer International Publishing.

Anderson, S.L. and Betz, N.E. (2001) Sources of social self-efficacy expectations: Their measurement and relation to career development. *Journal of Vocational Behavior* 58 (1), 98–117.

Andrews, S. (2003) Teacher language awareness and the professional knowledge base of the L2 teacher. *Language Awareness* 12 (2), 81–95.

Armor, D., Conry-Oseguera, P., Cox, M., King, N., McDonnell, L., Pascal, A., Pauly, E. and Zellman, G. (1976) *Analysis of the School Preferred Reading Programs in Selected Los Angeles Minority Schools*. Santa Monica, CA: Rand Corporation.

Ashton, P., Webb, R. and Doda, C. (1983) *A Study of Teachers' Sense of Efficacy*. Gainesville, FL: University of Florida.

Ashton, P., Buhr, D. and Crocker, L. (1984) Teachers' sense of efficacy: A self-or norm-referenced construct? *Florida Journal of Educational Research* 26 (1), 29–41.

Atay, D. (2007) Beginning teacher efficacy and the practicum in an EFL context. *Teacher Development* 11 (2), 203–219.

Avalos, B. (2011) Teacher professional development in teaching and teacher education over ten years. *Teaching and Teacher Education* 27 (1), 10–20.

Baldauf, R.B., Kaplan, R.B., Kamwangamalu, N. and Bryant, P. (2011) Success or failure of primary second/foreign language programmes in Asia: What do the data tell us? *Current Issues in Language Planning* 12 (2), 309–323.

Baleghizadeh, S. and Goldouz, E. (2016) The relationship between Iranian EFL teachers' collective efficacy beliefs, teaching experience and perception of teacher empowerment. *Cogent Education* 3, 1–15.

Ball, M. (2000) Preparing non-specialist language students for study abroad. *Language Learning Journal* 21 (1), 19–25.

Bandura, A. (1977) Self-efficacy: Toward a unifying theory of behavioral change. *Psychological Review* 84, 191–215.

Bandura, A. (1986) *Social Foundations of Thought and Action: A Social Cognitive Theory*. Englewood Cliffs, NJ: Prentice Hall.

Bandura, A. (1991) Human agency: The rhetoric and the reality. *American Psychologist* 46 (2), 157–162.

Bandura, A. (1993) Perceived self-efficacy in cognitive development and functioning. *Educational Psychologist* 28 (2), 117–148.

Bandura, A. (1997) *Self Efficacy: The Exercise of Control*. New York: W.H. Freeman and Company.

Bandura, A. (2001) Social cognitive theory: An agentic perspective. *Annual Review of Psychology* 52, 1–26.

Bandura, A. (2006) Guide for constructing self-efficacy scales. In F. Pajares and T.C. Urdan (eds) *Self-Efficacy Beliefs of Adolescents* (pp. 307–337). Greenwich, CT: Information Age.

Bandura, A. (2012) On the functional properties of perceived self-efficacy revisited. *Journal of Management* 38 (1), 9–44.

Bandura, A., Adams, N.E. and Beyer, J. (1977) Cognitive processes mediating behavioral change. *Journal of Personality and Social Psychology* 35 (3), 125–139.

Barahona, M. (2017) Exploring models of team teaching in initial foreign/second language teacher education: A study in situated collaboration. *Australian Journal of Teacher Education* 42 (12), 144–161.

Barcelos, A.M.F. (2006) Researching beliefs about SLA: A critical review. In P. Kalaja and A.M.F. Barcelos (eds) *Beliefs About SLA: New Research Approaches* (pp. 7–33). New York: Springer.

Basturkmen, H. (2012) Review of research into the correspondence between language teachers' stated beliefs and practices. *System* 40 (2), 282–295.

Basturkmen, H., Loewen, S. and Ellis, R. (2004) Teachers' stated beliefs about incidental focus on form and their classroom practices. *Applied Linguistics* 25 (2), 243–272.

Bautista, N.U. (2011) Investigating the use of vicarious and mastery experiences in influencing early childhood education majors' self-efficacy beliefs. *Journal of Science Teacher Education* 22 (4), 333–349.

Bautista, N.U. and Boone, W.J. (2015) Exploring the impact of teachme™ lab virtual classroom teaching simulation on early childhood education majors' self-efficacy beliefs. *Journal of Science Teacher Education* 26 (3), 237–262.

Bax, S. (2003) The end of CLT: A context approach to language teaching. *ELT Journal* 57 (3), 278–287.

Beauchamp, C. and Thomas, L. (2009) Understanding teacher identity: An overview of issues in the literature and implications for teacher education. *Cambridge Journal of Education* 39 (2), 175–189.

Beecham, S., Hall, T., Britton, C., Cottee, M. and Rainer, A. (2005) Using an expert panel to validate a requirements process improvement model. *Journal of Systems and Software* 76, 251–275.

Benesse Educational Research and Development Institute (2011) *Shogakko eigo ni kansuru kihon chosa (kyoin chosa) 2010 daijesuto [Basic Research about English in Elementary School (Teacher Perspectives) 2010 Digest]*. Tokyo: Benesse Corporation.

Berger, J.G., Boles, K.C. and Troen, V. (2005) Teacher research and school change: Paradoxes, problems, and possibilities. *Teaching and Teacher Education* 21 (1), 93–105.

Berliner, D.C. (1988) *The Development of Expertise in Pedagogy*. Washington, DC: AACTE Publications.

Berman, P., McLaughlin, M., Bass, G., Pauly, E. and Zellman, G. (1977) *Federal Programs Supporting Educational Change, Vol. VII: Factors Affecting Implementation and Continuation*. Santa Monica, CA: Rand Corporation.

Betoret, F.D. (2006) Stressors, self-efficacy, coping resources, and burnout among secondary school teachers in Spain. *Educational Psychology* 26 (4), 519–539.

Bolshakova, V.L., Johnson, C.C. and Czerniak, C.M. (2011) 'It depends on what science teacher you got': Urban science self-efficacy from teacher and student voices. *Cultural Studies of Science Education* 6, 961–997.

Bolt, M.A., Killough, L.N. and Koh, H.C. (2001) Testing the interaction effects of task complexity in computer training using the social cognitive model. *Decision Sciences* 32 (1), 1–20.

Bong, M. and Skaalvik, E.M. (2003) Academic self-concept and self-efficacy: How different are they really? *Educational Psychology Review* 15 (1), 1–40.

Borg, S. (2001) Self-perception and practice in teaching grammar. *ELT Journal* 55 (1), 21–29.

Borg, S. (2003) Teacher cognition in language teaching: A review of research on what language teachers think, know, believe, and do. *Language Teaching* 36 (2), 81–109.

Borg, S. (2006) *Teacher Cognition and Language Education: Research and Practice*. London: Continuum.

Borg, S. (2011) The impact of in-service teacher education on language teachers' beliefs. *System* 39 (3), 370–380.

Boyle, J. (1997) Native-speaker teachers of English in Hong Kong. *Language and Education* 11 (3), 163–181.

Braun, V. and Clarke, V. (2006) Using thematic analysis in psychology. *Qualitative Research in Psychology* 3 (2), 77–101.

Brewer, M.B. and Gardner, W. (1996) Who is this 'we'? Levels of collective identity and self representations. *Journal of Personality and Social Psychology* 71 (1), 83–93.

Brouwers, A. and Tomic, W. (2000) A longitudinal study of teacher burnout and perceived self-efficacy in classroom management. *Teaching and Teacher Education* 16 (2), 239–253.

Brown, J.D. and Yamashita, S.O. (1995) English language entrance examinations at Japanese universities: What do we know about them? *JALT Journal* 17 (1), 7–30.

Buehl, M.M. and Fives, H. (2009) Exploring teachers' beliefs about teaching knowledge: Where does it come from? Does it change? *The Journal of Experimental Education* 77 (4), 367–408.

Burns, A. (2017) Classroom English proficiency: What can be learned from the Vietnam experience? In D. Freeman and L. Le Dréan (eds) *Developing Classroom English Competence: Learning from the Vietnam Experience* (pp. 84–94). Phnom Penh: IDP Education.

Butler, Y.G. (2004) What level of English proficiency do elementary school teachers need to attain to teach EFL? Case studies from Korea, Taiwan, and Japan. *TESOL Quarterly* 38 (2), 245–278.

Butler, Y.G. (2011) The implementation of communicative and task-based language teaching in the Asia-Pacific region. *Annual Review of Applied Linguistics* 31, 36–57.

Cabaroglu, N. (2014) Professional development through action research: Impact on self-efficacy. *System* 44, 79–88.

Cameron, D. (2002) Globalization and the teaching of 'communication skills'. In D. Block and D. Cameron (eds) *Globalization and Language Teaching* (pp. 67–82). London: Routledge.

Cameron, D. (2012) English as a global commodity. In T. Nevalainen and E.C. Traugott (eds) *The Oxford Handbook of the History of English* (pp. 352–361). Oxford: Oxford University Press.

Canale, M. and Swain, M. (1980) Theoretical bases of communicative approaches to second language teaching and testing. *Applied Linguistics* 1 (1), 1–47.

Cantrell, P., Young, S. and Moore, A. (2003) Factors affecting science teaching efficacy of preservice elementary teachers. *Journal of Science Teacher Education* 14 (3), 177–192.

Capa Aydin, Y. and Woolfolk Hoy, A. (2005) What predicts student teacher self-efficacy? *Academic Exchange Quarterly* 9 (4), 123–128.

Caprara, G.V., Barbaranelli, C., Steca, P. and Malone, P.S. (2006) Teachers' self-efficacy beliefs as determinants of job satisfaction and students' academic achievement: A study at the school level. *Journal of School Psychology* 44 (6), 473–490.

Carless, D.R. (2006) Good practices in team teaching in Japan, South Korea and Hong Kong. *System* 34 (3), 341–351.

Carless, D. (2007) The suitability of task-based approaches for secondary schools: Perspectives from Hong Kong. *System* 35 (4), 595–608.

Carless, D. and Walker, E. (2006) Effective team teaching between local and native-speaking English teachers. *Language and Education* 20 (6), 463–477.

Chacon, C.T. (2005) Teachers' perceived efficacy among English as a foreign language teachers in Middle schools in Venezuela. *Teaching and Teacher Education* 21 (3), 257–272.

Chan, D.W. (2008) Dimensions of teacher self-efficacy among Chinese secondary school teachers in Hong Kong. *Educational Psychology* 28 (2), 181–194.

Chan, W.-Y., Lau, S., Nie, Y., Lim, S. and Hogan, D. (2008) Organizational and personal predictors of teacher commitment: The mediating role of teacher efficacy and identification with school. *American Educational Research Journal* 45 (3), 597–630.

Chang, M.-L. (2009) An appraisal perspective of teacher burnout: Examining the emotional work of teachers. *Educational Psychology Review* 21 (3), 193–218.

Chang, Y.-L. (2015) Examining relationships among elementary mathematics teacher efficacy and their students' mathematics self-efficacy and achievement. *Eurasia Journal of Mathematics, Science and Technology Education* 11 (6), 1307–1320.

Chen, C.-H. (2008) Why do teachers not practice what they believe regarding technology integration? *The Journal of Educational Research* 102 (1), 65–75.

Chen, Z. and Goh, C.C. (2011) Teaching oral English in higher education: Challenges to EFL teachers. *Teaching in Higher Education* 16 (3), 333–345.

Cheng, Y.C. (1994) Principal's leadership as a critical factor for school performance: Evidence from multi-levels of primary schools. *School Effectiveness and School Improvement* 5 (3), 299–317.

Chesnut, S.R. and Burley, H. (2015) Self-efficacy as a predictor of commitment to the teaching profession: A meta-analysis. *Educational Research Review* 15, 1–16.

Cheung, H.Y. (2006) The measurement of teacher efficacy: Hong Kong primary in-service teachers. *Journal of Education for Teaching* 32 (4), 435–451.

Cheung, H.Y. (2008) Teacher efficacy: A comparative study of Hong Kong and Shanghai primary in-service teachers. *The Australian Educational Researcher* 35 (1), 103–123.

Choi, E. and Lee, J. (2016) Investigating the relationship of target language proficiency and self-efficacy among nonnative EFL teachers. *System* 58, 49–63.

Choi, T.-H. (2015) The impact of the 'teaching English through English' policy on teachers and teaching in South Korea. *Current Issues in Language Planning* 16 (3), 201–220.

Choi, T.-H. and Andon, N. (2014) Can a teacher certification scheme change ELT classroom practice? *ELT Journal* 68 (1), 12–21.

Chong, W.H. and Kong, C.A. (2012) Teacher collaborative learning and teacher self-efficacy: The case of lesson study. *The Journal of Experimental Education* 80 (3), 263–283.

Chong, W.H., Klassen, R.M., Huan, V.S., Wong, I. and Kates, A.D. (2010) The relationships among school types, teacher efficacy beliefs, and academic climate: Perspective from Asian Middle schools. *The Journal of Educational Research* 103 (3), 183–190.

Chung, I.-F. and Cheng, H. (2009) The implementation of communicative language teaching: An investigation of students' viewpoints. *The Asia-Pacific Education Researcher* 18 (1), 67–78.

Cole, J. and Gonyea, R. (2010) Accuracy of self-reported SAT and ACT test scores: Implications for research. *Research in Higher Education* 51 (4), 305–319.

Collins, K.M.T., Onwuegbuzie, A.J. and Sutton, I.L. (2006) A model incorporating the rationale and purpose for conducting mixed-methods research in special education and beyond. *Learning Disabilities: A Contemporary Journal* 4 (1), 67–100.

Collins, K.M.T., Leech, N.L., Onwuegbuzie, A.J. and Slate, J.R. (2007) Conducting mixed analyses: A general typology. *International Journal of Multiple Research Approaches* 1 (1), 4–17.

Commission on the Development of Foreign Language Proficiency (2011) *Five Proposals and Specific Measures for Developing Proficiency in English for International Communication.* Tokyo: Ministry of Education, Culture, Sports, Science, and Technology.

Cook, M. (2009) Factors inhibiting and facilitating Japanese teachers of English in adopting communicative language teaching methodologies. *K@ta* 11 (2), 99–116.

Costello, A.B. and Osborne, J.W. (2005) Best practices in exploratory factor analysis: Four recommendations for getting the most from your analysis. *Practical Assessment, Research & Evaluation* 10 (7), 1–9.

Cramer, R.J., Neal, T. and Brodsky, S.L. (2009) Self-efficacy and confidence: Theoretical distinctions and implications for trial consultation. *Consulting Psychology Journal: Practice and Research* 61 (4), 319.

Cubukcu, F. (2008) A study on the correlation between self efficacy and foreign language learning anxiety. *Journal of Theory and Practice in Education* 4 (1), 148–158.

Dalton, R. and Shin, D.C. (2014) Growing up democratic: Generational change in East Asian democracies. *Japanese Journal of Political Science* 15 (3), 345–372.

Dastgahian, E.S., Turner, M. and Scull, J. (2018) Tensions and resistance during collaborative efforts for change: Facilitating the implementation of task-based pedagogy in Iran. In R. Chowdhury (ed.) *Transformation and Empowerment Through Education: Reconstructing Our Relationship With Education* (pp. 119–135). Oxford: Routledge.

De Oliveira, L. and Richardson, S. (2001) Collaboration between native and nonnative English-speaking educators. *CATESOL Journal* 13 (1), 123–134.

Dembo, M.H. and Gibson, S. (1985) Teachers' sense of efficacy: An important factor in school improvement. *The Elementary School Journal* 86 (2), 173–184.

Demir, K. (2008) Transformational leadership and collective efficacy: The moderating roles of collaborative culture and teachers' self-efficacy. *Eurasian Journal of Educational Research* 33, 93–112.

Desimone, L.M. and Le Floch, K.C. (2004) Are we asking the right questions? Using cognitive interviews to improve surveys in education research. *Educational Evaluation and Policy Analysis* 26 (1), 1–22.

Diallo, I. (2014) English in education policy shift in Senegal: From traditional pedagogies to communicative language teaching. *International Journal of Pedagogies and Learning* 9 (2), 142–151.

Edge, J. (1988) Applying linguistics in English language teacher training for speakers of other languages. *ELT Journal* 42 (1), 9–13.

Eiken Foundation of Japan (2016a) About eiken grade pre-1. See http://www.eiken.or.jp/eiken/en/grades/grade_p1/ (accessed February 25, 2016).

Eiken Foundation of Japan (2016b) Eiken grades. See https://www.eiken.or.jp/eiken/en/grades/ (accessed February 25, 2016).

Englert, C.S., Tarrant, K.L. and Rozendal, M.S. (1993) Educational innovations: Achieving curricular change through collaboration. *Education and Treatment of Children* 16 (4), 441–473.

Enochs, L.G. and Riggs, I.M. (1990) Further development of an elementary science teaching efficacy belief instrument: A preservice elementary scale. *School Science and Mathematics* 90 (8), 694–706.

Enochs, L.G., Scharmann, L.C. and Riggs, I.M. (1995) The relationship of pupil control to preservice elementary science teacher self–efficacy and outcome expectancy. *Science Education* 79 (1), 63–75.

Eslami, Z.R. and Fatahi, A. (2008) Teachers' sense of self-efficacy, English proficiency, and instructional strategies: A study of nonnative EFL teachers in Iran. *TESL-EJ* 11 (4), 1–19.

Evers, W., Tomic, W. and Brouwers, A. (2005) Does equity sensitivity moderate the relationship between self-efficacy beliefs and teacher burnout? *Representative Research in Social Psychology* 28, 35–46.

Faez, F. and Valeo, A. (2012) TESOL teacher education: Novice teachers' perceptions of their preparedness and efficacy in the classroom. *TESOL Quarterly* 46 (3), 450–471.

Fan, C. and Lo, Y.Y. (2015) Interdisciplinary collaboration to promote L2 science literacy in Hong Kong. In A. Tajino, T. Stewart and D. Dalsky (eds) *Team Teaching and Team Learning in the Language Classroom* (pp. 114–132). London: Routledge.

Fang, Z. (1996) A review of research on teacher beliefs and practices. *Educational Research* 38 (1), 47–65.

Farrell, T.S.C. and Bennis, K. (2013) Reflecting on ESL teacher beliefs and classroom practices: A case study. *RELC Journal* 44 (2), 163–176.

Feiman-Nemser, S. (2001) From preparation to practice: Designing a continuum to strengthen and sustain teaching. *The Teachers College Record* 103 (6), 1013–1055.

Fernandez, C. (2002) Learning from Japanese approaches to professional development: The case of lesson study. *Journal of Teacher Education* 53 (5), 393–405.

Fives, H. and Buehl, M.M. (2009) Examining the factor structure of the teachers' sense of efficacy scale. *The Journal of Experimental Education* 78 (1), 118–134.

Freeman, D. (2017) The English-for-teaching course in Vietnam: Who took it and what did they learn? A description of participants and their experience. In D. Freeman and L. Le Dréan (eds) *Developing Classroom English Competence: Learning from the Vietnam Experience* (pp. 44–54). Phnom Penh: IDP Education

Freeman, D., Katz, A., Garcia Gomez, P. and Burns, A. (2015) English-for-teaching: Rethinking teacher proficiency in the classroom. *ELT Journal* 69 (2), 129–139.

Gatbonton, E. (1999) Investigating experienced ESL teachers' pedagogical knowledge. *The Modern Language Journal* 83 (1), 35–50.

Ghaith, G. and Yaghi, H. (1997) Relationships among experience, teacher efficacy, and attitudes toward the implementation of instructional innovation. *Teaching and Teacher Education* 13 (4), 451–458.

Ghanizadeh, A. and Moafian, F. (2011) The relationship between Iranian EFL teachers' sense of self-efficacy and their pedagogical success in language institutes. *Asian EFL Journal* 13 (2), 249–272.

Ghanizadeh, A. and Jahedizadeh, S. (2016) EFL teachers' teaching style, creativity, and burnout: A path analysis approach. *Cogent Education* 3 (1).

Ghonsooly, B. and Ghanizadeh, A. (2013) Self-efficacy and self-regulation and their relationship: A study of Iranian EFL teachers. *The Language Learning Journal* 41 (1), 68–84.

Gibson, S. and Dembo, M.H. (1984) Teacher efficacy: A construct validation. *Journal of Educational Psychology* 76 (4), 569.

Gist, M.E. and Mitchell, T.R. (1992) Self-efficacy: A theoretical analysis of its determinants and malleability. *Academy of Management Review* 17 (2), 183–211.

Glasgow, G.P. (2012) Implementing language education policy to 'conduct classes in English' in Japanese senior high schools. In A. Stewart and N. Sonda (eds) *JALT 2011 Conference Proceedings* (pp. 399–407). Tokyo: JALT.

Glasgow, G.P. (2013) The impact of the new national senior high school English curriculum on collaboration between Japanese teachers and native speakers. *JALT Journal* 35 (2), 191–204.

Glasgow, G.P. (2014) Teaching English in English, 'in principle': The national foreign language curriculum for Japanese senior high schools. *International Journal of Pedagogies & Learning* 9 (2), 152–161.

Goddard, R. (2002) A theoretical and empirical analysis of the measurement of collective efficacy: The development of a short form. *Educational and Psychological Measurement* 62 (1), 97–110.

Goddard, R. and Goddard, Y. (2001) A multilevel analysis of the relationship between teacher and collective efficacy in urban schools. *Teaching and Teacher Education* 17 (7), 807–818.

Goddard, R., Hoy, W.K. and Woolfolk Hoy, A. (2000) Collective teacher efficacy: Its meaning, measure, and impact on student achievement. *American Educational Research Journal* 37 (2), 479–507.

Goddard, R., Hoy, W.K. and Woolfolk Hoy, A. (2004a) Collective efficacy beliefs: Theoretical developments, empirical evidence, and future directions. *Educational Researcher* 33 (3), 3–13.

Goddard, R., LoGerfo, L. and Hoy, W.K. (2004b) High school accountability: The role of perceived collective efficacy. *Educational Policy* 18 (3), 403–425.

Goddard, Y., Goddard, R. and Tschannen-Moran, M. (2007) A theoretical and empirical investigation of teacher collaboration for school improvement and student achievement in public elementary schools. *The Teachers College Record* 109 (4), 877–896.

Goddard, R., Goddard, Y., Kim, E.S. and Miller, R. (2015) A theoretical and empirical analysis of the roles of instructional leadership, teacher collaboration, and collective efficacy beliefs in support of student learning. *American Journal of Education* 121 (4), 501–530.

Göker, S.D. (2006) Impact of peer coaching on self-efficacy and instructional skills in TEFL teacher education. *System* 34, 239–254.

Göker, S.D. (2012) Impact of EFL teachers' collective efficacy and job stress on job satisfaction. *Theory and Practice in Language Studies* 2 (8), 1545–1551.

Gorber, S.C., Tremblay, M., Moher, D. and Gorber, B. (2007) A comparison of direct vs. Self-report measures for assessing height, weight and body mass index: A systematic review. *Obesity Reviews* 8 (4), 307–326.

Gorsuch, G. (1998) Yakudoku EFL instruction in two Japanese high school classrooms: An exploratory study. *JALT Journal* 20, 6–32.

Gorsuch, G. (2001) Japanese EFL teachers' perceptions of communicative, audiolingual and yakudoku activities: The plan versus the reality. *Education Policy Analysis Archives* 9 (10), 1–27.

Graham, S. (2011) Self-efficacy and academic listening. *Journal of English for Academic Purposes* 10 (2), 113–117.

Green, S.B. (1991) How many subjects does it take to do a regression analysis. *Multivariate Behavioral Research* 26 (3), 499–510.

Greene, B.A. and Miller, R.B. (1996) Influences on achievement: Goals, perceived ability, and cognitive engagement. *Contemporary Educational Psychology* 21 (2), 181–192.

Gresham, G. (2008) Mathematics anxiety and mathematics teacher efficacy in elementary pre-service teachers. *Teaching Education* 19 (3), 171–184.

Guillemin, F., Bombardier, C. and Beaton, D. (1993) Cross-cultural adaptation of health-related quality of life measures: Literature review and proposed guidelines. *Journal of Clinical Epidemiology* 46 (12), 1417–1432.

Guskey, T.R. (1988) Teacher efficacy, self-concept, and attitudes toward the implementation of instructional innovation. *Teaching and Teacher Education* 4 (1), 63–69.

Hallinger, P. and Heck, R.H. (2010) Collaborative leadership and school improvement: Understanding the impact on school capacity and student learning. *School Leadership & Management* 30 (2), 95–110.

Hamamoto, S. (2012) Shougakko eigoka no dounyuu ni okeru kyouin no kenkai [Elementary teachers' views on English teaching]. In A. Stewart and N. Sonda (eds) *JALT 2011 Conference Proceedings* (pp. 210–219). Tokyo: JALT.

Hamid, M.O. and Nguyen, H.T.M. (2016) Globalization, English language policy, and teacher agency: Focus on Asia. *International Education Journal: Comparative Perspectives* 15 (1), 26–43.

Hamid, M.O., Nguyen, H.T.M. and Baldauf, R.B. (2013) Medium of instruction in Asia: Context, processes and outcomes. *Current Issues in Language Planning* 14 (1), 1–15.

Hatipoglu, C. (2016) The impact of the university entrance exam on EFL education in Turkey: Pre-service English language teachers' perspective. *Procedia – Social and Behavioral Sciences* 232, 136–144.

Hato, Y. (2005) Problems in top-down goal setting in second language education: A case study of the 'action plan to cultivate "Japanese with English abilities"'. *JALT Journal* 27 (1), 33–51.

Hattie, J. (2003) Teachers Make a Difference: What is the Research Evidence? Paper presented at the Building Teacher Quality: What Does the Research Tell Us ACER Research Conference, Melbourne, Australia.

Hattie, J. (2012) *Visible Learning for Teachers: Maximizing Impact on Achievement*. Oxford: Routledge.

Hattie, J. (2015) The applicability of visible learning to higher education. *Scholarship of Teaching and Learning in Psychology* 1 (1), 79–91.

Hawley, W.D. and Valli, L. (1999) The essentials of effective professional development: A new consensus. In L. Darling-Hammond and G. Sykes (eds) *Teaching as the Learning Profession: Handbook of Policy and Practice* (pp. 127–150). San Francisco, CA: Jossey-Bass.

Hayes, A. (2018) Tacit rejection of policy and teacher ambivalence: Insights into English language teaching in Bahrain through actors' perceptions. *TESOL Journal* 9 (1), 114–137.

Henson, R.K. and Roberts, J.K. (2006) Use of exploratory factor analysis in published research: Common errors and some comment on improved practice. *Educational and Psychological Measurement* 66 (3), 393–416.

Hiep, P.H. (2007) Communicative language teaching: Unity within diversity. *ELT Journal* 61 (3), 193–201.

Hiver, P. (2013) The interplay of possible language teacher selves in professional development choices. *Language Teaching Research* 17 (2), 210–227.

Ho, I.T. and Hau, K.T. (2004) Australian and Chinese teacher efficacy: Similarities and differences in personal instruction, discipline, guidance efficacy and beliefs in external determinants. *Teaching and Teacher Education* 20 (3), 313–323.

Hoang, T. (2018) Teacher self-efficacy research in English as a foreign language context: A systematic review. *Journal of Asia TEFL* 15 (4), 976–990.

Hoffman, B. (2010) 'I think I can, but I'm afraid to try': The role of self-efficacy beliefs and mathematics anxiety in mathematics problem-solving efficiency. *Learning and Individual Differences* 20 (3), 276–283.

Hofstede, G. and Soeters, J. (2002) Consensus societies with their own character: National cultures in Japan and the Netherlands. *Comparative Sociology* 1 (1), 1–16.

Honigsfeld, A. and Dove, M.G. (eds) (2012) *Coteaching and Other Collaborative Practices in the EFL/ESL Classroom: Rationale, Research, Reflections, and Recommendations*. Charlotte, NC: Information Age.

Horng, J.-S., Hong, J.-C., ChanLin, L.-J., Chang, S.-H. and Chu, H.-C. (2005) Creative teachers and creative teaching strategies. *International Journal of Consumer Studies* 29 (4), 352–358.

Hu, G. and McKay, S.L. (2012) English language education in East Asia: Some recent developments. *Journal of Multilingual and Multicultural Development* 33 (4), 345–362.

Huff, L. and Kelley, L. (2005) Is collectivism a liability? The impact of culture on organizational trust and customer orientation: A seven-nation study. *Journal of Business Research* 58 (1), 96–102.

Humphries, S. and Burns, A. (2015) 'In reality it's almost impossible': CLT-oriented curriculum change. *ELT Journal* 69 (3), 239–248.

Hunt, S.M., Alonso, J., Bucquet, D., Niero, M., Wiklund, I. and McKenna, S. (1991) Cross-cultural adaptation of health measures. *Health Policy* 19 (1), 33–44.

Hymes, D. (1972) On communicative competence. In J.B. Pride and J. Holmes (eds) *Sociolinguistics* (pp. 269–293). Harmondsworth: Penguin.

Hyrkäs, K., Appelqvist-Schmidlechner, K. and Oksa, L. (2003) Validating an instrument for clinical supervision using an expert panel. *International Journal of Nursing Studies* 40 (6), 619–625.

İnceçay, G. and İnceçay, V. (2009) Turkish university students' perceptions of communicative and non-communicative activities in EFL classroom. *Procedia – Social and Behavioral Sciences* 1 (1), 618–622.

Japan Business Federation (2000) *Fostering of Human Resources in the Age of Globalization*. Tokyo: Japan Business Federation.

Johnson, K.E. (1995) *Understanding Communication in Second Language Classrooms*. Cambridge: Cambridge University Press.

Johnston, B. (1997) Do EFL teachers have careers? *TESOL Quarterly* 31 (4), 681–712.

Kahn, J.H., Schneider, K.T., Jenkins-Henkelman, T.M. and Moyle, L.L. (2006) Emotional social support and job burnout among high-school teachers: Is it all due to dispositional affectivity? *Journal of Organizational Behavior* 27 (6), 793–807.

Kamhi-Stein, L.D., Maggioli, G.D. and De Oliveira, L.C. (2017) *English Language Teaching in South America: Policy, Preparation and Practices*. Bristol: Multilingual Matters.

Karami, H., Mozaffari, F. and Nourzadeh, S. (2019) Examining the psychometric features of the teacher's sense of efficacy scale in the English-as-a-foreign-language teaching context. *Current Psychology*.

Karimi, M.N. (2011) The effects of professional development initiatives on EFL teachers' degree of self efficacy. *Australian Journal of Teacher Education* 36 (6), 50–62.

Karimi, M.N. and Nazari, M. (2017) The congruity/incongruity of EFL teachers' beliefs about listening instruction and their listening instructional practices. *Australian Journal of Teacher Education* 42 (2), 62–80.

Katz, A. (2017) The argument for developing teachers' classroom English proficiency. In D. Freeman and L. Le Dréan (eds) *Developing Classroom English Competence: Learning from the Vietnam Experience* (pp. 1–7). Phnom Pehn: IDP Education

Kawashima, T. (2013) The effects of exposure to non-native English on self-confidence of Japanese high school students. PhD thesis, Macquarie University.

Keith, T.Z. (2015) *Multiple Regression and Beyond: An Introduction to Multiple Regression and Structural Equation Modeling* (2nd edn). New York: Routledge.

Kennedy, K.J. and Hui, S.K.F. (2006) Developing teacher leaders to facilitate Hong Kong's curriculum reforms: Self-efficacy as a measure of teacher growth. *International Journal of Educational Reform* 15 (1), 137–151.

Kikuchi, K. (2006) Revisiting English entrance examinations at Japanese universities after a decade. *JALT Journal* 28 (1), 77–96.

Kikuchi, K. and Browne, C. (2009) English educational policy for high schools in Japan. *RELC Journal* 40 (2), 172–191.

Kim, S. (2008) Five years of teaching English through English: Responses from teachers and prospects for learners. *English Teaching* 63 (1), 51–70.

Kirkpatrick, R. and Bui, T.T.N. (2016) Introduction: The challenges for English education policies in Asia. In R. Kirkpatrick (ed.) *English Language Education Policy in Asia* (pp. 1–23). Cham: Springer International Publishing.

Kitao, K. and Kitao, S.K. (1985) Effects of social environment on Japanese and American communication (ERIC Document Reproduction Service No. ED260579).

Kitayama, S., Markus, H.R., Matsumoto, H. and Norasakkunkit, V. (1997) Individual and collective processes in the construction of the self: Self-enhancement in the United States and self-criticism in Japan. *Journal of Personality and Social Psychology* 72, 1245–1267.

Kizuka, M. (2006) Professionalism in English language education in Japan. *Language Teacher Education and Development* 9 (1), 55–62.

Klassen, R., Wilson, E., Siu, A.Y., Hannok, W., Wong, M., Wongsri, N., Sonthisap, P., Pibulchol, C., Buranachaitavee, Y. and Jansem, A. (2013) Preservice teachers' work stress, self-efficacy, and occupational commitment in four countries. *European Journal of Psychology of Education* 28 (4), 1289–1309.

Klassen, R.M. (2010) Teacher stress: The mediating role of collective efficacy beliefs. *The Journal of Educational Research* 103 (5), 342–350.

Klassen, R.M., Usher, E.L. and Bong, M. (2010) Teachers' collective efficacy, job satisfaction, and job stress in cross-cultural context. *The Journal of Experimental Education* 78 (4), 464–486.

Klassen, R.M., Tze, V.M.C., Betts, S.M. and Gordon, K.A. (2011) Teacher efficacy research 1998–2009: Signs of progress or unfulfilled promise? *Educational Psychology Review* 23 (1), 21–43.

Kleinsasser, R.C. (2014) Teacher efficacy in teaching and teacher education. *Teaching and Teacher Education* 44, 168–179.

Knoblauch, D. and Woolfolk Hoy, A. (2008) 'Maybe I can teach those kids': The influence of contextual factors on student teachers' efficacy beliefs. *Teaching and Teacher Education* 24 (1), 166–179.

Koçoğlu, Z. (2011) Emotional intelligence and teacher efficacy: A study of Turkish EFL pre-service teachers. *Teacher Development* 15 (4), 471–484.

Kormos, J., Kiddle, T. and Csizér, K. (2011) Systems of goals, attitudes, and self-related beliefs in second-language-learning motivation. *Applied Linguistics* 32 (5), 495–516.

Krashen, S.D. (1981) *Principles and Practice in Second Language Acquisition*. London: Prentice-Hall.

Kuncel, N.R., Credé, M. and Thomas, L.L. (2005) The validity of self-reported grade point averages, class ranks, and test scores: A meta-analysis and review of the literature. *Review of Educational Research* 75 (1), 63–82.

Kurihara, Y. and Samimy, K.K. (2007) The impact of a U.S. teacher training program on teaching beliefs and practices: A case study of secondary school level Japanese teachers of English. *JALT Journal* 29 (1), 99–122.

Kurt, T., Duyar, I. and Calik, T. (2011) Are we legitimate yet? A closer look at the casual relationship mechanisms among principal leadership, teacher self-efficacy and collective efficacy. *Journal of Management Development* 31 (1), 71–86.

Kurz, T.B. and Knight, S.L. (2004) An exploration of the relationship among teacher efficacy, collective teacher efficacy, and goal consensus. *Learning Environments Research* 7 (2), 111–128.

Kyriacou, C. (2001) Teacher stress: Directions for future research. *Educational Review* 53 (1), 27–35.

Lamie, J.M. (1998) Teacher education and training in Japan. *Journal of In-Service Education* 24 (3), 515–534.

Law, G. (1995) Ideologies of English language education in Japan. *JALT Journal* 17 (2), 213–224.

Leary, M.R. and Downs, D.L. (1995) Interpersonal functions of the self-esteem motive. In M.H. Kernis (ed.) *Efficacy, Agency, and Self-Esteem* (pp. 123–144). Boston, MA: Springer.

Lee, J.C.-K., Zhang, Z. and Yin, H. (2011) A multilevel analysis of the impact of a professional learning community, faculty trust in colleagues and collective efficacy on teacher commitment to students. *Teaching and Teacher Education* 27 (5), 820–830.

Lent, R.W., Lopez, F.G., Brown, S.D. and Gore Jr, P.A. (1996) Latent structure of the sources of mathematics self-efficacy. *Journal of Vocational Behavior* 49 (3), 292–308.

Li, D. (1998) 'It's always more difficult than you plan and imagine': Teachers' perceived difficulties in introducing the communicative approach in South Korea. *TESOL Quarterly* 32, 677–703.

Li, M. and Baldauf, R. (2011) Beyond the curriculum: A Chinese example of issues constraining effective English language teaching. *TESOL Quarterly* 45 (4), 793–803.

Little, J.W. (1990) The persistence of privacy: Autonomy and initiative in teachers' professional relations. *Teachers College Record* 91 (4), 509–536.

Little, J.W. (1993) Teachers' professional development in a climate of educational reform. *Educational Evaluation and Policy Analysis* 15 (2), 129–151.

Littlewood, W. (2007) Communicative and task-based language teaching in East Asian classrooms. *Language Teaching* 40 (03), 243–249.

Lortie, D.C. (1975) *School Teacher: A Sociological Inquiry*: Chicago, IL: University of Chicago Press.

MacCallum, R.C., Widaman, K.F., Zhang, S.B. and Hong, S.H. (1999) Sample size in factor analysis. *Psychological Methods* 4 (1), 84–99.

MacDonald, R., Nagle, J., Akerley, T. and Western, H. (2012) Double-teaming: Teaching academic language in high school biology. In A. Honigsfeld and M.G. Dove (eds) *Coteaching and Other Collaborative Practices in the EFL/ESL Classroom: Rationale, Research, Reflections, and Recommendations* (pp. 91–99). Charlotte, NC: Information Age.

MacIntyre, P.D., Ross, J., Talbot, K., Mercer, S., Gregersen, T. and Banga, C.A. (2019) Stressors, personality and wellbeing among language teachers. *System* 82, 26–38.

Mahoney, S. (2004) Role controversy among team teachers in the JET programme. *JALT Journal* 26 (2), 223–244.

Mak, S.H.-Y. (2011) Tensions between conflicting beliefs of an EFL teacher in teaching practice. *RELC Journal* 42 (1), 53–67.

Malinen, O.-P., Savolainen, H., Engelbrecht, P., Xu, J., Nel, M., Nel, N., et al. (2013a) Exploring teacher self-efficacy for inclusive practices in three diverse countries. *Teaching and Teacher Education* 33, 34–44.

Malinen, O.-P., Savolainen, H. and Xu, J. (2013b) Dimensions of teacher self-efficacy for inclusive practices among mainland Chinese pre-service teachers. *Journal of International Special Needs Education* 16 (2), 82–93.

Mangos, P.M. and Steele-Johnson, D. (2001) The role of subjective task complexity in goal orientation, self-efficacy, and performance relations. *Human Performance* 14 (2), 169–185.

Marjolein, Z. and Helma, M.Y.K. (2016) Teacher self-efficacy and its effects on classroom processes, student academic adjustment, and teacher well-being: A synthesis of 40 years of research. *Review of Educational Research* 86 (4), 981–1015.

Marsh, H.W. and Shavelson, R. (1985) Self-concept: Its multifaceted, hierarchical structure. *Educational Psychologist* 20 (3), 107–123.

Martinsen, R.A., Baker, W., Bown, J. and Johnson, C. (2011) The benefits of living in foreign language housing: The effect of language use and second-language type on oral proficiency gains. *The Modern Language Journal* 95 (2), 274–290.

Maslach, C., Schaufeli, W.B. and Leiter, M.P. (2001) Job burnout. *Annual Review of Psychology* 52, 397–422.

Matsui, T., Matsui, K. and Ohnishi, R. (1990) Mechanisms underlying math self-efficacy learning of college students. *Journal of Vocational Behavior* 37 (2), 225–238.

McKinley, J. and Thompson, G. (2018) Washback effect in teaching English as an international language. In J. Liontas, M. DelliCarpini and S. Abrar-ul-Hassan (eds) *TESOL Encyclopedia of English Language Teaching* (pp. 1–12). Hoboken, NJ: Wiley-Blackwell.

Meara, P. (1994) The year abroad and its effects. *Language Learning Journal* 10 (1), 32–38.

Mercer, S. (2008) Learner self-beliefs. *ELT Journal* 62 (2), 182–183.

Mercer, S. and Kostoulas, A. (2018) Introduction to language teacher psychology. In S. Mercer and A. Kostoulas (eds) *Language Teacher Psychology* (pp. 1–17). Bristol: Multilingual Matters.

Merkle, E.C. and Van Zandt, T. (2006) An application of the Poisson race model to confidence calibration. *Journal of Experimental Psychology: General* 135 (3), 391–408.

Mills, N. (2011) Teaching assistants' self-efficacy in teaching literature: Sources, personal assessments, and consequences. *The Modern Language Journal* 95 (1), 61–80.

Mills, N. and Allen, H. (2008) Teacher efficacy in native and non-native teaching assistants of French. In H.J. Siskin (ed.) *From Thought to Action: Exploring Beliefs and Outcomes in the Foreign Language Program* (pp. 213–234). Boston, MA: Heinle.

Mills, N., Pajares, F. and Herron, C. (2006) A reevaluation of the role of anxiety: Self-efficacy, anxiety, and their relation to reading and listening proficiency. *Foreign Language Annals* 39 (2), 276–295.

Ministry of Education (1999) *Kotogakko gakushu shido yoryo [The Course of Study for Upper Secondary School]*. Tokyo: Ministry of Education.

Ministry of Education, Culture, Sports, Science and Technology (MEXT) (2002) Chapter 2: Towards advancement of 'academic ability'. In *Japanese Government Policies in Education, Culture, Sports, Science and Technology 2002*. Tokyo: Ministry of Education, Culture, Sports, Science, and Technology. See http://www.mext.go.jp/b_menu/hakusho/html/hpac200201/hpac200201_2_015.html (accessed 19 November 2009).

Ministry of Education, Culture, Sports, Science, and Technology (MEXT) (2010) *Supaa ingurishu langeji haisukuru (SELHi) no jigyou gaiyou kaname oyobi seika [Outline of Points and Results of the SELHi Project]*. Tokyo: Ministry of Education, Culture, Sports, Science, and Technology. See http://www.mext.go.jp/a_menu/kokusai/gaikokugo/1293088.htm (accessed 25 June 2012).

Ministry of Education, Culture, Sports, Science, and Technology (MEXT) (2011a) *Eigo ga tsukaeru nihonjin' no ikusei no tame no kōdō keikaku (gaiyō to genjō) (Heisei 15-nen 3 tsuki sakutei [Action Plan for Fostering 'English-Speaking Japanese' (Overview and Current Situation) (Policy Formulated in March 2003)]*. Tokyo: Ministry of Education, Culture, Sports, Science, and Technology. See https://www.mext.go.jp/b_menu/shingi/chousa/shotou/082/shiryo/__icsFiles/afieldfile/2011/01/31/1300465_01.pdf#page=0001 (accessed 25 June 2012).

Ministry of Education, Culture, Sports, Science, and Technology (MEXT) (2011b) *Koutougakkou gakushuushidouyouryou [eigo katsudou] eiyaku han (kayaku) [Senior High School Government Course Guidelines (English Activities) English Translation Version (Tentative Translation)]*. Tokyo: Ministry of Education, Culture, Sports, Science, and Technology. See https://www.mext.go.jp/a_menu/shotou/new-cs/youryou/eiyaku/__icsFiles/afieldfile/2012/10/24/1298353_3.pdf (accessed 22 October 2012).

Ministry of Education, Culture, Sports, Science, and Technology (MEXT) (2012a) *Statistical Abstract 2012 Edition – Upper Secondary Schools: Full-time Teachers by Type of Position*. Tokyo: Ministry of Education, Culture, Sports, Science, and Technology. See http://www.mext.go.jp/component/english/__icsFiles/afieldfile/2013/08/09/1302888_05.pdf (accessed 30 July 2015).

Ministry of Education, Culture, Sports, Science, and Technology (MEXT) (2012b) *Statistical Abstract 2012 Edition – Upper Secondary Schools: Percentage of Full-Time Teachers by Age*. Tokyo: Ministry of Education, Culture, Sports, Science, and Technology. See http://www.mext.go.jp/component/english/__icsFiles/afieldfile/2013/08/09/1302888_06.pdf (accessed 30 July 2015).

Ministry of Education, Culture, Sports, Science, and Technology (MEXT) (2012c) *Statistical Abstract 2012 Edition – Upper Secondary Schools: Schools*. Tokyo: Ministry of Education, Culture, Sports, Science, and Technology. See http://www.mext.go.jp/component/english/__icsFiles/afieldfile/2013/08/09/1302888_01.pdf (accessed 30 July 2015).

Moafian, F. and Ghanizadeh, A. (2009) The relationship between Iranian EFL teachers' emotional intelligence and their self-efficacy in language institutes. *System* 37 (4), 708–718.

Mok-Cheung, H.M.A. (2001) The missing element of rational pedagogical reform: A critical analysis of the task-based learning English language syllabus. *Asia-Pacific Journal of Teacher Education & Development* 4 (2), 189–211.

Moodie, I. (2016) The anti-apprenticeship of observation: How negative prior language learning experience influences English language teachers' beliefs and practices. *System* 60, 29–41.

Moolenaar, N.M., Sleegers, P.J.C. and Daly, A.J. (2012) Teaming up: Linking collaboration networks, collective efficacy, and student achievement. *Teaching and Teacher Education* 28 (2), 251–262.

Moote, S. (2003) Insights into team-teaching. *The English Teacher: An International Journal* 6 (3), 328–334.

Moradkhani, S. and Haghi, S. (2017) Context-based sources of EFL teachers' self-efficacy: Iranian public schools versus private institutes. *Teaching and Teacher Education* 67, 259–269.

Moradkhani, S., Raygan, A. and Moein, M.S. (2017) Iranian EFL teachers' reflective practices and self-efficacy: Exploring possible relationships. *System* 65, 1–14.

Morgan, D.L. (1998) Practical strategies for combining qualitative and quantitative methods: Applications to health research. *Qualitative Health Research* 8 (3), 362–376.

Morling, B., Kitayama, S. and Miyamoto, Y. (2002) Cultural practices emphasize influence in the United States and adjustment in Japan. *Personality and Social Psychology Bulletin* 28 (3), 311–323.

Morris, D.B. and Usher, E.L. (2011) Developing teaching self-efficacy in research institutions: A study of award-winning professors. *Contemporary Educational Psychology* 36 (3), 232–245.

Morris, D.B., Usher, E.L. and Chen, J.A. (2016) Reconceptualizing the sources of teaching self-efficacy: A critical review of emerging literature. *Educational Psychology Review* 29 (4), 795–833.

Mulholland, J. and Wallace, J. (2001) Teacher induction and elementary science teaching: Enhancing self-efficacy. *Teaching and Teacher Education* 17 (2), 243–261.

Mulholland, J., Dorman, J.P. and Odgers, B.M. (2004) Assessment of science teaching efficacy of preservice teachers in an Australian university. *Journal of Science Teacher Education* 15 (4), 313–331.

Nagamine, T. (2007) Exploring teachers' beliefs through collaborative journaling: A qualitative case study of Japanese preservice teachers' transformative development processes in an EFL teacher education program. PhD thesis, Indiana University of Pennsylvania.

Nakamura, K., Hoshino, Y., Kodama, K. and Yamamoto, M. (1999) Reliability of self-reported body height and weight of adult Japanese women. *Journal of Biosocial Science* 31 (4), 555–558.

Nakata, Y. (2010) Improving the classroom language proficiency of non-native teachers of English: What and how? *RELC Journal* 41 (1), 76–90.

Nathans, L.L., Oswald, F.L. and Nimon, K. (2012) Interpreting multiple linear regression: A guidebook of variable importance. *Practical Assessment, Research & Evaluation* 17 (9), 1–19.

Nguyen, H.T., Fehring, H. and Warren, W. (2015) EFL teaching and learning at a Vietnamese university: What do teachers say? *English Language Teaching* 8 (1), 31–43.

Nguyen, N.T. and Ngo, N.D. (2017) Understanding teacher efficacy to teach English for specific purposes. *The Asian EFL Journal* (102), 4–16.

Nishino, T. (2008) Japanese secondary school teachers' beliefs and practices regarding communicative language teaching: An exploratory survey. *JALT Journal* 30 (1), 27–50.

Nishino, T. (2009) Communicative language teaching in Japanese high schools: Teachers' beliefs and classroom practices. PhD thesis, Temple University.

Nishino, T. (2011) Japanese high school teachers' beliefs and practices regarding communicative language teaching. *JALT Journal* 33 (2), 131–156.

Nishino, T. (2012) Modeling teacher beliefs and practices in context: A multimethods approach. *The Modern Language Journal* 96 (3), 380–399.

Nishino, T. and Watanabe, M. (2008) Communication-oriented policies versus classroom realities in Japan. *TESOL Quarterly* 42 (1), 133–138.

Nunan, D. (ed.) (1992) *Collaborative Language Learning and Teaching*. Cambridge: Cambridge University Press.

Nunan, D. (2003) The impact of English as a global language on educational policies and practices in the Asia-Pacific region. *TESOL Quarterly* 37 (4), 589–613.

O'Donnell, K. (2005) Japanese secondary English teachers: Negotiation of educational roles in the face of curricular reform. *Language, Culture, and Curriculum* 18 (3), 300–315.

Obaidul Hamid, M. (2010) Globalisation, English for everyone and English teacher capacity: Language policy discourses and realities in Bangladesh. *Current Issues in Language Planning* 11 (4), 289–310.

Olivella, J., Cuatrecasas, L. and Gavilan, N. (2008) Work organisation practices for lean production. *Journal of Manufacturing Technology Management* 19 (7), 798–811.

Onwuegbuzie, A.J., Bustamante, R.M. and Nelson, J.A. (2010) Mixed research as a tool for developing quantitative instruments. *Journal of Mixed Methods Research* 4 (1), 56–78.

Orafi, S.M.S. and Borg, S. (2009) Intentions and realities in implementing communicative curriculum reform. *System* 37 (2), 243–253.

Oxford, R.L. and Shearin, J.L. (1994) Language learning motivation: Expanding the theoretical framework. *The Modern Language Journal* 78 (1), 12–28.

Pajares, F. (1992) Teachers' beliefs and educational research: Cleaning up a messy construct. *Review of Educational Research* 62 (3), 307–322.

Pajares, F. (1996) Self-efficacy beliefs in academic settings. *Review of Educational Research* 66 (4), 543–578.

Pajares, F. (2002) Overview of social cognitive theory and self-efficacy. See http://www.des.emory.edu/mfp/eff.html (accessed 18 June 2012).

Pajares, F. and Miller, M.D. (1994) Role of self-efficacy and self-concept beliefs in mathematical problem solving: A path analysis. *Journal of Educational Psychology* 86 (2), 193–203.

Pajares, F. and Kranzler, J. (1995) Self-efficacy beliefs and general mental ability in mathematical problem-solving. *Contemporary Educational Psychology* 20 (4), 426–443.

Palmer, D.H. (2006) Sources of self-efficacy in a science methods course for primary teacher education students. *Research in Science Education* 36 (4), 337–353.

Pas, E.T., Bradshaw, C.P. and Hershfeldt, P.A. (2012) Teacher- and school-level predictors of teacher efficacy and burnout: Identifying potential areas for support. *Journal of School Psychology* 50 (1), 129–145.

Phan, N.T.T. and Locke, T. (2015) Sources of self-efficacy of Vietnamese EFL teachers: A qualitative study. *Teaching and Teacher Education* 52, 73–82.

Phillips, H. (1959) Problems of translation and meaning in field work. *Human Organization* 18 (4), 184–192.

Pintrich, P.R. and Schunk, D.H. (1996) *Motivation in Education: Theory, Research, and Applications*. Englewood Cliffs, NJ: Merrill/Prentice Hall.

Pituch, K.A. and Stevens, J.P. (2016) *Applied Multivariate Statistics for the Social Sciences* (6th edn). New York: Routledge.

Popov, V., Brinkman, D., Biemans, H.J.A., Mulder, M., Kuznetsov, A. and Noroozi, O. (2012) Multicultural student group work in higher education: An explorative case study on challenges as perceived by students. *International Journal of Intercultural Relations* 36 (2), 302–317.

Poulou, M. (2007) Personal teaching efficacy and its sources: Student teachers' perceptions. *Educational Psychology* 27 (2), 191–218.
Prapaisit de Segovia, L. and Hardison, D.M. (2008) Implementing education reform: EFL teachers' perspectives. *ELT Journal* 63 (2), 154–162.
Puchner, L.D. and Taylor, A.R. (2006) Lesson study, collaboration and teacher efficacy: Stories from two school-based math lesson study groups. *Teaching and Teacher Education* 22 (7), 922–934.
Ramezaney, M. (2014) The washack effects of university entrance exam on Iranian EFL teachers' curricular planning and instruction techniques. *Procedia – Social and Behavioral Sciences* 98, 1508–1517.
Rao, Z. and Chen, H. (2019) Teachers' perceptions of difficulties in team teaching between local- and native-English-speaking teachers in EFL teaching. *Journal of Multilingual and Multicultural Development*, 1–15.
Rastegar, M. and Memarpour, S. (2009) The relationship between emotional intelligence and self-efficacy among Iranian EFL teachers. *System* 37 (4), 700–707.
Raudenbush, S.W., Rowan, B. and Cheong, Y.F. (1992) Contextual effects on the self-perceived efficacy of high school teachers. *Sociology of Education* 65 (2), 150–167.
Richards, J.C. (2006) *Communicative Language Teaching Today*. Cambridge: Cambridge University Press.
Richards, J.C. (2017) Teaching English through English: Proficiency, pedagogy and performance. *RELC Journal* 48 (1), 7–30.
Richards, J.C. and Schmidt, R. (2002) *Dictionary of Language Teaching and Applied Linguistics* (3rd edn). Harlow: Pearson Education.
Riggs, I.M. and Enochs, L.G. (1990) Toward the development of an elementary teacher's science teaching efficacy belief instrument. *Science Education* 74 (6), 625–637.
Rosenberg, M. (1965) *Society and the Adolescent Self-Image*. Rahwah, NJ: Princeton University Press.
Rosenholtz, S.J. (1985) Effective schools: Interpreting the evidence. *American Journal of Education* 93 (3), 352–388.
Rosenholtz, S.J., Bassler, O. and Hoover-Dempsey, K. (1986) Organizational conditions of teacher learning. *Teaching and Teacher Education* 2 (2), 91–104.
Ross, J.A. and Gray, P. (2006) Transformational leadership and teacher commitment to organizational values: The mediating effects of collective teacher efficacy. *School Effectiveness and School Improvement* 17 (2), 179–199.
Ross, J.A., Bradley Cousins, J. and Gadalla, T. (1996) Within-teacher predictors of teacher efficacy. *Teaching and Teacher Education* 12 (4), 385–400.
Rots, I., Aelterman, A., Vlerick, P. and Vermeulen, K. (2007) Teacher education, graduates' teaching commitment and entrance into the teaching profession. *Teaching and Teacher Education* 23 (5), 543–556.
Rotter, J.B. (1966) Generalized expectancies for internal versus external control of reinforcement. *Psychological Monographs* 80, 1–28.
Ruan, J., Nie, Y., Hong, J., Monobe, G., Zheng, G., Kambara, H. and You, S. (2015) Cross-cultural validation of teachers' sense of efficacy scale in three Asian countries test of measurement invariance. *Journal of Psychoeducational Assessment* 33 (8), 769–779.
Rubie-Davies, C.M. (2010) Teacher expectations and perceptions of student attributes: Is there a relationship? *British Journal of Educational Psychology* 80 (1), 121–135.
Rubie-Davies, C., Hattie, J. and Hamilton, R. (2006) Expecting the best for students: Teacher expectations and academic outcomes. *British Journal of Educational Psychology* 76 (3), 429–444.
Saitoh, N. and Newfields, T. (2010) An interview with Shozo Kuwata: A pioneer of standardized rank scoring in Japan. *SHIKEN: JALT Testing & Evaluation SIG Newsletter* 14 (2), 2–5.
Sakui, K. (2004) Wearing two pairs of shoes: Language teaching in Japan. *ELT Journal* 58 (2), 155–163.

Sakui, K. (2007) Classroom management in Japanese EFL classrooms. *JALT Journal* 29 (1), 41–58.
Salanova, M., Llorens, S., Cifre, E., Martínez, I.M. and Schaufeli, W.B. (2003) Perceived collective efficacy, subjective well-being and task performance among electronic work groups: An experimental study. *Small Group Research* 34 (1), 43–73.
Sampson, R.J., Morenoff, J.D. and Earls, F. (1999) Beyond social capital: Spatial dynamics of collective efficacy for children. *American Sociological Review* 64 (5), 633–660.
Sato, K. and Kleinsasser, R.C. (1999) Communicative language teaching (CLT): Practical understandings. *The Modern Language Journal* 83 (4), 494–517.
Sato, K. and Kleinsasser, R.C. (2004) Beliefs, practices, and interactions of teachers in a Japanese high school English department. *Teaching and Teacher Education* 20 (8), 797–816.
Sato, K. and Takahashi, K. (2008) Revitalizing a program for school-age learners through curricular innovation. In D. Hayes and J. Sharkey (eds) *Revitalizing a Program for School-Age Learners Through Curricular Innovation* (pp. 205–237). Alexandria, VA: TESOL Inc.
Schunk, D.H. (1991) Self-efficacy and academic motivation. *Educational Psychologist* 26, 207–231.
Schunk, D.H. (1995) Self-efficacy, motivation, and performance. *Journal of Applied Sport Psychology* 7 (2), 112–137.
Schunk, D.H. and Meece, J.L. (2005) Self-efficacy development in adolescences. In F. Pajares and T. Urdan (eds) *Self-Efficacy Beliefs of Adolescents* (pp. 71–96). Greenwich, CT: Information Age.
Sharma, U., Loreman, T. and Forlin, C. (2012) Measuring teacher efficacy to implement inclusive practices. *Journal of Research in Special Educational Needs* 12 (1), 12–21.
Shavelson, R.J., Hubner, J.J. and Stanton, G.C. (1976) Self-concept: Validation of construct interpretations. *Review of Educational Research* 46 (3), 407–441.
Shi, Q., Zhang, S. and Lin, E. (2014) Relationships of new teachers' beliefs and instructional practices: Comparisons across four countries. *Action in Teacher Education* 36 (4), 322–341.
Shimazu, A., Okada, Y., Sakamoto, M. and Miura, M. (2003) Effects of stress management program for teachers in Japan: A pilot study. *Journal of Occupational Health* 45 (4), 202–208.
Shin, S.-K. (2012) 'It cannot be done alone': The socialization of novice English teachers in South Korea. *TESOL Quarterly* 46 (3), 542–567.
Shrauger, J.S. and Schohn, M. (1995) Self-confidence in college students: Conceptualization, measurement, and behavioral implications. *Assessment* 2 (3), 255–278.
Shulman, L. (1986) Those who understand: Knowledge growth in teaching. *Educational Researcher* 15 (2), 4–14.
Siegel, R.G., Galassi, J.P. and Ware, W.B. (1985) A comparison of two models for predicting mathematics performance: Social learning versus math aptitude–anxiety. *Journal of Counseling Psychology* 32 (4), 531–538.
Siwatu, K.O. (2011a) Preservice teachers' culturally responsive teaching self-efficacy-forming experiences: A mixed methods study. *The Journal of Educational Research* 104 (5), 360–369.
Siwatu, K.O. (2011b) Preservice teachers' sense of preparedness and self-efficacy to teach in America's urban and suburban schools: Does context matter? *Teaching and Teacher Education* 27 (2), 357–365.
Skaalvik, E.M. and Skaalvik, S. (2007) Dimensions of teacher self-efficacy and relations with strain factors, perceived collective teacher efficacy, and teacher burnout. *Journal of Educational Psychology* 99 (3), 611–625.
Skaalvik, E.M. and Skaalvik, S. (2010) Teacher self-efficacy and teacher burnout: A study of relations. *Teaching and Teacher Education* 26 (4), 1059–1069.

Skaalvik, E.M. and Skaalvik, S. (2014) Teacher self-efficacy and perceived autonomy: Relations with teacher engagement, job satisfaction, and emotional exhaustion. *Psychological Reports* 114 (1), 68–77.

Skaalvik, E.M. and Skaalvik, S. (2016) Teacher stress and teacher self-efficacy as predictors of engagement, emotional exhaustion, and motivation to leave the teaching profession. *Creative Education* 7 (13), 1785–1799.

Slaouti, D. and Barton, A. (2007) Opportunities for practice and development: Newly qualified teachers and the use of information and communications technologies in teaching foreign languages in English secondary school contexts. *Journal of In-service Education* 33 (4), 405–424.

Smylie, M.A. (1988) The enhancement function of staff development: Organizational and psychological antecedents to individual teacher change. *American Educational Research Journal* 25 (1), 1–30.

Somech, A. and Drach-Zahavy, A. (2000) Understanding extra-role behavior in schools: The relationships between job satisfaction, sense of efficacy, and teachers' extra-role behavior. *Teaching and Teacher Education* 16, 649–659.

Spooner-Lane, R., Tangen, D. and Campbell, M. (2009) The complexities of supporting Asian international pre-service teachers as they undertake practicum. *Asia-Pacific Journal of Teacher Education* 37 (1), 79–94.

Stajkovic, A.D. (2006) Development of a core confidence-higher order construct. *Journal of Applied Psychology* 91 (6), 1208–1224.

Swanson, P.B. (2008) Efficacy and interest profile of foreign language teachers during a time of critical shortage. *NECTFL Review* 62, 55–75.

Swanson, P.B. (2010a) Efficacy and language teacher attrition: A case for mentorship beyond the classroom. *NECTFL Review* 66, 48–72.

Swanson, P.B. (2010b) Teacher efficacy and attrition: Helping students at introductory levels of language instruction appears critical. *Hispania* 93 (2), 305–321.

Swars, S.L., Daane, C.J. and Giesen, J. (2006) Mathematics anxiety and mathematics teacher efficacy: What is the relationship in elementary preservice teachers? *School Science and Mathematics* 106 (7), 306–315.

Taguchi, N. (2002) Implementing oral communication classes in upper secondary schools: A case study. *The Language Teacher* 26 (11), 13–20.

Taguchi, N. (2005) The communicative approach in Japanese secondary schools: Teachers' perceptions and practice. *The Language Teacher* 29 (3), 3–12.

Tajino, A. and Tajino, Y. (2000) Native and non-native: What can they offer? Lessons from team-teaching in Japan. *ELT Journal* 54 (1), 3–11.

Takahashi, S. (2011) Co-constructing efficacy: A 'communities of practice' perspective on teachers' efficacy beliefs. *Teaching and Teacher Education* 27 (4), 732–741.

Takanashi, Y. (2004) TEFL and communication styles in Japanese culture. *Language, Culture and Curriculum* 17 (1), 1–14.

Tanaka, K. and Ellis, R. (2003) Study abroad, language proficiency, and learner beliefs about language learning. *JALT Journal* 25 (1), 63–85.

Tangen, D. (2007) A contextual measure of teacher efficacy for teaching primary school students who have ESL. PhD thesis, Queensland University of Technology.

The Japan Times (2013, December 7) English teachers to study abroad. Editorial. *The Japan Times*. See http://www.japantimes.co.jp/opinion/2013/12/07/editorials/english-teachers-to-study-abroad/#.Vm4uTDY_VBy (accessed 30 August 2015).

Thompson, G. (2018) Insights for efficacy development from an exploration of Japanese business management students' EAP self-efficacy beliefs. *The Asian ESP Journal* 14 (7.1), 244–284.

Thompson, G. and Yanagita, M. (2017) Backward yakudoku: An attempt to implement CLT at a Japanese high school. *Innovation in Language Learning and Teaching* 11 (2), 177–187.

Thompson, G. and Dooley, K. (2019a) Ensuring translation fidelity in multilingual research. In J. McKinley and H. Rose (eds) *The Routledge Handbook of Research Methods in Applied Linguistics*. Oxford: Routledge.

Thompson, G. and Dooley, K. (2019b) Exploring the key domains where teacher efficacy beliefs operate for Japanese high school teachers of English. *Asia Pacific Education Review* 20 (3), 503–518.

Thompson, G. and Woodman, K. (2019) Exploring Japanese high school English teachers' foreign language teacher efficacy beliefs. *Asia-Pacific Journal of Teacher Education* 47 (1), 48–65.

Thompson, G., Aizawa, I., Curle, S. and Rose, H. (2019) Exploring the role of self-efficacy beliefs and learner success in English medium instruction. *International Journal of Bilingual Education and Bilingualism*. See https://doi.org/10.1080/13670050.2019.1651819

Tomarken, A.J. and Waller, N.G. (2005) Structural equation modeling: Strengths, limitations, and misconceptions. *Annual Review of Clinical Psychology* 1, 31–65.

Tourangeau, R. (2004) Survey research and societal change. *Annual Review of Psychology* 55 (1), 775–801.

Tournaki, N. and Podell, D.M. (2005) The impact of student characteristics and teacher efficacy on teachers' predictions of student success. *Teaching and Teacher Education* 21 (3), 299–314.

Tran, Y. (2015) ESL pedagogy and certification: Teacher perceptions and efficacy. *Journal of Education and Learning* 4 (2), 28–42.

Tremblay, P.F. and Gardner, R.C. (1995) Expanding the motivation construct in language learning. *The Modern Language Journal* 79 (4), 505–518.

Tschannen-Moran, M. and Woolfolk Hoy, A. (2001) Teacher efficacy: Capturing an elusive construct. *Teaching and Teacher Education* 17 (7), 783–805.

Tschannen-Moran, M. and Barr, M. (2004) Fostering student learning: The relationship of collective teacher efficacy and student achievement. *Leadership and Policy in Schools* 3 (3), 189–209.

Tschannen-Moran, M. and Woolfolk Hoy, A. (2007) The differential antecedents of self-efficacy beliefs of novice and experienced teachers. *Teaching and Teacher Education* 23 (6), 944–956.

Tschannen-Moran, M. and McMaster, P. (2009) Sources of self-efficacy: Four professional development formats and their relationship to self-efficacy and implementation of a new teaching strategy. *The Elementary School Journal* 110 (2), 228–245.

Tschannen-Moran, M., Woolfolk Hoy, A. and Hoy, W.K. (1998) Teacher efficacy: Its meaning and measure. *Review of Educational Research* 68 (2), 202–248.

Tsui, K.T. and Kennedy, K.J. (2009) Evaluating the Chinese version of the teacher sense of efficacy scale (C-TSE): Translation adequacy and factor structure. *The Asia-Pacific Education Researcher* 18 (2), 245–260.

Tudor, I. (2001) *The Dynamics of the Language Classroom*. Cambridge: Cambridge University Press.

Underwood, P.R. (2012) Teacher beliefs and intentions regarding the instruction of English grammar under national curriculum reforms: A theory of planned behaviour perspective. *Teaching and Teacher Education* 28 (6), 911–925.

Underwood, P.R. (2013) Japanese teachers' beliefs and intentions regarding the teaching of English under national curriculum reforms. PhD thesis, Lancaster University.

Usher, E.L. and Pajares, F. (2008) Sources of self-efficacy in school: Critical review of the literature and future directions. *Review of Educational Research* 78 (4), 751–796.

Usher, E.L. and Pajares, F. (2009) Sources of self-efficacy in mathematics: A validation study. *Contemporary Educational Psychology* 34 (1), 89–101.

Valdes, A.I. and Jhones, A.C. (1991) Introduction of communicative language teaching in tourism in Cuba. *TESL Canada Journal* 8 (2), 57–63.

Van Someren, M.W., Barnard, Y.F. and Sandberg, J.A.C. (1994) *The Think Aloud Method: A Practical Approach to Modelling Cognitive Processes*. London: Academic Press.

Viel-Ruma, K., Houchins, D., Jolivette, K. and Benson, G. (2010) Efficacy beliefs of special educators: The relationships among collective efficacy, teacher self-efficacy, and job satisfaction. *Teacher Education and Special Education* 33 (3), 225–233.

Wada, K., Tamakoshi, K., Tsunekawa, T., Otsuka, R., Zhang, H., Murata, C., Nagasawa, N., Matsushita, K., Sugiura, K., Yatsuya, H. and Toyoshima, H. (2005) Validity of self-reported height and weight in a Japanese workplace population. *International Journal of Obesity* 29 (9), 1093–1099.

Ware, H. and Kitsantas, A. (2007) Teacher and collective efficacy beliefs as predictors of professional commitment. *The Journal of Educational Research* 100 (5), 303–310.

Ware, H.W. and Kitsantas, A. (2011) Predicting teacher commitment using principal and teacher efficacy variables: An HLM approach. *The Journal of Educational Research* 104 (3), 183–193.

Watzke, J.L. (2007) Foreign language pedagogical knowledge: Toward a developmental theory of beginning teacher practices. *The Modern Language Journal* 91 (1), 63–82.

Wheatley, K.F. (2002) The potential benefits of teacher efficacy doubts for educational reform. *Teaching and Teacher Education* 18 (1), 5–22.

Wheatley, K.F. (2005) The case for reconceptualizing teacher efficacy research. *Teaching and Teacher Education* 21 (7), 747–766.

Wiens, P.D., Andrei, E., Anassour, B. and Smith, A. (2018) Expanding circle: The case of Nigerien EFL teachers' English, training and career satisfaction. *TESL-EJ* 22 (2), 1–26.

Williams, M., Mercer, S. and Ryan, S. (2015) *Exploring Psychology in Language Learning and Teaching*. Oxford: Oxford University Press.

Woolfolk Hoy, A. (2000) Changes in Teacher Efficacy during the Early Years of Teaching. Paper presented at the Annual Meeting of the American Educational Research Association, New Orleans, LA.

Woolfolk Hoy, A. and Spero, R.B. (2005) Changes in teacher efficacy during the early years of teaching: A comparison of four measures. *Teaching and Teacher Education* 21 (4), 343–356.

Woolfolk Hoy, A. and Davis, H. (2006) Teacher self-efficacy and its influence on the achievement of adolescents. In F. Pajares and T. Urdan (eds) *Self-Efficacy Beliefs of Adolescents* (pp. 117–138). Greenwich, CT: Information Age.

Wyatt, M. (2010a) An English teacher's developing self-efficacy beliefs in using groupwork. *System* 38 (4), 603–613.

Wyatt, M. (2010b) One teacher's development as a reflective practitioner. *Asian EFL Journal* 12 (2), 235–261.

Wyatt, M. (2013a) Motivating teachers in the developing world: Insights from research with English language teachers in Oman. *International Review of Education* 59 (2), 217–242.

Wyatt, M. (2013b) Overcoming low self-efficacy beliefs in teaching English to young learners. *International Journal of Qualitative Studies in Education* 26 (2), 238–255.

Wyatt, M. (2014) Towards a re-conceptualization of teachers' self-efficacy beliefs: Tackling enduring problems with the quantitative research and moving on. *International Journal of Research & Method in Education* 37 (2), 166–189.

Wyatt, M. (2015) 'Are they becoming more reflective and/or efficacious?': A conceptual model mapping how teachers' self-efficacy beliefs might grow. *Educational Review* 68 (1), 114–137.

Wyatt, M. (2018a) Language teachers' self-efficacy beliefs: An introduction. In S. Mercer and A. Kostoulas (eds) *Language Teacher Psychology* (pp. 122–140). Bristol: Multilingual Matters.

Wyatt, M. (2018b) Language teachers' self-efficacy beliefs: A review of the literature (2005–2016). *Australian Journal of Teacher Education* 43 (4), 92–120.

Wyatt, M. and Dikilitaş, K. (2015) English language teachers becoming more efficacious through research engagement at their Turkish university. *Educational Action Research* 24 (1), 1–21.

Yamaguchi, S. (1994) Collectivism among the Japanese: A perspective from the self. In U. Kim, H.C. Triandis, C. Kagitcibasi, S.C. Choi and G. Yoon (eds) *Individualism and Collectivism: Theory, Method, and Applications* (pp. 175–188). Newbury Park, CA: Sage.

Yashima, T., Zenuk-Nishide, L. and Shimizu, K. (2004) The influence of attitudes and affect on willingness to communicate and second language communication. *Language Learning* 54 (1), 119–152.

Yilmaz, C. (2011) Teachers' perceptions of self-efficacy, English proficiency, and instructional strategies. *Social Behavior and Personality* 39 (1), 91–100.

Yonesaka, S. (1999) The pre-service training of Japanese teachers of English. *The Language Teacher* 23 (11), 9–15.

Yorimitsu, A., Houghton, S. and Taylor, M. (2014) Operating at the margins while seeking a space in the heart: The daily teaching reality of Japanese high school teachers experiencing workplace stress/anxiety. *Asia Pacific Education Review* 15 (3), 443–457.

Yung, K.W.-H. (2015) Learning English in the shadows: Understanding Chinese learners' experiences of private tutoring. *TESOL Quarterly* 49 (4), 707–732.

Zakeri, A., Rahmany, R. and Labone, E. (2015) Teachers' self-and collective efficacy: The case of novice English language teachers. *Journal of Language Teaching and Research* 7 (1), 158–167.

Zein, M.S. (2017) Professional development needs of primary EFL teachers: Perspectives of teachers and teacher educators. *Professional Development in Education* 43 (2), 293–313.

Zimmerman, B.J. (2000) Self-efficacy: An essential motive to learn. *Contemporary Educational Psychology* 25 (1), 82–91.

Zonoubi, R., Eslami Rasekh, A. and Tavakoli, M. (2017) EFL teacher self-efficacy development in professional learning communities. *System* 66, 1–12.

Index

Note: Page numbers in bold refer to information in figures and tables.

action research 39–40, 132
affective states 22, 26, 132
agency 17, 75
anxiety 17–18, 28, 81–2, 88–9, 134, 145
Ashton vignettes 45
assistant language teachers (ALTs) 3–4, 103, 121, 127
    communication with 64–5, 88, 90
    teaching with 65–6, 109, 124–5
atrophy of language skills 88–9, 91, 100, 138

Bandura, Albert 8–9, 11, 12–15, 16–17
    on efficacy beliefs 21, 26–8, 37, 117–18
    on efficacy scales 10, 35, 45–6, 51
behaviours 16
    predictors of 8, 19–20, 35, 46, 145
beliefs 84, 101, 104
    and behaviours 5–7, 10, 13

classroom practices
    communicative activities 5–6, 85, 126
    items on 70, 83–4
    and teacher efficacy 34, 107
    see also communicative language teaching (CLT)
cognitive mastery experiences 134–5, 137, 139–40, 143
collaboration 118–19, 139
    in language teaching 3–4, 11, 80–1, 82, 105–6, 120–7, 129, 137, 139–42
    materials design 103–4, 120, 121–3, 139, 140–1, 142
    professional development activities 116–17, 154–5
    see also team teaching
collaborative efficacy 117–20, 121, 127–30, 156, 158
    and personal efficacy 122–3
collective efficacy 15–16, 33, 71, 75, 139, 152
    and collaborative efficacy 117–20, 127–30, 156, 158
    and personal efficacy 80–1, 117–18, 122–3
Collective Teacher Efficacy Belief Scale (CTEBS) 33
communicative language teaching (CLT)
    communicative activities 5–6, 85, 126
    conceptual knowledge of 106–7
    and examination preparation 80, 103–4, 113
    experience with 95, 97, 98–9, 124, 136–7, 143–4
    implementation of 2–3, 32, 41, 148
    and L2 proficiency 82–4, 89, 93, 101, 108
    teacher efficacy beliefs 106–11
Communicative Teaching dimension 80, 93, 95–6, 104, 107–11, 149
confidence 6–7
    see also teacher efficacy
confirmatory factor analysis (CFA) 47, 102, 120
content 73
    content validity 60, 67, 68, 69–70
    knowledge of 25–6, 28–9, 42, 101–2
context 60, 73, 75–6, 99, 138–42, 149–50
    see also cultural context; domain specificity; school contexts
correlational analysis 48, 54

cultural context
    collectivist orientation 31, 33–5, 39, 84, 129, 139, 141
    instrument development 60, 102
    Japan 123–4, 126–7, 128–9, 141
    teacher efficacy 24, 38, 42, 131, 132–3, 139
cultural validity 60, 67, 68, 69–70
curriculum changes 41, 79, 121, 122, 127, 148
    school leadership 142

demographics 56–7, 78
    items **53–4**, 55, 66, 68, 70
discipline 81–2, 113–14
domain specificity 45–6, 57–9
    see also context

East Asian settings 31, 34–5, 39, 84, 139, 141, 148
efficacy see self-efficacy
efficacy scales 10, 14–15, 44–5, 47–9, 118, 152, 155
    see also Japanese Teacher of English Teacher Efficacy Scale (JTE-TES); Teacher Sense of Efficacy Scale (TSES)
effort 78–9, 148
Eiken test 39, 54, 57, 91–3, 96, 97
English language 2–3, 90
    as instructional language 4–5, 78, 79–80, 92–9, 108–9, 138, 148–9, 158
    maintaining ability 88–9, 91, 100, 138
    perceived proficiency 39, 57, 86–90, 96–9
    proficiency 4–5, 32, 41, 54, 79–80, 90–2, 94, 96–9, 148–9
    see also Eiken test; L2 efficacy
English language teaching (EFL/EAL) 3–4, 31–2, 87, 106
    East Asia 5, 38, 49, 89, 141, 144
    Middle East 34, 38, 40, 105–6, 119–20
    see also Japanese High School Teachers of English (JTEs)
English literature 107
evaluative cycle 55, 59–61, 67–71

examination preparation 6, 80, 83, 103–4, 140, 157
    academic level of schools 113–14
    knowledge requirements 75, 84, 111–12
expert panels 55, 59–61, 67–71, 73, 88–9
exploratory cycle 59–66
exploratory factor analysis (EFA) 47, 79–81, 87–8, 102, 120

factor analysis 47, 79–80, 87–8, 102, 120
feedback from colleagues 133
    collective efficacy 120
    and teacher efficacy 22, 24, 36–7, 38, 134, 140–2, 145
    see also social persuasion
Foreign Language Teacher Efficacy Scale (FLTES) 35, 47, 63, 74, 79
French language 32, 86
future orientation 18–19, 20, 42, 46, 68–70, 72

grammar-translation teaching method 3, 107, 111, 114–15
grammatical knowledge 75, 84

Hong Kong 4, 34, 102

individual efficacy see personal efficacy
innovation 41, 79, 129, 130
    resistance to 5, 126, 128
    see also curriculum changes
in-service experience 109, 111–12
    of communicative language teaching (CLT) 95, 97, 124, 136–7
instructional efficacy 102–6, 137
instrument development 50, 59–72
    misalignment with theory 44–5
interpretation of experience 22, 24, 56
interviews 49, 50–1, 61–6, 73
Iran 36, 40, 106, 119–20
items 51, 59, 63, **71**
    demographic items **53–4**, 55, 66, 68, 70
    review of 63–6, 67–71
    wording 42, 46

Japan 2–5, 51, 123–4, 128–9, 141

Japan Exchange and Teaching (JET)
    Programme 3–4
Japanese High School Teachers of
    English (JTEs) 88–9, 102–3
  efficacy beliefs 4–5, 40–2, 51,
      73–84, 90–2, 96–9, 131–2,
      149–50
    see also language teacher efficacy
        (LTE)
Japanese Teacher of English Teacher
    Efficacy Scale (JTE-TES) 52–5,
    60, 152
  efficacy dimensions **77**, 79–85, 88,
      104, **149**, 151–2
  and Eiken tests **91**
  instrument development 47, 50,
      59–72, 123
  items **52**
    see also items; research design
job satisfaction 33, 134

knowledge 25, 135, 143–4
Korea 4, 5, 88, 94, 99, 110, 141

L1 teachers 86
    see also assistant language teachers
        (ALTs)
L2 efficacy 9, 41, 119–20
  instructional 35, 78, 86–7, 102–6,
      108–9, 148–9
  perceived proficiency 9, 86–90, 125,
      135
  proficiency 9, 25, 90–2, 138, 154
    see also English language
language teacher efficacy (LTE) 1, 31–3
  development of 8, 36–40, 110–11,
      131–8, 143–4, 153–8
  dimensions 33–42, 47–8, 54, 64,
      73–5, 79–85, 151–3
  domains of challenge **64**, 74–6, 83–4,
      151–2
    see also Japanese High School
        Teachers of English (JTEs)
leadership 127–8, 129, 142
learners see students
learning experiences 137, 144, 155–6
linguistic validity 60, 67, 68–70
locus of control 12–13, 44–5
longitudinal case studies 49, 125, 153

Managing Workload dimension 81–2
mastery experiences 134–7
  cognitive pedagogic 111, 135
  enactive 36–8, 40, 96, 104, 112, 132,
      134, 139, 142
  and English proficiency 92, 98
  and teacher efficacy 21–3, 25–6, 29,
      36–8, 107, 132, 143–5
    see also personal experience
materials design 121–3, 139, 140–1, 142
mentorship 23, 135, 139, 143
Ministry of Education, Culture, Sports,
    Science and Technology
    (MEXT), Japan 2, 56, 91
motivation of students 9, 13, 18, 32

Nishino, T. 8, 41–2, 48, 63, 111
non-teaching duties 75, 81, 111–12,
    152–3
Norway 75, 82, 123, 152

observation 135, 136
Ohio State Teacher Efficacy Scale
    (OSTES) see Teacher Sense of
    Efficacy Scale (TSES)
outcome expectancy 13–14
overseas experience 98, 110, 137–8,
    155–6

path analysis 41–2, 48
pedagogic beliefs 82–3
pedagogic knowledge 32, 85, 101–2
  mastery experiences 25–6, 111, 135,
      140–1
personal efficacy 13, 117–18, 127–8
  and collaboration 121–3
    see also language teacher efficacy
        (LTE)
personal experience 28, 37, 136–8
  overseas 98, 110, 137–8, 155–6
    see also mastery experiences
personal variables 149–50
physiological states 21–2, 132, 134
pilot study 50–1
pre-service training 23, 25, 99
professional development
  collaboration 116–17, 128, 154–5
  and efficacy 23, 36–7, 39–41, 92, 105,
      106–7, 119–20, 134

requirements for 47–8, 81, 96, 109, 145, 158
see also mentorship

questionnaires 47, 50, 73

Rand Corporation study 12–13, 14
reflective thought 112
　and self-efficacy **17**, 28, 37, 105, 132, 143, 145
regression analyses 48–9, 54–5, 94–5, 108, 109
reliability 49, 51, 81
research design 46–51, 55–7
　see also Japanese Teacher of English Teacher Efficacy Scale (JTE-TES)
research methods 47, 50, 153

sample size 55, 56–7, 76, 152
school contexts 66, 133
　academic level 81, 93, 96, 103, 109, 113, 115, 149
　classroom practices 8, 16, 105–6
　and efficacy beliefs 15, 27–8, 116, 139–42, 145, 156
　private schools 38–9, 56
　public schools 38, 40, 93–4
self-beliefs 7, 12, 28–9
self-concept 19–21, 41, 44, 45, 132
self-doubt 18, 21, 28, 105, 154
self-efficacy 7, 25
　beliefs 17–18, 21–9
　and self-constructs 8, 18–21
　theory 12–16, 44–6
　　see also language teacher efficacy (LTE); teacher efficacy
self-esteem 19, 21, 45
self-knowledge 28–9
self-referent thought 16
simulated modelling 23–4, 26
Singapore 106, 133
social cognitive theory (SCT) 9, 12–18, 49, 95, 116
social context, teacher practice 138–42
social persuasion 19, 116, 138–42, 156–7
　collaborative practice 127–8
　L2 efficacy 100
　normative pressure 123–4
　teacher efficacy beliefs 21, 22–3, 24, 36, 38, 132–3
　see also feedback from colleagues
South Korea *see* Korea
stress 17–18, 28, 81–2, 88–9, 134, 145
structural equation modelling (SEM) 48–9, 109
Student Achievement dimension 80, 104, 111–14, 157
student centred teaching 38, 80, 83–4, 104
students 155–6
　achievement 8, 11, 13–14, 18, 48, 75, 111–14, 131, 157
　capabilities 41–2
　communicative competency development 2–3, 75, 80, 103–4, 148
　efficacy 18, 31, 90, 114, 117, 157
　engagement 34, 98, 102
　interaction with 88–9
　learning experiences 114–15
　motivation 9, 13, 18, 32, 76, 78, 152
　see also examination preparation
Super English language high schools (SELHi) 57, 66
surveys 50, 52–5, 66, **71**

task based learning 106–7, 111, 143
task demands
　collaborative practice 126
　contextual difficulties 69, 81, 105–6, 115
　and efficacy 27, 28
task specificity 7–8, 20, 46
teacher efficacy 1–2, 6–10, 16, 21, 117–18
　beliefs 8–10, 21–4, 131–5, 143–5
　and teaching practices 5–7
　see also collaborative efficacy; collective efficacy; language teacher efficacy (LTE); personal efficacy
Teacher Efficacy Scale (TES) 45–6
Teacher Sense of Efficacy Scale (TSES) 14–15, 46, 63, 73–4, 102–3
　application of 32, 33–5, 40, 47, 87, 98
teachers
　age 125–6, 127–8, 139, 142

attrition 82, 131, 145
cognition 5–6, 41
experience of learning 114–15
level of experience 37–8, 93, 97–8, 109, 111–12, 136, 153
specialist teaching language 89–90
  see also Japanese High School Teachers of English (JTEs); language teacher efficacy (LTE); teacher efficacy
team teaching 3–5, 15–16, 80–1
  with assistant language teachers (ALTs) 65–6, 103
  team dynamics 139, 156
  see also collaboration
Teamwork dimension 80–1, 117, 122–5, 139
Test in Practical English Proficiency (Eiken) *see* Eiken test
thematic analysis 63–4, 74, 119–20
translation 60, 66, 68–9, 70

triadic reciprocal causation 16, 42, 116, 139
Tschannen-Moran, M. 14–15, 27–8, 48, 96
Turkey 87, 105

Using English dimension 79–80, 88–9, 92, 96–8, 151

validity 35, 51, 59–60, 72
verbal persuasion *see* social persuasion
vicarious experiences
  modelling 107, 115, 132, 143–5, 145
  teacher efficacy beliefs 21, 23, 25–6, 36–7, 134, 136
  see also observation
Vietnam 38, 49, 133, 141, 144
virtual teaching environments 24

West Asian settings 31, 34, 148
wording 42, 46, 68–9, 70
workload 76, 78–9, 81–2, 103, 152

For Product Safety Concerns and Information please contact our EU Authorised Representative:

Easy Access System Europe

Mustamäe tee 50

10621 Tallinn

Estonia

gpsr.requests@easproject.com

www.ingramcontent.com/pod-product-compliance
Lightning Source LLC
Chambersburg PA
CBHW070611300426
44113CB00010B/1488